D1161486

The New Poor Law in the Nineteenth Century

Each volume in the "Problems in Focus" series is designed to make available to students important new work on key historical problems and periods that they encounter in their courses. Each volume is devoted to a central topic or theme, and the most important aspects of this are dealt with by specially commissioned essays from scholars in the relevant field. The editorial Introduction reviews the problem or period as a whole, and each essay provides an assessment of the particular aspect, pointing out the areas of development and controversy, and indicating where conclusions can be drawn or where further work is necessary. An annotated bibliography serves as a guide for further reading.

PROBLEMS IN FOCUS SERIES

The New Poor Law in the Nineteenth Century

EDITED BY
DEREK FRASER

St. Martin's Press   New York

362.5
N532

Copyright © 1976 David Ashforth, Anne Digby, Francis Duke,
M. W. Flinn, Derek Fraser, Norman McCord,
Audrey Paterson, Michael E. Rose

All rights reserved. For information, write:
St. Martin's Press, Inc., 175 Fifth Avenue, New York, N.Y. 10010
Printed in Great Britain
Library of Congress Catalog Card Number: 75-43484
First published in the United States of America in 1976

Contents

UNIVERSITY LIBRARIES
CARNEGIE-MELLON UNIVERSITY
PITTSBURGH, PENNSYLVANIA 15213

Introduction

DEREK FRASER

AFTER more than three decades of acute concern over England's system of poor relief Parliament in 1834 adopted a means of returning to the beloved 43rd of Elizabeth. The Poor Law Amendment Act released powerful forces whose impact is not yet spent. Part Malthusian, part Benthamite, the New Poor Law sought to reverse the trend which had carried poor relief from its legitimate empire of pauperism into the sacrosanct territory of poverty. Employing the apparently faultless logic of 'less-eligibility', reformers such as Chadwick assumed that voluntary paupers would now quit the class of pauper for the more rewarding condition of independent labour. To strengthen that incentive and to provide adequate institutional care for those labelled 'impotent' all relief would be channelled into a workhouse, and outdoor relief (the bane of the old system) would cease. In order to ensure equitable and efficient treatment of paupers in all areas a uniform administrative regime was attempted, under the guidance of a central Poor Law Commission. Less-eligibility, the workhouse test, uniformity and centralisation: such in outline were the main landmarks of the 1834 revolution.[1]

The New Poor Law is well known in image and theory. Contemporary polemics, novels and folk myths combined to sear upon the historical record the indelible image of a deterrent punitive system of poor relief. The actual practice of poor relief is less well known and is still in the process of exploration by historians. The aim of this book is to examine the actual operation of the New Poor Law in the mid-nineteenth century through a variety of themes (settlement, medical relief, education, philanthropy and politics) and a selection of geographic divisions (urban, rural and Scotland). In all these studies the philosophy of the Poor Law Amendment Act is discussed but the emphasis is upon administrative practice. Each chapter is based upon detailed research by the author, who also draws upon significant historical work by other scholars.

For Notes to the Introduction, see pp. 205–6.

I

In Chapter 1 Dr Michael Rose examines the complex problem of settlement. The basic legal framework is explained with special reference to legislation in 1846–8 and 1861–5 on the related questions of settlement and finance. The over-all paradox which emerges is the persistent survival of settlement and removal despite widespread criticism of the frauds, cruelties, delays, expense and litigation involved in the settlement system and the confused world which revolved around it. Even the 1834 *Report* recited all the familiar problems associated with settlement and concluded that it had long since served its day: 'in this instance, as in many others, like a patient who continues the use of remedies after the disease has ceased, we are suffering under laws of which the grounds have long been removed.'[2] Though most of the evils derived from the original 1662 Act of Settlement, the *Report* concluded that 'there are others greater and more extensive, which arise from the mere existence of a law of settlement whatever that law may be, which increases in intensity in proportion as the limits of the district which has to support what are called its own poor are restricted, and could be mitigated only by its extension and removed only by its entire abolition'.[3] A single qualification of birth and enlarged units of settlement were the only answers offered.

Settlement could vitally affect patterns of residence and mobility in rural England. It is true that the definition of so-called 'open' and 'close' parishes is difficult (see pp. 33 and 167), and it is equally true that residence and employment fundamentally depended on the state of agriculture. Nevertheless, settlement had given rise to a situation where small close parishes were able to keep strangers out and rely on labour at a distance. Again the *Report* was aware of this and wrote of landowners in close parishes that 'they may pull down every cottage as it becomes vacant and prevent the building of new ones . . . they may thus depopulate their own estates and cultivate them by means of the surplus population of the surrounding districts.'[4]

Urban areas, as magnets for migrating workers, did not have this problem but faced acute difficulties in relieving paupers or potential paupers without settlements. The growth of cities themselves, increased mobility, and sudden influxes of distressed Irish all created complex problems which revolved around settlement. Indeed so great was the mobility of early Victorian England that some urban political activists believed that towns were subsidising poverty which, according to settlement, was strictly rural. J. B. Smith, secretary of the Anti-Corn Law League, remarked that a full use of removal from Manchester would provide landlords with 'a very unpleasant exemplification of their dependence upon manufacturing prosperity', and he reported in 1839, 'There are thousands in this district who do not belong to our parishes and who dare not apply for relief lest the overseer should pass them to their own settlements in the agricultural parts of the country. These people cannot hold out much longer and if they be obliged to yield at last they must be sent in flocks for the landlords to support – it will then be seen of what benefit the *new* Poor Law is without a repeal of the Corn Laws.'[5] Smith hoped to link settlement reform with that of Corn Law repeal, and significantly the Poor Law Commission was at great pains in its 1839 *Report* to demonstrate how separate the Corn Law and Poor Law questions were.[6]

Though urban and rural areas might suffer different situations because of settlement they both faced the essential ambivalence posed by the condition of poverty and its relief within a settlement system. As employers, both farmers and manufacturers wished to maintain near at hand a labour force large enough to meet their most buoyant demands. This was as true of farmers facing the seasonal rhythm of agriculture as of manufacturers facing fluctuations in the trade cycle. Yet, as ratepayers, these same groups cavilled at the high poor rates necessary to maintain surplus labour in idleness when not required. Poor Law administration, as far as settlement and removal were concerned, was a shifting compromise between demands for labour and financial necessity. In practice, expedients such as non-resident relief were utilised to avoid removal and thus maintain the labour force. Yet ratepaying employers were unwilling in the last resort to give up removal as the ultimate defence against excessive claims by non-settled paupers. Implicit in J. B. Smith's remarks quoted above was the conclusion which experience confirmed, namely that threat of removal was a greater deterrent than the threat of the workhouse (see pp. 37 and 145).

The only rational final solution lay in a national Poor Law which relieved destitution no matter where it occurred. This would not only have been in breach of the centuries' long tradition that each area should maintain its own poor, but its implementation would also be inequitable without a national poor rate. Reformers, who by the late Victorian years were suggesting a national Poor Law, recognised that a national poor rate was a pre-requisite. Such a solution in 1834, above all, conflicted too much with the desire for local control which underlay resistance to such centralisation as was contained in the New Poor Law. For all its faults settlement provided a means for localities to maintain a vital discretion over its pauper clientele. In the last resort settlement and removal were practical symbols of the strength of local self-government in nineteenth-century England.

Settlement was much discussed in the nineteenth century and in the end was retained by design. In contrast the Poor Law medical service, which Professor Michael Flinn discusses in Chapter 2, evolved wholly by accident. Despite the 1834 *Report*'s specific exclusion of medical treatment from the provision that all relief must be in the workhouse, there is very little in the *Report* about sickness as a cause of pauperism and little in the way of a blueprint for a Poor Law medical service. Yet in spite of the absence of planning the middle decades of the nineteeth century witnessed the birth of a patchy and inadequate yet recognisable health service which in time came to serve pauper and non-pauper alike. In this, as in so much else, the New Poor Law merely confirmed and exaggerated tendencies which were clearly visible before 1834. G. W. Oxley's comment on medical relief under the pre-1834 Poor Law is equally apposite for the new: 'What began as an economy measure to reduce the dependence of the sick poor, expanded to take in the whole range of the poor and to bring within the range of the poor law others who had no claim for maintenance but who could not afford the treatment they needed. Along with this expansion in availability went a significant diversification of the services.'[7]

A number of interconnected developments aided the expansion of medical treatment within the New Poor Law. Poor Law unions appointed district medical officers who treated sick paupers in their own homes. These medical officers were often poorly paid and were responsible for extensive districts involving a heavy work load. They were often frustrated by the intervention of relieving officers whose authority was required for attendance upon a pauper. Although by the end of the century the status of the medical officer was enhanced, it was possible as late as 1910 for a district auditor to disallow the extra medical fees involved in the supply of an elastic stocking and a surgical sole because prior authority had not been obtained from relieving officer or guardians.[8] Similarly, medical officers found themselves the butt of some assistant commissioners, anxious to impress their superiors, who queried and sometimes challenged their medical decisions. Such was the case in Yorkshire in 1847 when an inspector cast doubt upon the necessity of the 'large quantity of wine and sugar given to the outdoor sick under the direction of the medical officers'.[9]

Notwithstanding these drawbacks more and more sick paupers were treated as outdoor-relief cases and indoor relief increasingly became a question of institutional care for the impotent rather than for the able-bodied. Workhouses, by accident, became hospitals of sorts; and indeed, from the 1860s were described as such in official terminology. An illustration of this tendency lay in the composition of the indoor pauper host. Though intended primarily for the shiftless able-bodied, workhouses were mainly populated by other groups. It was the adult able-bodied who were least in evidence.

TABLE I

The Composition of indoor paupers 1859–74 (on 1 Jan. each year)

	Adult able-bodied (per cent)	Adult non-able-bodied (per cent)	Children (per cent)
1859	16·13	45·25	37·60
1864	16·93	45·96	35·69
1869	17·71	44·56	34·55
1874	13·52	53·45	31·25

SOURCE: Local Government Board, *Fourth Annual Report* (1875), appendix, pp. 386–7. (The figures here exclude vagrants, who comprised between 1 and 3 per cent of the total.)

As Table I indicates, the adult able-bodied comprised significantly less than one-fifth of the indoor paupers. Indeed if male adult able-bodied paupers are separated out and non-able-bodied children included in the over-all non-able-bodied total, the figures are even more striking. On the basis of these official statistics, between 66 and 73 per cent of all indoor paupers were non-able-bodied, whereas adult male able-bodied paupers were never more than 6·7 per cent of the total.

The progress of the Poor Law medical service was further stimulated by developments which took medical officers beyond the boundary of pauperism into poverty. By a simple process of accumulated practice it became customary for non-pauper patients to receive treatment, for example, for confinements or accidents. A very elastic definition of pauper was utilised to determine whom the medical officer might treat, which could include those in work but on low wages. The role of the medical officer was in turn extended by the use of sickness as a means of getting around the official prohibition on outdoor relief. The Vaccination Acts consciously extended Poor Law provision to the population at large, simply because there was no other universally available medical service. The Poor Law was also drawn into preventive medicine by the designation of boards of guardians as public health agencies, especially in non municipal areas where the Poor Law was often the only comprehensive administrative organisation. Sometimes guardians acted in their official legal capacity, sometimes they simply stepped into the gap of local inactivity. In Leeds, during the second visitation of cholera in 1848, the guardians were the most active agent of public-health reform simply for lack of any other, while their public-health activity of the 1850s and 1860s was often beyond their legal authority. Similarly, Manchester guardians set up a special sanitary committee in 1848.

The very existence of a Poor Law medical service, particularly one which diversified its services and its clientele, posed acute problems in relation to Poor Law ideology. The key factor was the difficulty in reconciling decent medical treatment with the principle of less-eligibility (see p. 58). The Poor Law Commission recognised this as early as 1841: 'If the pauper is always promptly attended by a skilful and well qualified medical practitioner . . . if the patient be furnished with all the cordials and stimulants which may promote his recovery: it cannot be denied that his condition in these respects is better than that of the needy and industrious ratepayer who has neither the money nor the influence to secure equally prompt and careful attendance.'[10] However, it was often pointed out that the sick ought not to be subject to the deterrent less-eligibility principle. Even so, it required an authoritative statement by the President of the Poor Law Board in 1867 to formally release the sick poor from the less-eligibility straitjacket.

From the 1870s, therefore, the Poor Law medical service was able to develop in new directions, and the same decade witnessed new ideas on pauper education, which are examined in Chapter 3 by Francis Duke. Poor Law philosophy was geared to moral reformation. Hence it was believed that the New Poor Law would convert the idle into the industrious. In the case of pauper children, the Poor Law had adequate scope to eradicate those potential moral failings which brought adult paupers low. Pauper education was consciously geared to inculcating those habits and attitudes which would enable adult pauperism to be avoided.

The creation of a philosophy of pauper education and the design of a system to implement it were mainly the work of Dr James Kay (later Kay-Shuttleworth) and E. C. Tufnell, who each made significant contributions to the education of the poor. The underlying principle of the philosophy of pauper education was the physical separation of pauper children from the workhouse and other paupers. Child paupers would thus be immune to the debilitation of the workhouse and the demoralisation of adult pauperism. Kay was adamant that, as natural innocents, pauper children should not be subject to the constraints, stigma and deterrence of adult poor relief:

> A child should not be degraded in his own estimation by being a member of a despised class. A child cannot be a pauper in the sense in which that term is commonly understood, that is, he cannot be indigent as the consequence of his own want of industry, skill, frugality, or forethought and he ought not therefore be taught to despise himself. . . . it is the interest of society that the children should neither inherit the infamy, nor the vice, nor the misfortunes of their parents. This stigma, and consequent loss of self-esteem would be entirely removed if the children were taught at a District school.[11]

The district school system appeared to offer great benefits to society and pauper alike. However, for diverse reasons, fully discussed in Mr Duke's chapter, the district schools never developed as Kay and Tufnell hoped.

The large towns – for instance, Liverpool, Manchester and Leeds – ran their own industrial schools, but most unions continued with some form of workhouse education. Even workhouse schools benefited from Kay-Shuttleworth's 1846 Minutes under which government grants were available to finance salaries for suitably qualified teachers (see p. 74). Under the 1846 scheme five inspectors of Poor Law schools were appointed by the Committee of the Council which, until 1863, had responsibility for pauper and non-pauper schools. From that year tension between the Education Department and the Poor Law Board was resolved by restoring to the latter full responsibility for pauper education.

Pauper education, like medical relief, implicitly raised issues related to less-eligibility. Kay had conceded that pauper children's physical condition should not be elevated above that of the labourer's household, but he refused to allow the less-eligibility principle to inhibit the quality of education provided, since education was 'one of the most important means of eradicating the germs of pauperism from the rising generation'.[12] Hard-pressed ratepayers were doubtful of the equity in providing pauper schools, described by Dickens as superior to those available to the labouring poor. The overt industrial training within pauper education gave to the child born to pauperism a distinct advantage over the child born to mere poverty. Moreover, industrial training offended other tenets of classical economics in that it interfered with a free labour market. A line of demarcation could be drawn between industrial training, which instilled habits of application, diligence and discipline, and vocational training which prepared entrants for a specific trade. Yet the distinction was a fine one, as the daily dose of shoemaking at Leeds industrial school indicated.

Tufnell, despite all the setbacks, never lost faith in district schools, and in his final report in 1874 extolled their virtues by quoting the autobiography of a pauper boy, 'showing his ascent from the condition of a street arab to competence and respectability . . . it must not be considered as in any way exceptional but typical of the life of innumerable children who have been raised from the lowest grade of misery and heathendom to a state of complete and honest independence by the aid of a district school. . . . What is chiefly worthy of remark here is the pauperising effect of a town workhouse education, and the depauperising effect of a district school.'[13] Tufnell's retirement symbolised the dawning of a new age in pauper education. Criticism of 'barrack schools' was growing, and in the last quarter of the century efforts were made to integrate pauper children into the community. This process was aided by developments under the 1870 Education Act, whose role in pauper education was enhanced in 1873 when education was made a mandatory condition of outdoor relief. Clause 25 of the 1870 Act which empowered assistance for necessitous children gave to school boards and boards of guardians a shared responsibility for the education of the poor.

Indigent parents might choose to send their children to voluntary

schools, and so guardians in the 1870s were brought into closer
relationship with voluntary agencies. This was but one of many connections between the Poor Law and philanthropy, the subject of
Chapter 4. As Dr Norman McCord there shows, if we wish to understand the nineteenth-century Poor Law we must understand
nineteenth-century philanthropy. The Poor Law had always been
closely involved with voluntary institutions such as schools, hospitals,
asylums and reformatories. Overseers in the old system and guardians in the new made use of voluntary provision where official
provision was lacking. In the late eighteenth and early nineteenth
centuries, no less than 77 parishes subscribed to Manchester infirmary for their sick paupers; a century later Bradford guardians
maintained children in 35 voluntary institutions as far apart as
Southend and Kendal.

The nineteenth century witnessed a rapid extension of charitable
agencies and some felt that the very growth of philanthropy made
nonsense of the New Poor Law. As a Salford Tory critic remarked:
'Look round you on the charitable institutions of this town and you
may well ask is it to be believed that there is a law on the statute book
by which poverty is to be considered a crime.'[14] The remarkable
flowering of philanthropic endeavour sprang from many roots.
There was a genuine humanitarianism (often overlooked) in Victorian society which flowed from religious, especially evangelical,
commitment. Victorian society also made charity something of a
social imperative for the new urban elite, anxious to establish its role
as natural social leaders alongside the traditional landed paternalists.
Charity became the passing fashion, beautifully caricatured by a
Liverpool satirist:

> The most fashionable amusement of the present age is
> philanthropy. . . . We have the religious philanthropists, the social
> and moral philanthropists, the scientific philanthropists. Everyone
> who stands in need of the smallest assistance or advice from his
> neighbour, and a great many who do not, must become the pet or
> prey of some one or all of these benevolent classes . . . because
> [philanthropy] . . . elevates you, don't you see – makes you a
> patron and a condescending magnate and all that. . . . Take up
> Social Science as nineteen twentieths of Liverpool folk do, as
> something which makes a shopkeeper hail-fellow with a lord and
> flatters an alderman into believing himself a philosopher.[15]

Others took charity far more seriously, using it as a means of avoiding potential social revolution. This usually took three forms. First, it involved the relief of exceptional distress, such as that in the Lancashire cotton famine, in order to prevent revolution arising from desperation. Secondly, it aimed to counter that alienation and mutual hostility implicit in industrial society, consciously using charity as a social cement. Thus, in Leeds in 1839, citizens were encouraged to support charitable subscriptions so that 'the bonds of society will be more closely cemented amongst us'.[16] Similarly, a prominent Liverpool philanthropist urged the building of personal bridges between hostile classes:

> This alienation and mutual ignorance between rich and poor as classes, arising from the severance of the old lasting relations between individuals rich and poor – is at once a reproach to us as a Christian community, a peril to our interests as a free and powerful nation and an evil of ever increasing magnitude. . . . It is only by bringing the two classes once more into relations of personal kindness and friendly intercourse by service rendered without patronage and accepted without degradation that we can avert the danger of those terrible collisions between capital and labour.[17]

The third form of social insurance also involved personal contact between rich and poor in voluntary institutions, which aimed to amend the behaviour and attitudes of the poor. The sponsoring of charities such as the Mechanics' Institutes or moral reform societies was a device for using philanthropy as a means of social control by transmitting 'superior' social values to the poor.

The preceding analysis perhaps gives to Victorian philanthropy a rationality that is clearer to history than it appeared to contemporaries. What struck philanthropic reformers in the late 1860s and early 1870s was the complete absence of rationality in the plethora of charitable activity. In an endeavour to make philanthropy more scientific the Charity Organisation Society (C.O.S.) formally defined the boundaries between the empire of charity and that of the Poor Law. This was in truth merely a formalisation of aims that had always been implicit in charitable relief. Consciously, or unconsciously, supporters of charities wished to provide the means by which deserving groups could be protected from the stigma of pauperism. This was seen equally in the middle-class subscriptions in trade depressions and in working-class mutuality through trade-union charities. The

C.O.S. finally provided a rigorous discipline for what had previously been informally acknowledged; the deserving should be aided by charities, the undeserving by the Poor Law (see p. 102). As a staunch C.O.S. supporter explained: 'It would be the stern duty of the organisation to delegate to the care of the Poor Law officers all cases undeserving of . . . voluntary charity.'[18] What needs to be emphasised is that, both before and after this formal division of labour, the Poor Law was catering for only a minor part of the demonstrable need in Victorian England. The relief of poverty was channelled more through unofficial than official agencies.

Often the same people who ran the charities also ran the Poor Law, and control over the Poor Law involved the exercise of a political authority. Though one might not guess it from much of the research into the history of poor relief, the Poor Law was essentially a political institution. It is discussed as such in Chapter 5. The politicising of the Poor Law depended, like so much else, upon variable local factors. Differences in the local political situation determined that the political response to the New Poor Law should not be uniform. In Salford, where the local Whig elite were willing to introduce the new system, anti-Poor Law slogans became the shibboleths of the Tories. In the 1837 election William Garnett stood on an anti-Poor Law platform and his supporters were urged: 'If you value the rights of the poor – if you value the spirit of the 43rd of Elizabeth . . . vote for Garnett.' In short, a Tory vote in Salford in 1837 was a vote against the New Poor Law. Yet in Banbury in the same election the political equation was quite different. There Tory control of the New Poor Law drove the Whigs into the anti-Poor Law camp, as illustrated by this extract from an election squib:

Who Built the Great House, the Tory Bastile? The TORIES
Who separated Man and Wife? The TORIES.
Who separated Parent and Child? The TORIES.
Who drag Families from their Homes and Kindred? The TORIES.
Who treat Poverty as a Crime? The TORIES.[19]

In Oxfordshire this association of Tories and the Poor Law lasted many years, and several decades later an agricultural trade unionist commented: 'The Tories are responsible for all workhouse scandles, to vote for the Tories is to insult the Wounded and Poor of the Working Classes.'[20]

It was not simply at election time that the Poor Law became political, for it did so frequently in three other contexts. First, the Poor Law was an integral part of the local political structure, with important powers to exercise and patronage to dispense. The Poor Law guardian was an elected functionary and, as Keith Lucas has written, 'political feeling was often high, and the election of the guardians were in some cases as fiercely fought as those of borough councillors or Members of Parliament'.[21] Secondly, Poor Law policy and administration was politically controversial in many respects. The implementation of the New Poor Law was itself a political battle, and for many decades issues of poor relief such as centralisation or the building of workhouses raised the political temperature. 'Poplarism' is but a twentieth-century expression of a nineteenth-century concern. Thirdly, the Poor Law was officially and inextricably linked to the political system because of the connection of voting and poor rates. The parliamentary, municipal and even parochial franchise depended upon the payment of a poor rate, and so Poor Law officials occupied a key place in the local political system.

The workhouse question did much to politicise the Poor Law and this question figures prominently in Chapter 6, in which David Ashforth discusses the urban Poor Law. It was in towns that there was the greatest opposition to the New Poor Law and its administrative machine. Yet both before and after 1834 the most obvious characteristic of the urban Poor Law was its variety in organisation, function, policy and administration. While some Lancashire towns, such as Rochdale, were a permanent headache to the central authority because of their defiance, the Poor Law found in Manchester a model union which was fully imbued with the principles of 1834. David Ashforth cites the rectitude of the Manchester guardians in the 1860s (see p. 137), but, even before the introduction of the New Poor Law into the town, Manchester parochial authorities were sustaining Poor Law ideas. In the depression of 1837 they pronounced:

> Whilst this Board deeply sympathises with the suffering poor of this township they can never sanction the practice of indiscriminate relief . . . it would be holding out a most dangerous precedent to suppose that relief should be generally afforded from the parish fund because operatives may be reduced for a short period to the

necessity of only working half-time or may be temporarily unemployed . . . it is most desirable in a national as well as a moral
point of view to encourage and stimulate all classes of the community to lay by and be prepared against a season of distress and
to impress upon their minds the conviction that their last resource
should be an application to the parish fund.[22]

It was not only in methods but also in attitudes that many urban
parishes anticipated the New Poor Law.

Urban society found the concept and the practice of the workhouse
test emotive. Some urban guardians became obsessive about the improvement which might flow from the proper application of the
workhouse principle, which was superbly captured by the chairman
of the Sheffield board in 1855:

> The great object of the poor law board is to ensure a constant un-
> varying and efficient discipline during the entire residence of the
> pauper within the workhouse. He rises to the minute; he works to
> the minute; he eats to the minute. He must be clean, respectful, in-
> dustrious, obedient. In short the habits inculcated in the house are
> precisely those the possession of which would have prevented his
> becoming an inmate. . . . The pauper naturally enough concludes
> that the relief he received in the workhouse is a very inadequate
> return for the surrender of his liberty . . . the humiliation . . . and
> the painful consciousness that he has lost all self reliance and self
> respect. Who can wonder that the honest poor should make every
> effort to keep out of the workhouse?[23]

The last point is significant. It was in towns that the paradox was
most apparent wherein those who soldiered on manfully in desperate
poverty received no help because they were deterred from applying,
while those who displayed less resilience were aided. This struck the
Liverpool philanthropist William Rathbone most forcibly and he
identified the untended area of human need: 'It is beyond the om-
nipotence of Parliament to meet the conflicting claims of justice to
the community; severity to the idle and vicious and mercy to those
stricken down into penury by the visitation of God. . . . There is
grinding want among the honest poor; there is starvation, squalor,
misery beyond description, children lack food and mothers work
their eyes dim and their bodies thin to emaciation in the vain attempt
to find the bare necessities of life, but the Poor Law authorities have

no record of these struggles.'[24] The urban answer was to designate pauperism to the Poor Law and poverty to philanthropy. Here was the dichotomy which, in the days of Booth and Rowntree, would demonstrate the contrast between 3 per cent urban pauperism and 30 per cent urban poverty .

The towns often turned to the labour test as a substitute, though much disliked by both paupers and administrators. Again there was a variety of views. While a Manchester guardian in 1849 found humiliating task work 'unjust to the Poor, a great discouragement to honesty . . . (which) destroyed self respect, industrious habits and independent spirit', the Liverpool workhouse committee noted approvingly in 1859 that corn grinding was 'designedly distasteful . . . no other kind of labour . . . combines in itself so many of the essential qualities of the workhouse labour test'.[25] Significantly enough, working-class radicals often approved of the idea, though not the nature, of the labour test for fear of imposition and fraud. A committee in Leeds comprising Chartists and mid-Victorian radicals recommended the necessity of a labour test, though naturally enough they criticised humiliating unproductive labour, preferring work which would 'give the pauper himself and the ratepayer some prospect of his ultimately becoming self-sufficient and ceasing to be a burden on the rest of the community'.[26]

Urban critics of the labour test most frequently suggested sending outdoor paupers into the countryside for farm work while, *pari passu*, rural guardians looked to the towns to absorb their surplus labour. Though town and country faced different problems poor relief had some common characteristics. Dr Anne Digby identifies, in her review of the rural Poor Law in Chapter 7, two significant features: persistent variety and continuity in practice pre- and post-1834. Much the same emerges from David Ashforth's chapter on the urban Poor Law. The two great evils in the countryside exposed by the 1834 Commission had been outdoor relief and its distortion of the labour market. Both of these persisted in the new era. Outdoor relief survived because it was a logical way of dealing with a labour demand which was necessarily seasonal. Exploiting loopholes in the regulations, rural guardians pragmatically looked to outdoor relief to solve the problem of underemployment. The Poor Law Commission's optimistic reports about the abolition of outdoor relief were more propaganda than fact. Yet it would appear that they have seduced a recent rural historian into the false conclusion that 'the policy of denying outdoor relief to able bodied males was pushed through with remarkable resolution' and that outdoor relief was 'only comparatively rarely accorded to the most dangerous class, able bodied adult males'.[27] Dr Digby's calculation that never less than 64 per cent and as high as 87 per cent of able-bodied adults were in receipt of outdoor relief exposes the fallacy (see p. 162). More significantly, the high proportion of outdoor paupers in rural Norfolk was not markedly different from that in urban Merthyr Tydfil, where only 7 to 11 per cent of paupers were on indoor relief.

We have already noticed the role of settlement in the disputed question of open and close parishes. In a broader rural context recent research has discovered the continuation of the labour-allocation policies so much criticised in 1834. The key problem was that settlement regulations, at least until 1865, created the parish as the labour market. This severely limited labour mobility and the chances of employment. Furthermore, the very fact of poor relief vitally determined patterns of job opportunity. Whether a man was married, with or without children, single, settled or non-settled were the crucial factors in the search for work. Despite the desire of the classical economists to create a free market in labour, the New Poor Law, itself in many ways the child of classical economics, prevented the emergence of such a free market.

In this, as in other facets of poor relief, there were many local variations in practice. Though there was no organised rural anti-Poor Law movement, there was much bitterness in particular places depending on local factors. Similarly the role of the New Poor Law in reinforcing the natural cohesiveness of rural society was dependent on local variables. While it has been argued that the authority of natural social leaders was enhanced by the *ex officio* function of magistrates, it must be remembered how important elected guardians were, particularly in routine administration. An important variable in all these matters was the structure of the union itself. Some rural unions were in fact amalgamations of an agricultural area with a perhaps quite sizeable market town; and some urban unions, such as Bradford or Gateshead, had a substantial rural hinterland. In both urban and rural areas this created much tension between conflicting interests, sometimes leading to the break up of the union (see p. 144). Such variables as the geographic nature of unions help to explain the enormous variety of provision in both institutions and services which characterised the rural Poor Law.

Of course, the most significant local variations examined in this book were those to be found in Scotland, described in Chapter 8 by Dr Audrey Paterson. Scotland had a quite separate system, and its New Poor Law introduced in 1845 was markedly different from that in England and Wales. Even so, and despite the conscious separation of their two legal systems, there were always important connections between poor relief in Scotland and England. English Poor Law reformers in the early nineteenth century were much impressed by the ideas of the Glasgow minister Thomas Chalmers. His achievements in parochial poor relief may not have been quite as impressive as he claimed but his views were strongly echoed in the New English Poor Law (see p. 172). Towards the end of the century the Scottish practice of boarding out pauper children much appealed to English educational reformers and was widely introduced south of the border.

Perhaps the most obvious initial contrast between Scotland and England was the absence of an anti-Poor Law movement, largely because the controversial issues of England in 1834 were not introduced into the Scottish scheme of 1845 (see p. 176). In the course of time, however, the practice of social administration brought the two systems more into line. The two central authorities had remarkably similar roles by the latter part of the century. In England the Poor Law Commission claimed central powers from which it gradually retreated; in Scotland the Board of Supervision did not claim powers at the outset but gradually accumulated centralised functions. Equally significant was the fact that, though the English system was avowedly uniform and the Scottish avowedly variable, they both had a similar range of variations in practice. Even the fundamental difference of Scotland having no workhouse test did not significantly alter the pattern of indoor relief. Although in 1868 the 6·45 per cent of Scottish paupers on indoor relief was lower than the English figure, by 1894, when 12·64 per cent of Scottish paupers were maintained indoors, the two countries were marching broadly in step with each other.

Two really significant differences were important. First, the Scottish system formally defined a role for voluntarism where in England this was merely informal and implicit. Chalmers had been opposed to legal relief through institutions, preferring voluntary charity if properly organised. The 1845 Scottish system combined Chalmers's ideology and traditional practice by allowing parishes to preserve the voluntary system if they so wished. The pressures on voluntarism, especially those of finance, gradually undermined the principle, so that, while in 1845 only 25 per cent of parishes had a formal assessment for a poor rate, by 1894 only 5 per cent did not need one. The second major difference lay in the Scottish denial of relief to the able-bodied, the scourge of the English system. In practice, elastic regulations might secure relief to this class but in strict legality the able-bodied were outside the pale of poor relief. In Scotland relief was officially restricted to those who were disabled and destitute. Essentially the Scottish Poor Law catered solely for the non-able-bodied.

II

The fruits of much research have been gathered in these studies. Much remains still to be done, yet it is possible to draw from the chapters of this book some tentative conclusions which may be tested out in future historical research.

It would appear that the 1870s were something of a watershed in the history of the Poor Law. Following the Goschen Minute of 1869 it was in the early 1870s that the Local Government Board battled against the abuse of outdoor relief. In the same period the C.O.S. formalised the relationship between Poor Law and philanthropy, adopting a stern tone with the undeserving. Yet the same decade also witnessed more positive new dimensions in education and medical relief. In another sphere the extension of caucus politics into the minor institutions of local government politicised in a more intense way the guardians' elections of the 1870s. Beyond this chronological dimension three more fundamental general points emerge, concerning (1) the relationship of principle and practice in poor relief; (2) the conflict of the image and the reality of the New Poor Law; and (3) the place of the New Poor Law in Victorian society.

(1) Three essential principles were explicit in the origins and creation of the New Poor Law. These were uniformity, the abolition of outdoor relief, and less-elegibility. Poor Law practice severely compromised all three. At no time in the nineteenth century did the poor relief system achieve even the semblance of uniformity. Variety was the essence of the New Poor Law as of the old, and the full range of that variety has only partly emerged. We need many more local studies of poor relief by historians, both amateur and professional, since firm general conclusions must depend on comprehensive local

research. It is already clear that further research will reveal a wider range of provision within the Poor Law at local level. Perhaps there was some uniformity in the simple rejection of the principle of abolishing outdoor relief, on which so much Poor Law theory rested. In both urban and rural areas the abolition of outdoor relief was at once impracticable and inappropriate. However much magistrates, guardians and relieving officers might sympathise with the social theory underpinning the abolition of outdoor relief, the harsh necessities of their practical problems forced them to abandon metaphysics for pragmatism. The estimate offered in Chapter 6 that somewhere between 6 and 15 per cent of urban paupers were in receipt of indoor relief is supported by national Poor Law statistics. Even in the case of able-bodied adult males the vast majority were on outdoor relief (cf Table I, p. 5).

TABLE II

Indoor relief in England and Wales, 1859–74 (1 Jan. of each year)

	Able-bodied adult male paupers on indoor relief (per cent)	All paupers on indoor relief (per cent)
1859	19·24	14·44
1864	14·77	12·14
1869	21·80	13·86
1874	28·64	15·46

SOURCE: Local Government Board, *Fourth Annual Report* (1874–5).

Table II points unequivocally in one direction: the overwhelming majority of paupers, even able-bodied adult males, never saw the inside of the workhouse.

If the compromise on the abolition of outdoor relief was justified by the practicalities of the situation, the Poor Law authorities were much more reluctant to abandon the logic of less-eligibility with its promise of moral reform. Yet less-eligibility posed an insoluble dilemma for the Poor Law. How could relief be provided at a level below that of the labouring poor which, at the same time, could be considered humane and decent in a civilised society? It was difficult enough merely in the area of food and physical environment. The standard of living of depressed urban handworkers or of starving farm labourers was so low that it was quite impossible for less-eligibility to operate. To maintain paupers below such a level was un-thinkable. Critics of poor relief were reminded time and again that the food, income and accommodation of paupers was often superior to that of their poorest independent neighbours. In more subtle fields, such as medical relief or education, less-eligibility was even more difficult to operate. The more reformers sought to raise the standards of Poor Law infirmaries or schools, the greater became the gap between the provision for those in pauperism and those in poverty.

(2) This contrast between principle and practice is similar to that between the image and the reality of the New Poor Law. One of the most powerful images of the 1834 system was the principle of centralisation. It was this which bound together in one movement in the late 1830s both the potential dispensers of relief and potential paupers. Typical of an attitude which survived beyond the 1830s was this 1838 comment on 'the tyrannical and arbitrary power of the Central Board of the irresponsible commissioners which completely nullifies and destroys the representative system so congenial to the feelings of the people of this country – so essential to their liberties and so indisputably the cause of all the prosperity of England – and places the individuals whom the people may elect to regulate their af-fairs entirely and helplessly subject to the baneful coercion of govern-ment hirelings.'[28] Elected guardians as malleable pawns in the hands of despotic commissioners were a powerful image, but the reality was otherwise. Considerable powers of discretion remained in local hands, which accounts for the variety of experience already referred to. It soon became clear that, tactically, it accorded better with reality for opponents of the New Poor Law to adopt it and shape it to their needs rather than refuse to implement it altogether. The image of a centralised Poor Law stuck, while the reality confirmed the impor-tance of local control over poor relief.

A frequent accusation relating to the central authority was that it was bent on 'grinding the poor down'. The image of the administra-tion tarred the institution as a whole, and it was commonly said that the whole of the New Poor Law was an inhuman machine geared to crushing the poor. The evidence hardly points exclusively in this direction. It is true that the Commission in London frequently dis-played absolute indifference to the condition of paupers in their charge; and the bureaucracy was on occasion prone to pettifogging intervention over such trifles as whether the porridge was too thick or whether paupers were given too much beer. Nevertheless, the most frequent battle between central and local administration was that between a reforming bureaucracy anxious to raise standards and parsimonious guardians bent on economy. This was especially true of the middle ranks of the bureaucracy, that is the inspectors and assistant commissioners working the system. One recalls the work of Kay and Tufnell in education or of the little-known T. B. Browne, who wanted pauper children to be taught poetry. In the medical field Dr Edward Smith was especially keen to raise standards, though here external medical opinion in the 1860s pushed the Poor Law Board initially. The ordinary regional inspectors were also anxious about improvements in provision and wished to counter local parsimony.

Such was frequently the case in battles over new workhouses. Often the local inspector wished a new workhouse to be built solely because existing accommodation was below standard. The worst indoor conditions were to be found not in new purpose-built, well-regulated workhouses but in the old squalid, insanitary township or parochial institutions. Furthermore, it was invariably the condition of the impotent poor which the inspector had in mind rather than the able-bodied. Such was the case in Leeds when in 1845 Charles Clements, the assistant commissioner, tried to shame the guardians into action on a workhouse which was 'without proper accommodation for the aged and infirm and the sick'. Clements urged them 'to render the workhouse tolerably creditable where the aged and infirm can be accommodated with decent comfort, the sick properly attended to, the helpless idiot sufficiently protected and the unruly and shiftless able-bodied male pauper kept apart from the vicious and abandoned of the other sex'.[29] The 'shiftless' male might resent the enforced separation from the 'abandoned' female, but this was hardly 'grinding the poor down'.

Yet the image of the workhouse, the most powerful of all, was too well entrenched to be modified by reality. Especially when so few paupers were on indoor relief, the wild rumours of 'bastilles' found a ready audience among the poor. Pretty well all the scandals (the Victorian equivalent to the mental-home scandals of our own day) have been found to be grossly exaggerated and invariably the result of local rather than central policy. Workhouses were depressing and life inside them was monotonous, yet it is doubtful if they ever really became the harsh prisons of popular myth. Nevertheless, there was great psychological cruelty inflicted alike on those who did apply for relief and those who were deterred from applying. Though we should recall that, in practice, threat of removal was a greater deterrent than fear of the workhouse, we have no reason to doubt William Rathbone's conclusion on the workhouse test: 'It is felt so deeply to degrade the pauper that the best of the working class will rather starve – often do rather starve – than apply for it. . . . It does succeed in deterring those who can support themselves from applying for parish support; it does diminish pauperism, it has effectively checked the rapid progress of demoralization and ruin under the old Poor Law of Elizabeth. But as a system of public charity it fails altogether.'[30] The image became the reality and fear of the workhouse became a cultural inheritance which has survived the generations.

(3) The third area where general conclusions emerge from these studies is in the relationship of the Poor Law with other aspects of Victorian society. The New Poor Law was built upon an unshakeable belief in the distinction between pauperism and poverty. Pauperism was not taken to be one end of a spectrum centred on poverty whose other end might be moderate working-class affluence. Pauperism was seen as a quite separate condition from poverty and the pauper qualitatively different from the poor. The physical separation of the pauper from the rest of the community naturally presumed a Poor Law which was a discrete institution separate from the rest of society. The isolation of pauperism was thus to be aided by the insulation of the Poor Law itself. Unfortunately much research on the history of the Poor Law proceeds on this assumption and the greatest defect of such research is that it wrenches the Poor Law out of its historical and social context and examines it in a vacuum. Hopefully these chapters redress the balance by restoring the Poor Law to its proper place within Victorian society.

It was never possible to maintain the Poor Law in isolation, not least because legislative action interwove it into a complex fabric of administration. The Poor Law had important public-health functions; it administered the Vaccination Acts; it was the agent for civil registry; it was the source of electoral machinery; it was bound up with police, justices and highways. It was in short an all-purpose administrative agency which accumulated functions largely because it was universally available. In fact, in the middle decades of the century, non-poor-relief expenditure accounted for between 28 and 40 per cent of the disbursement of funds, as shown in Table III. A breakdown of non-poor-relief expenditure for one year (Table IV) demonstrates the range of administration with which the Poor Law was concerned.

TABLE III

Poor Law expenditure in England and Wales, 1844–74

	Total expenditure (£ million)	Percentage expended on poor relief
1844	6·99	72·69
1854	7·32	72·82
1864	9·68	66·80
1874	12·85	59·64

TABLE IV

Non-poor-relief expenditure, 1865

Percentage expended on:	
Police	61·6
Highways	15·7
Constables/J.P.s	1·2
Registration	2·2
Vaccination	1·7
Election lists	1·1
Surveys and valuations	1·8
Other	14·7

Total £3·41 m., representing 35·54 per cent of total Poor Law expenditure.

SOURCE (both tables): *Local Government Board, Fourth Annual Report* (1874–5), appendix, pp. 352–3.

Apart from this legal intermingling, the administration of poor relief was inevitably bound up with the wider society. Through settlement it related to the labour market; through the Poor Law medical service it catered to the generality of the poor; through its provisions for lunacy it was in partnership with the Lunacy Commission; through its educational activities it was hitched to the Board of Education; but most important of all the Poor Law was inextricably linked both formally and informally with philanthropy. If the honest and independent poor were to avoid the humiliation of poor relief they would have to be able to call upon voluntary resources in time of need. There was an implicit alliance of official and unofficial relief agencies each reinforcing the other. By the late 1860s and early 1870s reformers such as William Rathbone and Octavia Hill were devising liaison committees to formalise the relationship. Rathbone wished to 'combine organization and individual effort, state supervision and local management so that the one should support and stimulate without fettering the other'.[31] The many voluntary hospitals, asylums, children's homes and like institutions which accommodated paupers confirmed that the Poor Law was no island in the Victorian Lake. Poor relief was enmeshed in a complex web of administration, and its wider impact was felt throughout that society of which it was so characteristic a part.

In the longer historical perspective the New Poor Law assumes a central though ambivalent place. The ambivalence flows directly from that conflict between principles and images on the one hand and practices and realities on the other (of which some mention has already been made). In the practice of poor relief elementary universal agencies were created which could cater for a great range of social needs and conditions. From a twentieth-century vantage point the Victorian Poor Law appears grossly inadequate; a comparison with early nineteenth-century possibilities gives a different perspective. Considering that *circa* 1820 there was widespread support for the total abolition of the Poor Law, what had been achieved by 1880 assumes more heroic proportions. As Professor Flinn points out in Chapter 2, the Poor Law medical service set Britain, however hesitatingly, on the road that led to Bevan's National Health Service.

That these minimal but universal provisions did not become the foundations of a more splendid edifice, but became ruins alongside which a welfare state was constructed, was due to the unacceptable social price demanded by the Poor Law. So great was popular resentment at the stigma of pauperism that more generous provision for the poor inevitably came beyond the Poor Law and not within it. As social sensibility became more attuned to the demands of poverty rather than to those of pauperism, so categories of social need were gradually withdrawn from the fiat of the Poor Law. The sequence is now familiar as the sick, the unemployed and the old came to be maintained on terms socially more acceptable than those prevailing within the Poor Law. Where, earlier, philanthropy sought to protect people from the stigma of pauperism, by the late Victorian and Edwardian era this function was implicit in official social policy. The aim was to ensure that relief to deserving cases whose social condition was no fault of their own should no longer carry with it a punitive *quid pro quo.* It was wholly typical of this new attitude that the little known Cleansing of Persons Act of 1897, which allowed local authorities to defray out of the poor rate the cost of a free service for cleansing and disinfecting people affected with vermin, should include this important rider: 'The use of such apparatus shall not be considered to be parochial relief or charitable allowance to the person using the same, or to the parent of such person, and no such person or parent shall by reason thereof be deprived of any right or privilege or be subject to any disqualification or disability.'[32]

In time the principles of the New Poor Law necessitated a new practice of poor relief.

1. Settlement, Removal and the New Poor Law

MICHAEL E. ROSE

'T H E whole business of settlements, even in its present amended form, is utterly contradictory to all ideas of freedom. The parish persecution of men whose families are likely to become chargeable, and of poor women who are near lying-in, is a most disgraceful and disgusting tyranny.' In these forthright terms, the Reverend T. R. Malthus condemned the laws relating to the settlement and removal of the poor. His words echoed those of Adam Smith, who more than twenty years earlier had maintained that 'there is scarce a poor man in England of forty years of age . . . who has not in some part of his life felt himself most cruelly oppressed by this ill contrived law of settlements'.[1]

Although earlier statutes had introduced the notion of settlement, the law which attracted the wrath of Adam Smith and T. R. Malthus was that of 1662 (13 & 14 Charles II cap. 12), and its numerous subsequent accretions. To judge from its preamble, the Act of 1662 seems to have been something of a panic reaction to the economic distress and threatened social upheaval following the Restoration. The Act empowered magistrates to order the removal back to their parish of settlement of any person coming into a parish to inhabit a tenement with a yearly value of less than £10 upon a complaint being made to a magistrate, within forty days of the person's intrusion, by the churchwardens or overseers of the parish.

Later critics of the law of settlement condemned the 1662 Act as a confused ill-drafted piece of legislation rushed through Parliament at the request of a few wealthy parishes, particularly those in London, who feared an invasion by hosts of ragged paupers intent on preying upon their ample parochial resources. Despite its dubious origins and ramshackle structure, however, the Act became as integral a part of the English Poor Law as the 43rd of Elizabeth of 1601. Over the

For Notes to Chapter 1, see pp. 206–7; for Bibliography, see pp. 195–6.

next 150 years, numerous additions were made to it both by statute and case law until, as one writer pointed out, it became 'the bulkiest title in the law books'.

Backed by this extensive and complex legal provision, parish officers kept a look-out, particularly in periods of economic distress, for those without a settlement in the parish who might apply to it for poor relief. Those likely to become a burden on the parish might be persuaded to move on, either illegally by the use of cash payment or brute force, or legally by obtaining an order of removal from the magistrates under which the poor man and his family could be conveyed back to their parish of settlement. This apparently simple legal device was, however, greatly complicated by the fact that the parish of settlement of the person to be removed had to be discovered before a removal order could be issued. A man's settlement, like his surname, was inherited from his father. A woman, on marriage, took her husband's name and also his place of settlement, while children aged under sixteen followed the settlement of their parents. These regulations prevented the family from being broken up in the event of a removal. On reaching sixteen years of age, the young man or woman retained the settlement derived from his or her father until he or she acquired a settlement in some other parish by, for example, being hired for a year to an employer in a particular parish, completing the service of an apprenticeship in a parish, paying parish rates or acting as a parish officer, renting a tenement of the annual value of £10, purchasing an estate, or even, before 1795, merely residing in a parish for forty days after giving due notice of intention to do so. In each case the most recently acquired settlement was the operative one which cancelled earlier acquired or derivative settlements. Thus, to find a person's parish of settlement might require a search through a number of acquired settlements to discover the most recent. If no settlement had been acquired, then the paternal settlement had to be discovered, or (failing that) the maternal one. In the event of neither derivative settlement being discovered, recourse had to be made to the place of birth as the parish of settlement. Thus, the removal of a poor person might well involve long and complex searches in some cases extending back over several generations. George Elson recounted how, on the death of his father in 1837, his mother and her four children were taken into Northampton workhouse and were then removed to Lutterworth, where his grandfather had acquired a settlement by serving an apprenticeship in the parish.[2] This settlement he passed on to his son who, in his turn, passed it on to his wife and children. Poor relief recipients and administrators alike found themselves enmeshed in a tangle of almost inextricable legal complexity.

Three years before Malthus issued his condemnation of the law of settlement, a major statutory amendment had been made to it by an act of 1795 (35 Geo. III cap. 101). Under the terms of this, no order of removal could be taken out against any person until he actually applied to the parish for relief. This linked the law of settlement even more closely to the system of poor relief, since only actual rather than potential paupers were now removable. This considerable limitation of its scope, however, might seem to be the beginning of the end for the system of settlement. Not only had it been censured by Adam Smith and T. R. Malthus, two of the greatest seminal influences on nineteenth-century social and economic policy; it was also severely criticised by the influential parliamentary select committee on the Poor Laws of 1817. Between 1819 and 1832, a whole series of bills were introduced in Parliament, some of them aimed (like Thomas Wood's scheme of 1822) at the abolition of the power of removal. Despite the failure of these attempts at reform, it seemed unlikely that the laws of settlement and removal would long survive. Like the apprenticeship and wage-fixing statutes, they would be swept away because they constituted a hindrance to the workings of a free economy by restricting labour mobility.

Yet the law of settlement survived not only the attempted legislative reforms of the 1820s, but also the Royal Commission's enquiry of 1832 and the Act of 1834 – the New Poor Law – which was based on its work. In 1840, 11,000 removal orders involving, it was estimated, 32,000 English paupers were issued by justices in England and Wales. In 1849, 13,867 orders covering perhaps 40,000 paupers, nearly 4 per cent of all those relieved, were issued. Once the crisis years of the 1840s were over, the number of removal orders issued fell off; in 1856, 6800 for 16,546 persons were issued, and in 1867, 4600 for 9900 paupers and their families. In the first decade of the twentieth century, the Royal Commission on the Poor Laws (1905–9) discovered that in 1907 12,000 paupers were removed, while, in 1905, the expenses involved in obtaining and executing removal orders amounted to over £21,000. Although those removed constituted only a very small portion of all those relieved, the Royal Commission noted that some of the larger Poor Law unions were employing full-time officers to enquire into the settlement of those who applied for relief and to effect their removal if necessary. It is the purpose of this essay to examine the reasons for the long survival of the law of settlement and removal, and to see why its reform was to prove so difficult.

The long continuation of the settlement and removal laws was not due to any lack of attention being bestowed upon them by legislative reformers. The 1832 Royal Commission on the Poor Laws, albeit devoting less time to settlement than to other aspects of the poor-relief system, recommended the simplification of the law so that birth in a parish would become the sole means for claiming a settlement in it. As with so many of the Royal Commission's proposals, the Act of 1834 ignored this suggestion. Instead it limited reform to the abolition of hiring for a year, serving a parish office and apprenticeship in the merchant navy as modes of acquiring a settlement. It also improved the system of giving notice of, and appealing against, removals, and contained a permissive section giving boards of guardians the right to request that the union rather than its constituent parishes be made the area of settlement. This latter provision, which required the unanimous consent of the guardians, proved to be almost wholly null and void.[3]

The economic and social distress of the 1840s – coupled with a growing realisation among Poor Law reformers that the law of settlement was proving a greater barrier to the establishment of a rational, efficient and more uniform system of poor relief than they had at first thought it to be – brought pressure for a more thorough-going reform of the law than had been achieved by the Poor Law Amendment act of 1834. Attention centred particularly on three questions. The first was that of making the Poor Law union rather than the parish the area of settlement, thus transferring the responsibility for applying for, and executing orders of, removal from parish overseers to boards of guardians and their officers. Next came the idea of rendering those who had been resident in a parish for some considerable time immune from the danger of being removed back to their parish of settlement if they applied for relief. Finally, there was the aim of simplifying settlement law by abolishing the acquired settlements and making birth in a parish the basis for settlement.

The Poor Law Commission devoted a considerable amount of space in its ninth annual *Report* of 1843 to the reform of the law of settlement. In response to the recommendations contained in the report, the government introduced reform legislation in 1844, 1845 and 1846. The only fruit of this, as far as the law of settlement was concerned, was the short Act of 1846 (9 & 10 Vic. cap. 66) which introduced a new concept, that of irremovability, into the already tangled law of settlement. Persons continuously resident for five years in a parish were not to be removed to their parish of settlement if they applied for poor relief. Widows were also to be irremovable for twelve months after the deaths of their husbands as were those who applied for temporary relief on account of sickness or accident. An Act of the following year (10 & 11 Vic. cap. 110), called Bodkin's Act after its sponsor Sir William Henry Bodkin (M.P. for Rochester and secretary of the Society for the Suppression of Mendicity) transferred the cost of the relief of these irremovable paupers from the parish to the common fund of the union to which all its constituent parishes contributed in proportion to their expenditure on poor relief. Bodkin's Act was a temporary emergency measure designed to apply for one year only. However, its provisions were confirmed and extended by an Act of 1848 (11 & 12 Vic. cap. 110), thus making an important step forward towards the idea of union chargeability.

In the stormy parliamentary climate of 1846, however, the 'Irremovability Bill' had a rough passage, calm discussion on it being hindered by the lengthy debates and strong emotions engendered by Corn Law repeal and Irish coercion. On the resignation of Peel's ministry, the new Home Secretary, Sir George Grey, took up the 'mangled remains' of the Bill and piloted it through its remaining stages in the closing weeks of the parliamentary session. There thus emerged on the statute book a short but confusing piece of legislation containing, as one peer remarked, 'an appeal in every line'.

In recognition of the failure of the 1846 Act to make any fundamental alteration in the law of settlement and removal, the Whig government obtained the appointment in 1847 of a parliamentary select committee to investigate the operation of the law. After examining witnesses, several of whom were highly critical of the practice of removal and in favour of a more rational system involving union rather than parochial settlement and rating, the committee began to prepare its report. Its members were unanimous in their opinion that the existing system was unjust and that the power of removal ought to be abolished. However, they differed strongly over the feasibility of introducing a system of union settlement and rating, and ended by merely reporting the evidence they had heard without making any specific recommendations to Parliament.[4]

In 1849 the Poor Law Board conducted its own enquiry into the problems of settlement and removal by asking a number of its inspectors to report on the operation of the system in their areas. These reports, published in 1850, were in the main strongly critical of the law of settlement, and particularly of the encouragement it was thought to give to the establishment of 'close' parishes, whose landowners discouraged new residents.[5] In a supplementary report George Coode, formerly an assistant secretary to the Poor Law Commission, produced a devastating historical and theoretical criticism of 'the most stringent, despotic and searching law that ever controlled the domestic condition and industrial habits of a nation'.[6] The following year saw the publication of the barrister Robert Pashley's *Pauperism and Poor Laws*, which echoed many of Coode's criticisms of the settlement law and made suggestions for their reform.[7] Other powerful voices for reform included those of Sir Edmund Head, a former Poor Law Commissioner, in an article published in the *Edinburgh Review* in 1848, and of another former Poor Law Commissioner, Sir George Nicholls, in a memorandum written prior to his resignation as secretary of the Poor Law Board in November 1850.[8]

Backed by these weighty criticisms, Matthew Talbot Baines, the President of the Poor Law Board, introduced a bill in 1854 to abolish removal and place the whole cost of poor relief upon the common fund of the Union. In addition the bill contained provisions for the gradual introduction of union rating. As with Sir James Graham's proposed measures of 1844 and 1845, however, the bill was withdrawn. One of the main stumbling blocks to its passage was a threatened revolt by Irish M.P.s who demanded that the bill be amended to provide some protection for Irish immigrants against removal back to Ireland. A select committee was appointed to enquire into the vexed question of the removal of Irish and Scottish persons, but no legislative action was taken on its recommendation that no person whether English, Irish or Scottish be removed from a parish in which he had resided for three years continuously.[9] A further select committee set up in 1857 spent three years looking into the problem of those rendered irremovable by the Act of 1846, and their enquiries led to the Act of 1861 (24 & 25 Vic. cap. 66) under which a three-year residence rather than a five-year one conferred irremovability.[10] The 1861 Act also required parishes to contribute to the union common fund on the basis of their rateable value rather than their relief expenditure. It was not until 1865, however, that the important but often little noticed Union Chargeability Act (28 & 29

Vic. cap. 79) at last took all powers over settlement and rating out of the hands of the parish and made them the responsibility of the union and its board of guardians. One year's continuous residence in a union gave immunity against removal from it.

Despite this major reform, the law of settlement continued to call for the attention of legislative reformers. In 1876 the Divided Parishes Act (39 & 40 Vic. cap. 61) created a new method of acquiring a settlement, namely a continuous residence of three years in a union. In 1878 a parliamentary select committee enquired once more into the law of settlement, and recommended that compulsory removals should be abolished.[11] This recommendation was ignored, however, so that even in the first decade of the twentieth century several thousand people were being removed every year from the Poor Law union in which they were resident, and a considerable amount of time and money was being spent on matters involving settlement and removal. An Act of 1927 tidied up the law and repealed some of its more obsolete clauses. Not until 1948, however, did the law of settlement and removal finally disappear from the statute book.

As can be seen from this necessarily sketchy review of nineteenth-century settlement legislation, the law of settlement and its defects were kept constantly in the public and parliamentary mind, particularly during the middle decades of the century. Powerful voices, such as those of Edwin Chadwick, Sir George Nicholls and George Coode, were raised in favour of its abolition or drastic reform. Not only were the voices powerful; the arguments they advanced were, in theory at least, weighty ones. To judge from the arguments advanced in favour of reform, the law of settlement offended against some of the most sacred economic, social and political principles of Victorian England.

In the realm of economics the law of settlement conflicted with the principle that labour, like other factors of production, ought to be free to respond to market forces. A worker, however, might be deterred from moving from the parish in which he had a settlement to one in which there was a greater demand for his labour because of the fear that if, due to sickness or unemployment, he applied for poor relief he might be summarily removed back to the parish with which he had severed his former ties. One of the hopes of Poor Law reformers in 1834 was that, by ending the system of outdoor-relief allowances in aid of low wages, the New Poor Law would force redundant agricultural labourers to move from their villages to the labour-hungry manufacturing areas of northern and central

England. To prime the pump for this movement, the Poor Law Commission was persuaded in 1835 to appoint agents in Leeds and Manchester whose task was to put local manufacturers seeking workers in touch with parish overseers or guardians in southern villages burdened by large numbers of unemployed or underemployed able-bodied paupers.[12] The collapse of this scheme in the depression of 1837, and the growing realisation that the New Poor Law had not greatly stimulated the free movement of labour, may well have directed the attention of Poor Law theorists like Nicholls and Chadwick to the influence of the unreformed settlement law in restricting the movement of labour.

Much of the criticism of the law of settlement in the 1840s and 1850s concentrated on its restrictive effect on the labour market. Numerous references were made to rural labourers being like medieval or eastern European serfs, bound to the soil of their native village by the law of settlement. It was argued that this not only hindered the long-distance movement of labour but, more importantly, that it created rigidity and inefficiency in the local market for agricultural labour. As Edwin Chadwick told the Select Committee of 1847, the first question put to a man when he applied to a farmer for a job was 'To what parish do you belong?' Priority was usually given, it was argued, to labourers settled in the employer's parish, however inefficient they might be, since if they were not given work they and their families would become a burden on the parish and increase the rates which the farmer would have to pay. 'This is essentially a condition which I call a condition of slave labour', pronounced Chadwick, 'labour without interest and without the proper motives of the freeman'.[13] Labourers who did break out of this condition and move to manufacturing areas might, when unemployed, be sent back to the village from which they had migrated. Thus, it was argued, rural parishes were being made to bear an unfair share of the burden of industrial depression. The answer to many of these problems was, it would seem, the abolition or drastic reform of the law of settlement which would help to create a more perfect market for labour.

Economic arguments constituted only a part of the case against the law of settlement. The moralistic humanitarianism which was such a powerful element in Victorian social reform was also aroused by some aspects of the law. The practice of removal, Sir Francis Head pointed out, 'touched to the quick the happiness of the poor from one end of England to another', and he cited the sad case of a pauper immured in a southern workhouse whose removal from Wigan where he had lived for more than twenty years had cast him into a deep melancholy.[14] Not only did legal removals cause distress amongst those uprooted from their homes and transported to parishes in which they or their parents were long forgotten; the system also gave rise to illegal removals involving the bribery or bullying of unfortunate victims. The Act of 1846, which created the notion of irremovability, was held by some critics to have increased the practice of putting pressure on poor people to move from a parish before they completed the required five-year residence and thus became irremovable by legal methods. In 1852 the Poor Law Board ordered their inspector in the area to carry out an enquiry into the case of John Ince, a blind pauper, who had been harried from one parish to another in the Great Boughton Union of Cheshire. The enquiry revealed the appalling lengths to which parochial officers were prepared to go in order to prevent the cost of a pauper's relief falling upon their parish. The inspector, Andrew Doyle, expressed the hope that the Poor Law Board would obtain from Parliament 'salutary modifications of the law of settlement' in order to guard against the recurrence of such cruelties.[15]

A more specific area of concern to which attention was particularly drawn by the reports of the Poor Law Board's inspectors in 1850 was the effect of the system of 'close' and 'open' parishes on the morals and well-being of the rural labourer (see p. 167). Where the property in a parish was all owned by one or two landlords, it was argued that the law of settlement held out an inducement to them to destroy cottage property in the parish in order to prevent labourers and their families residing there and thus acquiring a settlement or, after 1846, irremovability, which would have given them a claim to poor relief at the expense of the parish. Labourers were thus prevented from living near the farms on which they were employed and were forced to find accommodation in 'open' villages, where the cottage property was in the hands of a number of small owners, or in adjacent market towns. This involved many of them having to walk several miles each day to and from their work to the detriment of their health and their efficiency as workers. The itinerant nature of agricultural labour which settlement created was held to stimulate the system under which labour gangs, often composed of women and children, were recruited in towns and 'open' villages by gang masters and hired out on a contract basis to farmers. Despite the claims of gang masters that those employed by them were closely supervised, the idea of large numbers of both sexes working in close proximity in the fields disturbed the Victorian moral conscience. Even more disturbing were the reports of housing conditions in 'open' villages and urban areas where high rents brought overcrowding in squalid conditions which rapidly demoralised those who dwelt in them. Gilbert à Beckett reported that in Bury St Edmunds labourers were paying up to £5 a year for two damp, dirty and ill-ventilated rooms in which vain attempts were made 'to preserve decency' by dividing up sleeping apartments with curtains. Throughout the reports of à Beckett and his fellow investigators there ran veiled hints of sexual immorality and perversion resulting from overcrowding, which was itself exacerbated by the operation of the law of settlement.[16]

Another frequent complaint against the law of settlement was that it caused parishes considerable expense in discovering settlements and effecting removals, particularly where this involved them in litigation with other parishes. This, in its turn, held out opportunities for corruption and a temptation to remove paupers by illegal methods. Thus the system militated against the Victorian ideal of cheap and uncorrupt government. Lawyers, remarked George Coode, himself a member of the Inner Temple, were 'the only interest which, as yet, this law has never wholly ceased to favour'. One of the most common complaints of parish officials to the Royal Commission of 1832 was over the expense involved in settlement cases. These do not, however, seem to be borne out by the returns of expenditure made to the Commission. Manchester in 1831 spent only £1400 of the £31,500 it raised in poor rates on removal expenses and settlement litigation. Spilsby in Lincolnshire raised £783 in rates in the same year, but spent only £13 on settlement and removal.[17] Even in the early 1840s, when removals from manufacturing areas were particularly heavy, Stockport spent just over £600 a year on removals, about 5 per cent of its total relief expenditure.[18] The real complaint perhaps lay in the fact that the expenses of settlement and removal could not easily be estimated. Settlement litigation might drag on, involving one parish after another, until a considerable bill for legal costs had been run up. It took seven years for a case brought by the township of Carlton in Yorkshire against Marsden in Lancashire to be settled, and when the Court of Queen's Bench finally decided the issue in 1849, the 142 ratepayers of Carlton were left with a legal bill of over £300.[19] Even in cases where expenditure was not so high enquiries as to the settlement of applicants for relief could take up much of a Poor Law officer's time. In Manchester it was estimated that thirty cases had to be investigated for every one actually removed.[20] In 1844 a Halifax overseer ran up a bill of £50 contesting a removal order for a family from nearby Elland. His enquiries involved him in travelling to Sowerby Bridge, Luddenden Foot, Skircoat, Elland, Bradford, Pontefract and Manchester.[21] Thus, as critics of the law of settlement were not slow to point out, it was often cheaper to relieve a pauper than to remove him. Abolition of settlement, particularly of the power of removal, would not only reduce costs but would also release officers for more useful types of Poor Law investigation. A substantial gain in cheapness and efficiency might therefore be achieved.

Yet, despite the weighty arguments and the powerful authorities ranged against it, the continual delays in effecting any substantial reform of the law of settlement would seem to suggest that the case against it was less clear cut in practice than it appeared to be on paper. Labour mobility, for example, was far less restricted by settlement law than its critics from Adam Smith onwards had inferred. As the union clerk of Stockport told the Select Committee of 1847, the industry of the town would be seriously damaged if workers were dispersed in every trade depression. It was often preferable to maintain an unemployed man on outdoor relief for a short period of time in the hope that he could resume work once trade revived. This policy was facilitated by the system of non-resident relief which was widely practised particularly in industrial areas (see p. 145). If a man applied for poor relief and was found not to have a settlement in the parish where he was resident, this parish, or the union in which it was situated, would seek out and contact the parish in which the applicant had a settlement. The parish of settlement would be asked to agree to reimburse the parish of residence for relief payments made to the applicant. Faced with the alternative of having the applicant and his family sent back to them under the removal order with little prospect of their being able to support themselves once removed, the parish of settlement would often agree to meet the quarterly bills sent to them for relief payments made to these non-resident poor. A complex system of inter-parochial and inter-union accountancy sprang up. Between 1846 and 1859 the Chorlton-on-Medlock Union was reimbursing thirty-six unions and parishes, and was at the same time in receipt of payments from about one hundred unions or parishes on behalf of their non-resident paupers. In Leeds when a person resident there, but settled elsewhere, applied for relief, a copy of the relieving officer's report on the case was sent to the parish of settlement together with a letter asking permission 'to relieve on your account according to the necessities of the case'.[22]

Despite the disapproval of the Poor Law Commission, who felt that such a system of relief made strict controls impossible and opened the door to graft and corruption, non-resident relief continued to operate on a large scale in areas of continuous labour migration. Between 1839 and 1846 about 20 per cent of those relieved in the West Riding of Yorkshire were non-resident paupers. After 1846, when those with a five-year residence in a parish became irremovable, the parish of residence could no longer claim reimbursement for the irremovable poor from parishes of settlement. In order to alleviate the sudden financial burden thrown on some parishes by this measure, Bodkin's Act of 1847 transferred the cost of relieving the irremovable poor from the parish account to the common fund of the union. A return in 1855 revealed that in some counties a high proportion of total relief expenditure was being paid to irremovable poor, long resident outside their parishes of settlement. Relief to the irremovable constituted 37 per cent of total relief expenditure in Lancashire, and 33 per cent of that in the West Riding, as compared with 14 per cent in Herefordshire.[23]

The introduction of the concept of irremovability did not end the practice of non-resident relief, which continued even after 1865 when one year's continuous residence in a union was sufficient to render a person irremovable. As late as 1906 over £270,000 was being received by boards of guardians in repayments for non-resident paupers; and nearly 22,000 persons, about half of them old people, were in receipt of this type of relief.[24]

The continued operation of the non-resident relief system and the large proportion of irremovable poor to be found in some parts of the country would seem to suggest that the practice of settlement and removal was no great barrier to labour mobility. E. H. Hunt has recently shown that labour in nineteenth-century Britain was far less immobile than has sometimes been supposed.[25] Given its flexibility, the poor relief system was not a major factor in inducing even such immobility as existed.

If settlement and removal were far less inhibiting to labour mobility than their critics suggested, it may also be true that they were allotted too much of the blame for the creation of 'open' and 'close' parishes in rural areas. Robert Weale, one of the inspectors who reported to the Poor Law Board on the operation of the law of settlement in 1849, remarked that he thought that the allegations against close parishes had been overstated. A witness to the Select Committee of 1847 pointed out that there were considerations other than those of poor relief expenditure to make a large landowner restrict the number of dwellings on his estate. If cottages did not harbour poachers, they would almost certainly contain children, who might get into woods, disturb game, break down palings and commit other depredations. Whilst recent studies (that of D. R. Mills on Lincolnshire, for example), have pointed out some connection between poor relief systems and settlement patterns, B. A. Holderness has indicated the difficulty of defining the terms 'open' and 'close' parish in any meaningful way, and has suggested that the number of 'close' parishes in mid-nineteenth-century rural England may well have been far less than was implied by critics of the law of settlement.[26] W. T. Hawley, investigating Northumberland for the Poor Law Board's enquiry of 1849, sent a circular to parish overseers asking them to state whether their parish was a 'close' or an 'open' one. A 'close' parish he defined for them as 'a parish where the property is in the hands of one or very few proprietors and *where cottages have been pulled down and building is not encouraged*' (our italics).[27] Not surprisingly, therefore, Hawley reported that the system of 'close' parishes led to the pulling down of cottages and the restriction of new building. In their anxiety to make out a case for the reform of the law of settlement some of its critics were none too careful with the evidence.

Whatever the truth as to the effects of the law of settlement in rural areas, Poor Law authorities in urban or industrial areas regarded it as a useful defence against undue pauper pressures, especially in periods of trade depression. The threat of removal acted as a deterrent against applying for poor relief. 'The actual penalty falls on few, the fear of it afflicts and deters all', argued George Coode, pointing out that with an average removal rate of two per parish per annum, most people must at least have witnessed the effects of the removal system. Given the propensity of the urban working class to move from one parish to another within the town, it was difficult for them to obtain even the limited protection given by the status of irremovability after 1846. Thus many may have shrunk from applying to the guardians for relief lest they be threatened with removal back to their parish of settlement. For those who did apply, the threat of removal was often enough to keep them from going forward with their application. Between 1840 and 1846, Stockport guardians ordered the removal of 2190 families who had applied for relief. In the event, however, only 656 families were actually removed, since the others withdrew their application for relief and were left, in the words of the union clerk, 'to shift for themselves'.[28]

In years like 1842 or 1848 when applicants for relief pressed heavily upon them, guardians, overseers and relieving officers saw their powers of removal as a useful protection against overwhelming pauper demands. The Poor Law Commission's argument, that an efficient workhouse constituted a far better test of pauperism, fell on deaf ears in unions where workhouses would be filled to overflowing in periods of trade depression and then stand half empty once trade revived. Threat of removal seemed a much more flexible, less expensive form of test. The ratepayers of Manchester were opposed to the abolition of removal, William Royston, the assistant clerk to the Manchester Union told the Select Committee of 1847, 'simply because they think they would be losing the most important test they have'.[29] Of the 52,000 removal orders granted by magistrates in England and Wales between 1845 and 1849, 29,000 were taken out in Lancashire as urban parishes sought to protect themselves against a run on their rates.[30]

A particular fear of parish and union authorities in years of distress like the late 1840s was the invasion of their area of responsibility by hordes of pauper vagrants attracted by tales of easy relief. The 'terror of the tramp' still aroused the same fears as it had done in 1662, particularly in towns like Liverpool, Manchester and Bradford which were experiencing a large influx of ragged Irish refugees from the Great Famine.

Constituting as they did the poorest and most insecure sector of the urban population, the Irish posed a large and unwelcome problem for urban Poor Law authorities in the mid-nineteenth century. Those born in Ireland possessed no settlement in England and Wales and, given their poor circumstances, few immigrants acquired one. An Act of 1833 (3 & 4 Wm IV, cap. 40), regularly renewed in the first half of the nineteenth century, empowerd magistrates, on receipt of a complaint from the parish authorities, to enquire into the settlement of any person born in Ireland, Scotland, the Isle of Man or the Isles of Scilly. If they were found to have acquired no settlement in England or Wales, they could be removed back to their country of origin. Under this legislation, many thousands of Irish paupers and their families were shipped back to Ireland in the early nineteenth century, despite the protests of Irish M.P.s, parish authorities and charitable organisations that these wretched people were being indiscriminately dumped at ports of entry and left to find their way back to their native parish as best they could.

After some initial hesitation, it was decided that the Act of 1846 was applicable to those born in Ireland who had completed a five-year unbroken residence in an English parish. This ruling, however, only increased the determination of some parish officials to remove Irish applicants for relief before they completed the residence necessary to claim irremovability, and to resist any amendments in the law of settlement which might deny them this protection against Irish pauperism. If powers of removal were abolished, William Royston told the Select Committee of 1847, 'there would have to be some measure to protect English towns from being inundated by Irish in the same way as they have been of late'.[31] As late as 1878 when only 88 Irish paupers were removed back to Ireland from Liverpool as compared with 15,000 thirty years earlier, Liverpool's vestry clerk told a select committee that memories of the famine period still haunted the ratepayers and Poor Law authorities, and that protective legislation was still required against the possibility of any such invasion in the future.[32] In deference to such sentiments, the Select Committee, while generally recommending the abolition of removal, suggested that special privileges be given to relief authorities in ports of entry like Liverpool which might be subject to a sudden influx of pauper immigrants. 'Sometimes I beat off Irish applicants for a good while', a London relieving officer told Robert Pashley; 'they have universally a great dread of being sent back to Ireland. . . . All that we want is not to see them again.'[33]

The Irish were not, however, the only type of pauper applicant whom relieving officers wished to see disappear from their sight. It was often to their advantage and that of the ratepayers to use the power of removal against relief applicants who might prove troublesome or a long continued burden on the parish. Widows with dependent children or single women with illegitimate children were prominent amongst these. The 58 cases removed from Leeds in 1841 included eleven widows, ten single women with a bastard child each and another single woman who was pregnant. In 1878 in Birmingham 34 of the 118 paupers removed were single or widowed women and 30 more of them were women with dependent children.[34] Henry Higgins, assistant clerk to St Pancras parish, pleaded before the Select Committee of 1878 for the retention of powers of removal for parishes like his own which contained within its boundaries three of London's major railway termini. Every year, he claimed, about 200 young women, many of them pregnant, applied to the parish for aid. Under existing legislation, St Pancras could remove them back to their native parishes in the country, thus rescuing the unfortunates from descent into prostitution and crime, and the parish from having to bear the cost of relieving them and their illegitimate offspring.[35] To officers like Higgins the theoretical and humanitarian arguments for the abolition of settlement and removal were of little weight compared with their practical value as a device for saving trouble and expense.

It was, in fact, the question of expense, of the financial structure of the Poor Law, which played the most important role in ensuring the survival of the system of settlement and removal. As has been seen (p. 28), the Act of 1834, which established unions of parishes under boards of guardians for the purposes of relief administration, left considerable powers to the constituent parishes of each union. Decisions over removal remained the responsibility of the parish overseer, and paupers could thus be removed from one parish to another within the same union: a procedure which often led to ill feeling and quarrels between rival guardians at board meetings of the union. Each parish remained responsible for the assessment and collection of its own poor rate. Out of the sum collected it had to meet the cost of relief to paupers settled in it, whether this was given in the workhouse or in the form of outdoor-relief payments ordered by the guardians. In addition each parish had to pay a share of the common fund of the union, which was used to meet expenses like the running costs of the workhouse or the salaries of union officers. The proportion of the common fund which each parish had to pay was calculated on the basis, not of rateable value, but of relief expenditure, not on the property of a parish, but on its poverty. Not surprisingly, considerable inequalities resulted. In Carlisle Union, the township of Caldewgate, a working-class district (inhabited by Irish labourers) in the centre of the city, had an annual relief expenditure equal to one-quarter of that of the whole union, whilst its rateable value was only one-ninth of the union total. It contributed £1400 a year to the union common fund whilst the rural parish of Cummersdale which had greater rateable value paid only £41, and the 'close' parish of Grinsdale, which had no settled poor, paid nothing.[36]

The 'irremovability' Act of 1846, which was intended to alleviate financial inequities by relieving rural parishes of responsibility for settled paupers who had migrated from them and resided in an urban parish for five years or more, did not always have this effect. Working-class townships in inner urban areas now found that they could no longer recoup the cost of relieving immigrants from other parishes by non-resident relief. A proviso in the Act stating that time spent in receipt of poor relief did not count towards the five-year residence qualification for irremovability was held, in the legal confusion following the passage of the Act, not to be retrospective. Thus paupers who had been in receipt of non-resident relief and who had resided in a parish since 1841 suddenly became the financial responsibility of that parish. Leeds found that £3000 or £4000 was likely to be added to its annual relief bill as a result. Market towns at the centre of mainly rural unions were also hard hit. Kendal lost £1000 a year in non-resident relief payments, and Doncaster £500.[37] Conversely, some 'close' parishes in rural areas were relieved even of the small burdens they had previously borne. Lord Egerton of Tatton was estimated to have gained £150 a year as a result of the cancellation of non-resident payments to paupers with settlements in parishes on his estate but resident in nearby Knutsford.[38]

A new burden was thrown on to the relief funds of parishes and townships in urban, industrial areas at a time when demands for relief were already increasing as a result of economic depression and Irish immigration. In the confusion surrounding the application of the Act, there were threats of indiscriminate removals, of cuts in, or refusal of, relief to applicants without a settlement in the parish, and of the break up of unions in which guardians of urban and of rural parishes found themselves increasingly at loggerheads over the question of settlement and non-resident relief. As has been seen, Bodkin's Act of 1847 (see p. 29) attempted to alleviate this situation by transferring the cost of relieving irremovable paupers from individual parish accounts to the common fund of the union. However, the unequal mode of distributing the burden of the common fund meant that parishes with a large working-class population still bore the heaviest burden of poor relief.

Given the inequalities and uncertainties of Poor Law finance, parishes clung to removal as a protection against increased poor rates. Heavily burdened urban parishes, with the experience of 1846 in mind, feared that any move towards abolition of settlement and of their powers of removal might bring with it a rapid increase in applications for poor relief. Low-rated rural or suburban parishes had no wish to increase their contribution to the finances of the union. Thus they opposed any attempt to implement the clause in the 1834 Act allowing for union, rather than parochial, settlement and rating. Despite constant recommendations by Poor Law experts and parliamentary select committees that union settlement and rating should become compulsory, it was not until thirty years after the passage of the Poor Law Amendment Act that this was implemented.

The Acts of 1861 and 1865 did not, however, provide any final solution to the problem. Poor relief was still on a local base, albeit a rather broader one than before. Removals were fewer, but non-settled paupers were still liable to be removed. Financial inequalities remained, especially between inner urban unions with large working-class populations and outer suburban unions, or between unions in the East and West End of London. Removals within unions ceased, but many removals were still over comparatively short distances. Of the 118 removals from Birmingham Union in 1878, almost one-third were into the adjacent Aston, King's Norton and Walsall Unions; and of the 991 removals from St Pancras in 1875, 577 were to other parishes or unions in the metropolis.

The practice of settlement and removal reflected the intensely local nature of the English poor relief system. The desire to preserve this constituted one of the greatest barriers to any drastic reform of the law of settlement. Much of the opposition to the introduction of union settlement and rating sprang from a fear that it was the thin end of a wedge for the abolition of settlement and removal, and for the financing of poor relief from national rather than local funds. Ideas for such a system of national Poor Law finance to accompany a repeal of the law of settlement were floated but were generally re-jected as being subversive of traditional English rights of local self-government. Relief of the poor from a national fund would remove the check of local experience and knowledge. Those who provided the funds for poor relief would no longer be intimately concerned with its expenditure as they were in a system where parish and union officials were either elected or nominated by ratepayers. Not only would a door be opened to fraud and reckless expenditure, but the hands of centralisers like Edwin Chadwick would be strengthened to squeeze the life from local self-government. Even Robert Pashley, staunch critic of settlement and removal though he was, rejected the idea that abolition of settlement should be accompanied by national provision for poor relief out of the Consolidated Fund. 'Its gigantic injustice is only equalled by its stupendous folly', he remarked, and went on to outline a complex scheme of his own whereby settlement might be abolished and parochial rates made more equal, without removing local responsibility for finance. Matthew Talbot Baines, President of the Poor Law Board, likewise rejected any idea of a national poor relief fund when introducing measures for the reform of settlement and removal in the House of Commons in 1854. 'One of my chief objections to any such scheme', he announced, 'is that I verily believe it would be fatal to the principle of local self-government in the administration of the Poor Laws'.[40] So inextricably woven into the context of parochial self-government and taxation had the law of settlement become that any drastic alteration of it threatened the whole fabric of the local rate and its local expenditure.

Despite their flouting of Victorian economic and humanitarian ideals, settlement and removal remained an integral part of the nineteenth-century Poor Law system. Given that they were capable of being operated more flexibly in practice than appeared possible in theory, local Poor Law administrators found them a useful deterrent against importunate or excessive claims for relief. The notion of settlement, of belonging to and being the responsibility of a particular parish, appeared to maintain a degree of stability in a rapidly changing and increasingly mobile industrial society. Most important of all, it guaranteed local responsibility for poor relief against those who wished to increase the powers of central government. All these elements combined to ensure that Robert Pashley's confident assertion in 1852 that 'the law of settlement and removal is finally doomed, that its days are numbered and that it must soon be abolished for ever' was to prove an empty prophecy.

TABLE V

Removals – England and Wales

Year	(1) Removal orders granted by J.P.s	(2) Number of persons involved	(3) Total number relieved	(4) Percentage (2) of (3)
1845	7116	21,348*	995,218†	2·15
1846	6564	19,692*	1,007,940†	1·95
1847	14,124	42,372*	992,405†	4·27
1848	9837	29,511*	1,059,757†	2·78
1849	13,867	41,601*	1,088,659†	3·82
1853–4 (year ending Lady Day)	4923	11,786	864,617‡	1·36
1854–5 ,,	5025	12,475	897,686‡	1·42
1856–7 ,,	6803	16,546	885,010‡	1·87
1862–3 ,,	6055	13,989	1,079,382‡	1·30
1867–8 ,,	4657	9908	992,640‡	1·00
1881–2 ,,	4241	8915	788,289‡	1·13

* Calculated from Removal Orders × 3 – 'I take three as the average number of persons comprised in each order. I believe it is a low average.' M. T. Baines, *Hansard* (10 Feb. 1854) col. 451. Whilst this is obviously too high a multiple for the later period, the decline in the number of persons included in a removal order may indicate a change during the century in the type of case removed, that is from a predominance of young married persons with families to one of single elderly persons or single women with an illegitimate child.

† Calculated from *Total Relief Expenditure* – see Webb, *English Local Government, English Poor Law History,* part II, vol. II, appendix II, pp. 1036–41.

‡ Mean of total number relieved on 1 January and 1 July.

SOURCE: *P.P.* 666, L (1850); 489, LV, pt 1 (1854); 436, XLIX (1856); 506, XLIX (1857–8); 12, XLVIII (1865); 477, LX (1867–8); 366, LVIII (1882).

TABLE VI

Irish paupers removed from England and Wales

Year	Number removed
1845–9	29,079
1853–4 (Year ending Lady Day)	5349
1854–5 ,, ,,	5725
1856–7 ,, ,,	3436
1862–3 ,, ,,	416
1867–8 ,, ,,	508
1881–2 ,, ,,	248

SOURCE: As for Table V above.

2. Medical Services under the New Poor Law

M. W. FLINN

SICKNESS has always been a prime cause of poverty. It prevents bread-winners from earning their families' keep, and calls for expenditure over and above the normal on drugs and the services of doctors and nurses. The more advanced the forms of social and economic organisation, the more acute the problems it raises. The Industrial Revolution, by polarising rural society, and by increasing the proportion of urban dwellers in the population as a whole, made new demands on society's resources of social organisation. The relative decline of smaller village communities in which the closeness of personal relationships made it difficult to ignore a family's problems arising out of sickness, and the relative rise of large, impersonal and unhealthy cities where any sense of corporate responsibility was slow to develop, intensified a problem that had always of necessity made heavy demands on social organisation.

From the strictly economic point of view, sickness was never a problem for the wealthy. Doctors commonly adjusted their fees shrewdly to patients' incomes, and the middle and upper classes were usually comfortably placed to cope with the temporary cessation of earnings, if, indeed, sickness actually did lead to this. For the lower-income groups in society, however, sickness immediately created economic problems of immense, and often insuperable magnitude. Wages were so low that savings were out of the question, even to the extent of the few pence of weekly subscriptions to a 'club', the mutual health-insurance organisation of the day: there was, therefore, an immediate problem of income, if the wage-earner's family was not to starve. The fees of doctors and nurses and the cost of drugs were beyond the pockets of all classes below the better-paid skilled workers, while the most effective cure was often the prescription of high-quality foods and stimulants whose price placed them even

For Notes to Chapter 2, see pp. 207–8; for Bibliography, see pp. 196–8.

further from the workers' reach in times of sickness. Thus, if the sick poor were not to be deprived of even the little that the limited medical skill of the day could do for them, and their families were not to be allowed to starve, society must intervene and offer help.

From the sixteenth century this help had been institutionalised in the Poor Law. Subject to certain conditions, society, acting from a judicious mixture of humanitarian and political motives, was prepared to provide both financial assistance in these circumstances and, as time progressed, some rudimentary medical services. The proportion of people in society whose economic insecurity forced them to accept, through the Poor Law, the ministrations of the wealthier members of society in times of need such as periods of sickness, is not easy to estimate. But at some periods and in some areas it may have reached, if not exceeded, half of the population – the large element in both rural and urban society known as 'the poor'. 'The poor' were those whose sources of livelihood were either so slender or so insecure as to oblige them, in situations of need, to turn to 'the parish' for assistance. When not, through sickness, old age or unemployment, actually in need, they supported themselves independently. When they crossed the line from 'independence' to acceptance of relief from the parish, the poor became, temporarily or permanently, 'paupers', 'paupers' being those actually in receipt of relief from the parish overseers. Moreover, the condition upon which parochial relief was given was that 'pauperism' should be a condition of deprivation, a stigma signified in the brutal sixteenth century sometimes by actual branding, in the marginally more humane eighteenth century by badges, and in the nineteenth century by loss of pride or status which could, on occasion, be more wounding than the physical insignia. Apart from certain specific deprivations, such as disfranchisement (not very significant until the franchise was pushed lower down the social scale in the later nineteenth century), the principal impact of pauperism was, therefore, a social stigma against which the pride of the 'respectable' poor rebelled.

By the early nineteenth century, then, the long-run pressures of social need and humanitarianism had combined with the shorter-run impact of industrialisation to produce a rudimentary medical service for the poor, administered by the Poor Law authorities and tightly bound up with a status system that both limited the liability of the wealthy and abetted the existing mechanisms of social control. This dual function of answering the call of humanitarianism and bolstering the system of social relationships of the day was to be an important determinant of the path taken in the developments of the early Victorian period.

The medical services that had evolved by the last years of the Old Poor Law took the form of the appointment by the overseers in many parishes of a medical officer, and in a very few, exclusively urban, parishes, of the institutional care of the sick either in an infirmary ward of a workhouse, or in a separate workhouse infirmary. Parish medical officers were engaged for an annual fee to attend the sick in the parish. 'As far as I have been able to ascertain,' said George Cornewall Lewis, a Poor Law commissioner in the early days of the New Poor Law, 'the practice of giving medical relief systematically arose in the latter half of the last century; parishes at that time began to appoint Medical Officers regularly.'[1] He went on to point out, however, that this practice was common only in the Midlands, the south and east, and was little known in the north and west. An example of the workhouse infirmary is provided by the parish of Marylebone in London. A large urban parish with a population equal to that of some of the major provincial towns, Marylebone had already by the 1770s provided a building separate from its workhouse to house the sick. When a new workhouse was built in 1775, the sick were moved into the more commodious premises of the old workhouse, where standards of care resulted, according to one claim, in a death rate half that prevailing in the best hospitals of that period. In spite of this claim, a series of bad epidemics obliged the select vestry to move the infirmary to a new site, and in 1792 a new building with 300 beds was built and brought into use. In 1799 this infirmary had, in addition to a physician and a surgeon, a resident apothecary, a matron and four paid nurses.[2]

In spite of the importance of sickness as a cause of poverty and as a drain on the poor rates, the problems associated with it drew surprisingly little comment in the *Report* that led to the Poor Law Amendment Act. In later years Joseph Rogers recalled that C. P. Villiers, one of the 1832–4 commissioners of enquiry and subsequently a President of the Poor Law Board, told him that 'although a variety of subjects was referred to them (the Poor Law commissioners) in connection with the administration of the Poor Laws, yet the question of sickness as a factor in the production of pauperism was not referred to them, and if it had not been for the pertinacity of Dr. G. Wallis and some others, that this important sub-

ject would have been passed over altogether'.[3] The *Report* had concluded, with little supporting evidence, that medical attendance was
'adequately supplied, and economically, if we consider only the price
and the amount of attendance'. The commissioners were, of course,
obsessed with other aspects of the problem and were wilfully, as it
might seem, determined not to confront most of the real issues. This
is particularly ironic in view of the fact that it was not to be very long
before Chadwick, one of the chief authors of the *Report* and architects
of the 1834 Act, was to build the whole public-health reform movement on the assertion that sickness resulting from insanitary en-
vironments was a major charge on Poor Law expenditure. The
specialised treatment of the sick poor in separate institutions had certainly formed a part of Chadwick's broad scheme for the categorisa-
tion and segregation of the different types of pauper, and the *Report*'s
recommendation that the able-bodied poor be denied outdoor relief
explicitly allowed for the 'indoor' treatment of the 'really impotent'.[4]
But Chadwick's broader vision was somehow suppressed in the
urgency, as both he and his fellow commissioners saw it, of solving
the problem of the able-bodied poor, and the *Report* had little to say
about sickness. Nor did the 1834 Act do much to repair the omission.
The possibility of medical relief was mentioned only in one clause
which gave the Justices of the Peace power to order medical relief to
be given in cases of sudden illness. There was no explicit provision
for regular medical relief, though this seems to have been assumed by
the inclusion of medical practitioners in an 'interpretation' clause
dealing with the appointment and qualification of 'officers'.

Through this narrow legislative chink, however, there quickly
emerged one of the more remarkable social developments of the Victorian period. Almost all the newly constituted boards of guardians
quickly appointed medical officers on a scale judged adequate to
provide for the populations of the new unions. As the union
workhouses came to be built during the later 1830s provision was
mostly made for sick wards. Within a few years so rapid and extensive
were the developments in all parts of the country that the central
authority was obliged to take cognisance of them. Following a formal
enquiry into the operation of relief in 1838,[5] a General Medical
Order of 1842 endeavoured to standardise practice and offer some
measure of guidance in this new area of relief.

Though in the field of medical relief the New Poor Law was simply
building on foundations inherited from the previous legislation, the
expansion in the late 1830s was really very remarkable. Yet it was un-

intended and unplanned, a spontaneous development in which neither legislators nor central administrators played any part. It was an accident of history which only the most pressing social need could have engineered. And if the need was there in the 1830s but had only been met skeletally before 1834, we can only assume that it was the new flexibility and enhanced financial strength of the unions compared with the feebleness of the old parish authorities that was responsible for releasing the potential. This was something for which the 1834 Act, for all its defects and lack of intent, must be given credit.

The key figure in the medical service as it was formalised after 1842 was the district medical officer. Unions were to be divided into districts which would embrace a population not too numerous for a single doctor to attend nor dispersed over an area so extensive as to involve the doctor in too much travelling or the patients in too long a walk to the doctor. By 1844 there were over 2800 district medical officers in England and Wales. Within their districts the medical officers were required to treat all the sick paupers and to supply all necessary drugs. In some cases they would also have the responsibility of attending the 'indoor' sick in the workhouse. Strictly, the medical officer treated only the paupers who were referred to him by the union's relieving officer, the salaried official whose duty it was to determine entitlement of relief. This arrangement, necessitated by the whole philosophy of the New Poor Law, proved to be a running sore in the side of its medical service. 'The power to grant medical relief', commented Richard Griffin, an experienced district medical officer and seasoned campaigner for reform, 'is almost entirely in the hands of the relieving officers, who give or withhold orders as judgment prompts or caprice dictates'.[6] Medical officers insisted, not without justice, that relieving officers were not competent to judge whether an applicant for relief genuinely needed medical treatment or not: relieving officers, on the other hand, backed by the guardians, claimed that medical officers took too little account of the many moral and economic factors involved in determining whether or not an applicant was a fit recipient of the proceeds of the poor rates. The patients, for their part, complained that it was often difficult enough in a poor state of health to make the journey to a doctor's house that could, in rural districts, be some way from their own homes, without the added burden of first visiting the relieving officer, whose office was not necessarily located near the doctor's. For the elderly and the chronic sick the bureaucratic formalities were somewhat reduced by the issue of yearly 'tickets' which authorised continuing medical relief without repeated prior visits to the relieving officer. Relieving officers were kept under pressure by the guardians to revise their list of 'tickets' frequently.

Medical officers were paid at first either on a *per capita* basis according to the number of patients treated, or else by an annual stipend. Guardians tended to find that the former method was more costly, and came to prefer the latter, particularly since, by putting the position up for tender, they were able to allow competition to beat the price down. Doctors were willing to bid competitively for the posts partly because the profession was often over-stocked and partly because Poor Law appointments were the means of establishing a wider practice of paying patients: 'they are really and fully paid by the experience they acquire which brings them credit and private patients', as one of the commission's inspectors, E. C. Tufnell, expressed it.[7] No doctor expected to live entirely on the meagre stipend and a Poor Law practice was only possible in combination with a private practice. To make matters worse, the district medical officer was commonly expected to supply drugs gratis to patients from his stipend. To counter-balance this there was usually an arrangement by which a separate fee was payable for attendance at childbirths in the workhouse, although, to keep a check on this expense, it was left to the workhouse master or matron to decide whether the medical officer's services were really necessary rather than those of the cheaper midwife.

An alternative to expenditure from the rates on the services of a district medical officer was the encouragement of the system of dispensaries which had developed since the late eighteenth century for the care of the sick poor (see p. 90). A dispensary was a kind of group clinic in which a number of doctors in a district attended at stated times for consultation and the dispensing of medicines. Costs were met by a combination of charity and the weekly subscriptions of the poor themselves. In some areas guardians chose to subscribe to existing dispensaries and even to initiate the establishment of new ones on the assumption that this would reduce the pressure on the district medical officers and hence indirectly on the rates. Dispensaries agreed to treat patients sent by the relieving officer in proportion to the amount subscribed by the guardians. In the absence of fixed surgery hours by the district medical officers, this arrangement offered certain advantages to both the patients and the doctors. It also bypassed the relieving officer and took the stigma of pauperism out of medical treatment. But dispensaries never became widely integrated into the Poor Law medical service and their contribution was never more than marginal.

The medical officer's contract sometimes included an obligation to attend the sick in the workhouse infirmary. In smaller unions or workhouses this may have involved the care of no more than a handful of patients in a single ward for each sex: in others, however, this might have consumed a considerable proportion of the medical officer's time each day. Only the larger infirmaries appointed separate physicians or surgeons. Whether the medical superintendence lay with the district medical officer or its own physician, the workhouse infirmary came quickly to provide a comprehensive service, with provision, often in separate wards, for children, midwifery cases, fever and other infectious-disease cases, the insane, the chronically ill, the disabled and the aged. Only in the larger unions, where the scale of the problem became unmanageable, were the insane poor farmed out to separate asylums which were often commercially run.

The medical services that evolved in these ways after 1834 were run on a shoe-string. It was the constant endeavour of most guardians to minimise the rates. Accordingly, out of a total expenditure of £4·5 million in 1840, medical relief accounted for a mere £150,000. Even the development of the medical services in the ensuing thirty years involved no disproportionate increase in the medical share of total expenditure: in 1871 medical relief still accounted for less than £300,000 out of a total bill of just under £8 million.

Not the least of the virtues of the New Poor Law, at least in the eyes of governments of the day, was the national coverage of the network of unions to which the central Poor Law Commission offered direct administrative access by the government and over which some degree of uniformity could, in theory, be enforced. In the absence of effective local government outside the boroughs, the guardians remained the only administrative network with a national coverage of both urban and rural areas until the creation of the county councils in 1888. Not surprisingly, the guardians became a tempting peg on which to hang further administrative functions as the needs of advancing social reform demanded, particularly when these needs could be shown to have a link with health. The first imposition of this kind was vaccination. An act of 1840 provided, through the Poor Law, a vaccination service for the entire population: district medical officers were to be the vaccinators, paid, as in midwifery cases, by a separate *per capita* fee. The association of a basic health service, essential to all classes in the nation, with the Poor Law was regretted but recognised as unavoidable. A special act of the following year expressly asserted the non-pauperising nature of the vaccination service. When vaccination was made compulsory in 1853, and particularly when this compulsion was tightened up in 1867, the work involved for the medical officers was further increased.

When, by the Nuisance Removal and Diseases Prevention Act of 1846, the guardians in all areas outside the boroughs were held to be responsible for removing 'nuisances' and controlling epidemics, their medical functions were extended from the fairly finite world of curative medicine to the unlimited sphere of preventive medicine or public health. The guardians showed themselves to be both ideologically and administratively unequal to this new burden. In the cholera epidemic of 1848–9 – the first test of their powers as epidemic authorities – they were uniformly supine and ineffective. By the time of the third outbreak of cholera in 1853–4, however, in the City of London at least under the insistent prodding of the City's Medical Officer, John Simon, the guardians reluctantly met some of their obligations for medical relief. Nuisance-removal authorities were expected to make and enforce regulations governing the deposit and removal of any 'noxious matter' that might constitute a threat to health. Since this included virtually the whole field of drainage, sewage disposal and refuse collection, it is hardly surprising that, in the words of Dr H. W. Rumsey, one of the most active of the Poor Law medical reformers, 'Boards of guardians have not shown themselves the most hearty promoters of sanitary improvements',[8] or, in the stronger language of Simon at a meeting of the Privy Council in 1865, the guardians in their capacity of nuisance authorities had generally been guilty of 'an absolutely inexcusable neglect of duty'.[9] Consequently the Nuisance Removal Act of 1855 relieved the guardians of these duties by passing them on to the vestries. But by 1860 the need to find some less dormant and more professionally staffed authorities competent, even if unwilling, to take on public-health responsibilities in rural areas forced Parliament to restore these duties to the rural guardians. When the whole sanitary system was reviewed by the 1869 Royal Sanitary Commission, the logic of involving the rural guardians in the public-health system was unanswerable: '1. They are representative; 2. They exist everywhere;

3. They have a complete organisation in their offices, and a staff of executive officers . . . ; 4. Through their Medical Officers they possess a knowledge of the state of disease in the unions . . . ; 5. . . . Communications on sanitary questions are continually passing between the Poor Law and Sanitary Authorities . . . ; 6. Within limits . . . the same staff may render assistance in both services.'[10] Thus, in spite of the fact that the Royal Sanitary Commission had itself commented that 'Boards of guardians . . . seldom seem aware that the removal of nuisances in country places is entrusted to them',[11] the 1872 Public Health Act redesignated the rural guardians as sanitary authorities with a wide range of public-health duties and powers.

The public-health arena demonstrated that, for all the temptation the guardians offered to legislators unwilling to create yet more centralised bureaucracies, there were limits to their willingness and capabilities. A closer look at their existing medical services in the 1850s and 1860s, moreover, would have shown that, in fact, they had already bitten off a great deal more than they could chew even before Parliament began to push them unwillingly into the wider field of public health. The truth of the matter was that a health service of the degree of comprehensiveness attempted after 1834 was simply not compatible either with the underlying ideology of the New Poor Law or with the willingness, let alone capacity, of the ratepayers to finance it. Finance and ideology, in other words, stood between the Poor Law medical service and efficiency. The miracle is that somehow the hamstrung service limped along until the slow but persistent sniping of the reformers prodded public opinion sufficiently to improve conditions within the service and to provide the bare minimum of adequate finance. But these conditions were not obtained until the late 1860s and early 1870s.

The failure of the medical service was not merely, as Chadwick (as ever using two words where one would do) wrote in 1866, because 'the evil conditions which are manifest as prevalent now, were on examination condemned at the time of our inquiry in 1834; and that such administration has hitherto been continued in contravention of the provisions of the Poor Law Amendment Act'.[12] There was also a fundamental gap between the needs of the poor and the willingness of the ratepayers. The key, it was said earlier, to the post-1834 Poor Law medical service was the district medical officer: yet his position and conditions of work were so profoundly unsatisfactory that it is astonishing that the service did not collapse as quickly as it had been expanded. The 2825 district medical officers of 1844 received in payment a total of £151,442 in salaries and fees.[13] Given the derisory rates of pay it was hardly to be expected that the better-qualified medical men would seek to enter the service, but if public money was to be spent on purchasing medical skill for the poor, the guardians would be right to insist on some evidence of that skill in the shape of recognised qualifications. This requirement, as we have seen, was built into the 1834 Act, and by the time of the 1842 General Medical Order an attempt was made by the Commission, under pressure from the medical profession, to ensure that guardians appointed only doctors possessing at least two qualifications, one of which should be from one of the Colleges of Physicians or Surgeons, while the other might be from a university or the Society of Apothecaries.

But practice did not invariably follow precept. On the one hand, experienced practitioners, anxious for reasons connected with practice-building to take on Poor Law contracts, too often tended to delegate the actual work to poorly paid and inadequately qualified assistants. On the other hand, the guardians, searching always for ways of reducing expenditure, were too often unwilling to offer a stipend sufficient to attract the full-time services of a well-qualified doctor. While the establishment of the General Medical Register in 1858 went some way towards simplifying the confusion over medical qualifications, and rates of stipend improved slowly, decade by decade, the professional position of the district medical officer remained unsatisfactory throughout the nineteenth century.

The parsimony of the guardians further prejudiced the efficient operation of the service in their allocation of districts. The 1842 General Medical Order laid down a maximum population of 15,000 in a district with a single medical officer. Not all people in a given population were potential patients for the district medical officer, of course, since the middle and upper classes normally made use of private practice, while many of the working classes, particularly the better paid, provided for medical care through friendly societies or 'clubs'. But in some areas at least one-half of the population may have come within the orbit of the district medical officer, so that in districts with maximum populations the medical officer was likely to be seriously stretched. Whether or not these huge numbers might be served satisfactorily depended to some extent on the geographical dispersion of the practice. Recognising this, the 1842 Order laid down a further maximum of 15,000 acres as the limit of a district to be served by a medical officer. Both these limits, however, conflicted with the guardians' need for economy, and in practice they were often exceeded. Griffin reported in 1861 that there were no less than 583 districts with more than 15,000 acres, some of an extent between 80,000–100,000 acres; and 120 districts with populations in excess of 15,000, some with up to 40,000.[14] Given the autonomy of the guardians, only persistent pressure from the profession and the Poor Law Board would have reduced the size of districts to a point of adequacy over the whole country.

If the 'outdoor' sick got less than a proper share of the medical officer's attention, the 'indoor' sick were cared for in conditions that were mostly a standing reproach to a nation which thought of itself as civilised. Workhouse infirmaries were a double charge on the ratepayers in so far as they called for both capital and current expenditure. If there was a reluctance on the part of the guardians to provide sufficiently for the day-to-day medical care of the indoor sick, there was an additional hostility to capital expenditure on buildings and equipment. Wherever possible, therefore, old buildings were utilised for workhouse infirmaries, and when new building was unavoidable, specifications were pared to the absolute minimum. Beds were crowded together and patients were sometimes put two or three to a bed. 'Public opinion', wrote Dr Ernest Hart in 1866, 'will not tolerate that the sick convict shall have less than 1,000 cubic feet of air, and the sick soldier 1,200, while the sick pauper is limited to from 350 up to 500 feet of air'.[15]

Conditions in the wards matched this degree of parsimony. 'The same rough beds . . .', wrote Frances Cobbe of workhouse infirmaries in 1861, 'which are allotted to the rude able-bodied paupers, are equally given to the poor, emaciated, bed-ridden patient whose frame is probably sore all over, and whose aching head must remain, for want of pillows, in a nearly horizontal position for months together. Hardly in any workhouse is there a chair on which the sufferers from asthma or dropsy, or those fading away slowly in decline, could relieve themselves by sitting for a few hours, instead of on the edges of their beds, gasping and fainting from weariness.'[16] She added that there were no washing utensils, no towels, and that even in new rural workhouses the walls and floor were of bare stone while the windows were without shutters and curtains. In Paddington workhouse infirmary in 1866 there was one towel to every 24 to 31 patients. In the Strand workhouse the supply of soap was limited since 'it might readily be wasted'. Urban workhouse infirmaries were almost always situated in the poorer parts of towns and subject, therefore, to all the health dangers of those districts – lack of light and ventilation, and the stink and infection arising from ill-kept privies, slaughter-houses, unregulated industrial processes and mountains of uncollected refuse. Joseph Rogers, one of the hardiest fighters for Poor Law medical reform, described conditions in the Strand union workhouse infirmary of which he was medical officer: 'The workhouse of which the infirmary was a part found remunerative employment for its able-bodied paupers beating carpets. . . . This work was done in a yard immediately outside the ward's only window so that constant rising dust obliged them to keep the windows permanently closed. Persistent protests from the medical officer failed to persuade the workhouse master either to give up this work or find somewhere else to pursue it.'[17] Maternity wards were no better. Dr Rogers found the 'nursery' ward a 'wretchedly damp and miserable room, nearly always over-crowded with young mothers and their infant children. That death relieved these young women of their illegitimate offspring was only what was to be expected, and that frequently the mothers followed in the same direction was only too true. I used to dread to go into this ward, it was so depressing. Scores and scores of distinctly preventable deaths of both mothers and children took place during my continuance in office through their being located in this horrible den.'[18]

Given an able and energetic nursing force, some of these terrible conditions could perhaps have been overcome: but the greatest handicap under which the Poor Law infirmaries laboured in their early decades was a complete absence of trained nurses. It was assumed from the start that the infirmaries could be tolerably served by the able-bodied women paupers. Their chief merit was, of course, that they required no payment. They were unlikely from their situation to be among the cleaner, most patient and dedicated members of society. 'Of the able-bodied women . . . in the workhouse', wrote Louisa Twining in 1866 with all the moral overtones without which middle-class comment on the working classes was almost impossible at that time, 'it is sufficient to say that they are the persons now employed as nurses; the young and physically efficient ones must have morally defective characters for it is well known that hardly any others resort to these institutions – and to train the elderly women for this occupation would surely be a hopeless task.'[19] Though the beginnings of the professional training of hospital nurses dates from this period, workhouse infirmaries were at the bottom of the scale and it was inevitable that they would be the last to benefit from the new type of nurse when she emerged.

It is easy in retrospect to regard all this parsimony and inhumanity as part and parcel of the general callousness of the age or of the indifference of the wealthy towards the poor. However, the conditions of the Poor Law medical service which appear excessively austere to a later generation were the product of an ambivalence which pervaded the whole service from its beginnings. So far as the able-bodied poor were concerned, the New Poor Law had no difficulty in determining its theoretical principles. Its aim was to cure what the ruling classes in 1834 saw as the moral evils of 'dependence' on parochial relief by a system of deterrence. Deterrence was to be provided by the 'workhouse test' in which the applicant's real destitution would be judged by his willingness to abandon everything and accept relief inside the workhouse. The effectiveness of this test of destitution was ensured by requiring that the condition inside the workhouse were 'less-eligible' than those of the lowest-paid worker outside. These simple principles were, however, inoperable because they did not correspond to the realities of nineteenth-century poverty. The standards of feeding and comfort that could be provided in some of the lower-paid occupations, even by those in regular work, were so low that not even the guardians in pursuit of 'less-eligibility' could decently offer less to paupers. In practice, the pauper's condition was often necessarily more 'eligible' than that of the lowest-paid worker outside the workhouse.

The correct principles for dealing with the sick were even more difficult to determine. The New Poor Law never denied that it had an obligation to treat the destitute sick, though it demurred when it came to the sick poor – a distinction sufficiently fine as to be extremely difficult to draw in practice. Ideally, the Poor Law should be so poised that the merely 'poor' would be encouraged to be 'independent'. As the Rev. E. J. Howman, a Norfolk guardian, expressed it: 'I think the first object is to induce people to render themselves independent, and the narrower you can fairly draw the limit of medical relief, the sooner you will make them independent.'[20] 'Independence' in regard to sickness meant membership of a sick club which, through the payment of weekly subscriptions, provided for medical attention and hospitalisation in a voluntary hospital. The destitute that remained would then be cared for. This ideal, however, was founded on a failure to appreciate the facts of life for much of the working class during the nineteenth century. Sickness rates were far higher among the poor than in the middle class. Sick clubs predominantly catered for the subscriber – the wage-earner – and not for his family; and a majority of wage-earners could never, for one reason or another, become subscribers to a sick club. Most clubs were local, and migration, necessarily high in a period of rapid economic growth, ruled out membership for many even of those who could afford it. In Liverpool, Wolverhampton and Gloucester in the 1840s, club members amounted therefore only to about one in twelve of the population, and in Bath, Cheltenham, Shrewsbury and Worcester they were only about one in thirty.[21] And there remained, under the most favourable circumstances, a large section of society whose incomes were so low or so irregular that any kind of regular provision for sickness through thrift was totally out of the question.

The ideal, then, was unattainable: some compromise was unavoidable. If an effective destitution test would exclude many of the sick poor that the guardians found themselves, in practice, unable to turn away, how should a line be drawn? It could only be a matter of judgement in individual unions and individual cases. In practice this involved some form of 'less-eligibility'. There had, of course, been nothing in either the *Report* or the 1834 Act to suggest that 'less-eligibility' should apply to the sick pauper. But as early as 1841 the Poor Law Commission had supported its refusal to provide more fully for medical services with the argument that, if it did, 'This superiority of the condition of the paupers over that of the independent labourers as regards medical aid will . . . encourage a resort to the poor-rates for medical relief . . . and will thus tempt the industrious labourer into pauperism.'[22] The Webbs observed that 'although the Principle of Less Eligibility had . . . in the 1834 Report been explicitly applied only to the able-bodied, we note a constant tendency to think of it as applicable to all recipients of relief. The "independent labourer" of the lowest grade did not, at that date, usually obtain for himself or his family, either efficient medical treatment or skilled nursing; and the consciousness of this fact was always standing in the way of any attempt to get the guardians to provide for the inmates of the workhouse or for the still larger number of those maintained on Outdoor Relief, either the one or the other.'[23]

So the instinct of guardians generally was to sail as close to 'less-eligibility' as their strained humanity permitted them. Workhouse infirmaries must not, therefore, compete at the level of service and amenities with the voluntary hospitals: when the persistence of the reformers looked like beginning to bear fruit in more lavish Poor Law hospitals in 1866, Dr Ernest Hart was obliged to comment that 'the schemes of erecting the new infirmaries on a large scale has excited fears which I regard as exaggerated, if not entirely chimerical, that these new institutions will drain the voluntary hospitals of patients, and by supplying state institutions of a satisfactory kind will decrease the principal incentives to charitable contributions by benevolent persons'.[24] Similarly, district medical officers must be relatively difficult of access, protected by the stony barrier of the relieving officer, and their innate generosity with drugs and 'extras' (nutritious food) must be strictly curbed. In the last resort, the Poor Law always retained a weapon which was effective without reducing the quality of the service – the stigma of pauperism. Everyone accepting relief of any kind, including medical relief, automatically became a pauper for the duration of the treatment, and pauperism, as we have seen, involved both deprivation and stigma. It acted as an additional deterrent. Voters were known to have refused to allow members of their families to apply for medical relief for fear of being struck off the register as paupers.

From the start, then, the Poor Law medical service was torn by conflicting pressures. The guardians, for the most part with the articulate middle and upper classes behind them and in general enjoying either the tacit or overt support of the Commission and Board, sought consciously to restrain development, to starve the service of resources, and to stress the need for 'deterrence'. These tendencies were resisted, however, by a small group of reformers drawn at first almost exclusively from the ranks of the Poor Law doctors. Armed with a detailed familiarity of the operations and philosophy of the service and supported by a resilient humanity and almost unbelievable persistence, they struggled skilfully and unceasingly in the face of persecution, obstruction and immense hostility for improvement of the system.

At first the Poor Law medical officers worked through their existing medical associations. Agitation through the Provincial Medical and Surgical Association and the first British Medical Association contributed towards the inclusion of some valuable provisions in the first Medical Orders of the Poor Law Commission in 1842 and 1847. The Provincial Association, which, in its relations with the government, represented local Medical Officers of Health as well as the Poor Law doctors, operated mainly through its Poor Law Committee until 1845 when it spawned off the Convention of Poor Law Medical Officers which then took on the particular functions of representing the interests of the Poor Law medical officers. The Convention, however, enjoyed only limited success, and by the 1850s had ceased to be an effective pressure group. The cudgels were taken up again in the mid-1850s by a Poor Law Medical Relief Association formed largely through the exertions of Dr Richard Griffin, Medical Officer to the Weymouth Union. In its reconstituted form as the Poor Law Medical Officers' Association, still under the leadership of Griffin, this body was very active throughout the 1860s. Meanwhile, under a threat of injurious measures from the Poor Law Board, Dr Joseph Rogers hastily formed an Association of Metropolitan Workhouse Medical Officers in 1866 which after two years merged with its parent body, the Poor Law Medical Officers' Association. The rather complex history of bodies formally representing the Poor Law medical officers is important since they were a major influence on the legislative development of the medical service. By 1869, when, after Griffin's death, Rogers had succeeded as President, the Poor Law Medical Officers' Association had become a powerful body boasting no less than 89 M.P.s pledged to support it.

The medical officers' campaign for reform was aided by the British Medical Association, which had grown out of the Provincial Medical and Surgical Association in 1856, by other non-medical bodies such as the Workhouse Visiting Society, by influential lay individuals like Florence Nightingale, Louisa Twining and Edwin Chadwick, and, above all, by the medical press. The radical *Lancet*, in particular, was a vigorous and tireless supporter of the Poor Law medical reform movement, making a major contribution in 1865–6 when it appointed its own private 'commission' consisting of three well-known doctors to investigate and report on the state of workhouse infirmaries. The agitation was carried on through the conventional channels of the nineteenth century – petitions and deputations to Parliament and the President of the Poor Law Board, letters to the press, articles in the weeklies and quarterlies and, above all, memoranda and evidence to the select committees that sat endlessly on one aspect or another of poor relief.

What did the reform movement achieve? This is very difficult to assess since there were other influences also at work. Change there certainly was, and the medical service was significantly different in the 1870s from what it had been in the 1830s. The reformers needed to attack on three fronts: there was a perpetual guerrilla warfare at union level as individual medical officers struggled to drag their mostly unyielding guardians into the nineteenth century; most efforts to secure improvement at national level had to be directed to the Poor Law Commission and Board, which possessed considerable delegated power though frequently protesting that they lacked the legislative authority to coerce boards of guardians in some important areas; and, in the last resort, only Parliament could ultimately prod the dinosaur of the Poor Law into movement. Pressure on the first of these at local level mostly achieved very little except, as in the case of Dr Rogers at the Strand Union, the dismissal on trumped-up charges of the offending would-be reformer. Under adverse publicity some minor details might be adjusted, but, bolstered by an impregnable ideology and the knowledge that all reform was likely anyway to add to the burden of the rates, the guardians contrived in the main to re-main insensitive and immovable. The central authority, on the other hand, particularly after the replacement in 1847 of the Commission by the Board with a President accessible in Parliament, was bound to be a little more responsive to the pressure groups. Its main instru-ment was the Order – a form of delegated legislation. But, in the event, the two main Orders affecting the operation of the medical service before the late 1860s – the General Medical Order of 1842 and the General Consolidated Order of 1847 – conceded very little to the pressure of the reformers. In the early days the medical officers had concentrated their principal efforts on methods of appointment and payment of district medical officers, yet the 1842 Order made no provision for standardisation in these respects, leaving both in the hands of the individual boards of guardians. Cornewall Lewis, one of the commissioners, had pointed out to the Select Committee of 1844 that though an early Committee of 1838 had recommended the abolition of tendering and the limitation of the size of districts, Parliament had chosen not to act in the matter. The Commission, he said, had passed these recommendations on to boards, though it was true that most boards ignored them. In the Maidenhead Union, for example, the guardians had replied that they had 'no desire to make any alteration'.[25] The General Consolidated Order of 1847, though it regulated comprehensively all aspects of medical relief and formed the basis of the service for the next twenty-five years, was merely a codification of existing practice and changed little. Some minor gains were registered through this channel, however. In the early 1860s Simon was able to bring some medical pressure from the Privy Council to bear on the Poor Law Board and persuade it to sharpen up its control of the public vaccination procedure. Under pressure in 1865, the Board at last appointed a medical inspector to supplement the lay inspectorate that had previously acted in all enquiries into the operation of all aspects of poor relief. The appointee, Dr Edward Smith, was immediately ordered to conduct the Board's enquiry into workhouse infirmaries in answer to the revelations of the *Lancet*'s private 'commission'.

The government, for its part, responded to the pressure of the reformers with the traditional delaying tactics of select committees. At intervals of approximately ten years, committees heard evidence from representatives of the medical associations and other pressure groups. Guardians and the Board were also allowed to express their satisfaction with the way things were. The final recommendations were seldom radical and rarely led to legislation. After three years of deliberation, for example, the Select Committee of 1861–4 decided that 'there are no sufficient grounds for materially interfering with the present system of medical relief'.[26] As a result there were no major legislative changes before the late 1860s.

Nursing was one of the most intractable of the problems on which the reformers focused their attention. For improvement to take place, not only had the guardians to overcome their reluctance to pay for services that had hitherto been freely available, but institutions for the training of nurses had to be established: indeed, a whole new concept of nursing training had to be accepted. The work of Florence Nightingale in the 1860s was crucial to this latter development, and though the benefits of her labours were slow to filter down to the workhouse infirmaries, the door was thereby opened to the possibility of improvement. A start was made in 1864 when William Rathbone, an enlightened philanthropist, overcame the hostility of the Liverpool guardians by offering to put a team of trained nurses into their infirmary for three years at his own expense. Under the inspired guidance of Agnes Jones, one of the unsung heroines of the Victorian age, whose brief career was terminated by typhus contracted in the workhouse ward, these nurses demonstrated the enormous advantages to all of clean and efficient wards. At the end of the three years the guardians accepted the cost of retaining the trained nurses. So long as the supply of trained nurses remained small, however, pauper nurses remained predominant in workhouse infirmaries, and it was not until the 1870s that trained nurses really began to take over in the Poor Law hospitals.

In the mid-1860s, after thirty years of campaigning that had until then produced only the most trifling of gains, the reform movement seemed to gather momentum. It is not easy to explain why the atmosphere should have changed at this point in time. Certainly, the anti-centralisation campaign that had so effectively hindered social reform at the national level in the decade after 1848, destroying the central Board of Health in the process, lost its fire and was no longer such a barrier by the 1860s. The Webbs believed that 'a growing public alarm as to infectious disease' may have contributed, though they do not mention the fourth cholera epidemic of 1866–7 in this context. There may have been some cumulative impact of the constant revelations of deficiencies and inhumanities ceaselessly published by the reformers. The new status of the medical profession after the act of 1858 may have proved to be the strength behind the vigour with which the medical officers' organisations went to work, while the foundation of the National Association for the Promotion of Social Science in 1857 provided a new annual forum that brought amateur social scientists and doctors into contact with politicians and influential public figures. The failure of the government to respond in any effective way to the *Report* of the Select Committee that had been gathering evidence for three years between 1861 and 1864 added fuel to the fires, and the widely reported deaths of two sick paupers in London workhouse infirmaries in circumstances that indicated culpable neglect may have proved to be the final spur.

Whatever the impulse, every propaganda weapon in the reformers' armoury was trained on parliament and government from 1865. The *Lancet* announced its 'commission' to enquire into workhouse infirmaries; the Poor Law Medical Officers' Association petitioned the President of the Poor Law Board; a newly formed Association for the Improvement of Workhouse Infirmaries, bringing some of the leading medical reformers together, sent a deputation to the Board's President; Hart, one of the three *Lancet* 'commissioners', placed articles in the *Fortnightly Review*, and Chadwick did likewise in *Fraser's Magazine*; and Florence Nightingale dispatched a memorandum to the Select Committee on Metropolitan Local Government. The immediate focus of attention was the workhouse infirmaries of the metropolis. C. P. Villiers, the President of the Poor Law Board in Russell's Liberal government of 1865–6, who, as Chairman of the Select Committee of 1861–4, had listened to three years of criticism, showed signs of responding to the pressure, but found himself out of office before he could draft legislation. It was left to Gathorne Hardy in the new Derby Conservative government to take the credit for action. Though President of the Poor Law Board, he had the courage to repudiate its existing philosophy. 'The evils complained of', he said (in the House of Commons), 'have arisen from the workhouse management, which must, to a great extent, be of a deterrent character, having been applied to the sick, who are not proper objects for such a system'. The result of all this pressure was an act of 1867 variously known as the Metropolitan Poor Law Amendment Act, the Metropolitan Poor Law Act, or the Metropolitan Asylums Act. This Act was important because it began the process of taking the hospitals out of the workhouses, because it at last eroded the administrative structure that had so effectively withstood the opposition of the reformers since 1834, and because it paved the way for further development in the provinces. It required the Poor Law Board to amalgamate the medical services of all the metropolitan unions into a single unit or into a small number of large units. In the event a combination of these alternatives was chosen. The Metropolitan Asylums Board became the unified hospital authority for the treatment of typhus, smallpox and insanity for the whole of Greater London. It was to be financed by a Common Poor Fund into which all member unions would contribute according to their rateable values, thus ensuring that the wealthier unions with low demands on the workhouse infirmaries would help out the poorer unions which tended to make much heavier demands on the service. For all other forms of medical treatment, the London unions were to be grouped into 'sick asylum districts' in which the sick poor were to be treated in hospitals that were to be separated from the workhouses. Finally, the hospital system was to be supplemented by a network of dispensaries for out-patients.

Not all the provisions of this sweeping Act were realised. The dispensaries mostly fell by the wayside; but the new Metropolitan Board and asylum districts got to work reorganising and building the new hospitals necessary to give effective implementation to the Act, though the discovery of how expensive a business this was quickly led to modifications to the initial ambitious plans. In the following year a parallel Act encouraged provincial guardians to create separate hospitals, though since there was no provision for the merging of unions outside London there was no Common Poor Fund to make them financially attractive.

The 1867 Act was important, above all, because it was 'the first explicit acknowledgement that it was the duty of the state to provide hospitals for the poor'.[27] It did not, of course, immediately transform the Poor Law hospitals into palaces: nursing personnel could not change overnight, and the hospitals were still operated, technically as detached workhouses, by the Poor Law authorities. But the hospitals, in London at least, were separated from the workhouses and had a chance to develop in their own way free from the inhibiting pettiness and cheese-paring of the workhouse masters. The Poor Law Board was at considerable pains to insist to guardians that there had been a change of policy and that 'less-eligibility' was no longer to apply to the sick poor. Under the impulse of this direction from the centre a new style of hospital developed: able-bodied pauper women were replaced in the wards by trained nurses; buildings and equipment evolved to meet the changing needs of advancing standards and medical skill; and consultants and resident medical officers were appointed. With the advantage of a central, indirectly financed Board, the metropolis led the way in these developments. Provincial unions were much slower to implement the separation of hospitals from workhouses and much still remained to be done when the second great enquiry into the state of the Poor Laws got under way in 1905. Gradually, and starting with the specialist hospitals of the Metropolitan Asylums Board, the requirement of destitution was eased, so that hospitals began to lose the stigma of pauperism and so became more attractive to the poor. The phrase 'state medicine' had already been used by the medical reformers in respect of the Poor Law medical service before 1867: after the Act of that year the term 'state hospitals' began to be substituted quite deliberately for the separated workhouse infirmaries. It took longer to destroy the last vestiges of 'less-eligibility', however. Not until 1885 did the Medical Relief (Disqualification Removal) Act allow the recipient of medical relief to retain his or her right to vote.

The 1867 Act had not, of course, touched the conditions under which the district medical officers administered 'outdoor' medical relief. This aspect of the medical service continued unchanged, hardening into an even more changeless routine when the Poor Law administrators from the Board took over the effective control of the new Local Government Board in 1871. Official policy in this area, indeed, tended to become even less enlightened after 1867, in marked contrast to the enthusiasm for the new hospitals. Even late in the nineteenth century, a German observer commented that 'in many districts, especially in the country, the medical treatment is quite inadequate; many of the medical officers being deficient in the scientific knowledge undoubtedly required'.[28]

If the Acts of 1867 and 1868 opened new doors to better hospitals, they also, more importantly, broke through the ideological casing that had shielded the guardians throughout the early Victorian period. By divorcing the hospitals from the workhouses they took an important branch of medical relief out of the immediate ambience of pauperism. Making the infirmaries no longer repellent to the working classes went hand in hand with regenerating them physically and medically. These Acts could not transform the infirmaries overnight, of course, but they made it possible, ideologically as well as financially, for the transformation to begin in a way that would have been quite impossible previously. And by the late 1860s the change was long overdue. The 1834 Act had been directed almost entirely towards the problem of the able-bodied poor, but in the ensuing thirty years the compulsion of sheer necessity had transmuted practice imperceptibly until, by the 1860s, the workhouses were being used for purposes quite other than those for which they were designed. Instead of a population of able-bodied paupers sitting out a trade depression or summoning up the resolution to migrate in search of work, as the commissioners of 1832–4 had intended, they housed instead a mass of the sick and aged, orphans, the insane and the fever-ridden. They had, willy-nilly, become hospitals – general hospitals, fever hospitals, paediatric, geriatric and mental hospitals. And in becoming hospitals their relevance to the Poor Law was diminished if not destroyed. The guardians, on the whole, acting in the spirit of 1834, had striven unavailingly to resist the change. The Board, indifferent, hardly cared one way or the other. Only Parliament, in the end, recognised the metamorphosis, decreed that it was acceptable, and made provision, albeit cautiously and inadequately, for the emergence of 'state hospitals' freed from the shackles of the workhouses. In doing so it set the Poor Law medical service on the road that was to lead, hesitatingly but inevitably, to Bevan's National Health Service of the 1940s.

3. Pauper Education

FRANCIS DUKE

'Well! You have come here to be educated and taught a useful
trade . . .'
'So you'll begin to pick oakum tomorrow morning at six o'clock.'
Oliver Twist

To provide an appropriate if rudimentary education for pauper
children was a major concern of the Poor Law throughout the
nineteenth century. Pauperism was held to be an hereditary disease,
endemic among a substantial section of the labouring class. A sound
basic education, preparing them for their future station in life, was
the most effective way of breaking this chain of hereditary pauperism,
at least among the children resident in workhouses. The much larger
number of pauper children whose families received relief outside the
workhouse were more difficult to accommodate and tended in practice to be left out of serious account. For orphaned and deserted
children who would spend their entire childhood in a Poor Law institution education needed to encompass all aspects of a child's
upbringing. A curriculum which centred upon oakum picking, the
economically worthless task-work imposed on the adults, might in-
culcate habits of industry and docility, useful virtues for a well-
conducted working class, but in all other respects it was defective. It
provided no kind of skill or useful information, and it was considered by Poor Law reformers to be bad moral and social training,
for it made work seem distasteful and punitive, rather than useful
and satisfying. To teach genuine industrial skills, diligent habits and
an appreciation of the circumstances and duties of their future social
role was a very different matter, to which much attention was devoted
by the Poor Law authorities after 1834.

The Poor Law *Report* of 1834 made little direct reference to
education, although the final paragraph stressed its importance in

For Notes to Chapter 3, see pp. 208–9; for Bibliography, see pp. 198–9.

general terms. The detailed evidence appended to the *Report* is much more informative. Assistant commissioners reporting from a number of localities emphasised the inadequacy, or total absence, of provision in many parishes. A few large parishes, notably Leeds, Birmingham and a number in London, possessed schools of industry, which, while instructing children in the 'three Rs', devoted most attention to teaching them a trade. More commonly, parish workhouses contained only a handful of children. In most cases they appear either to have received nominal instruction from an adult pauper, or to have been sent out to a local day school. To judge from the reports of the assistant commissioners, neither alternative had much to recommend it. In general there was a lack of proper supervision; at a local school the pauper children were likely at best to be neglected in favour of more rewarding and remunerative pupils; in the workhouse any benefits were likely to be outweighed by the circumstances of their education. The majority of parishes did not do even this much, for they possessed no workhouse and made no regular provision at all for the education of pauper children, although a number of orphans must have been sent to 'child farms' or foundling hospitals. At the earliest suitable age most of these orphaned children would be apprenticed to whichever employer demanded the lowest premium to take them off the hands of the parish. One major objective after 1834 was to destroy the parish apprenticeship system, by moulding the children into valuable employees who could hold their own in a genuinely free labour market.

Shortly after its formation the Poor Law Commission laid down regulations which in the circumstances were ambitious, though they were in keeping with the spirit of the Poor Law report. Each union was to set up a properly constituted school, with a salaried schoolmaster and schoolmistress. They must provide a minimum of three hours schooling each day in the 'three Rs' and the principles of religion. The children were also to receive additional, but undefined, industrial training to 'fit them for service, and train them to habits of usefulness, industry and virtue'.[1] The commissioners probably assumed that the school would be established on a self-contained site, to conform with the segregation of different categories of paupers recommended in the 1834 report. This of itself was expected to ensure a substantial improvement in the provision of schooling. Instead the general workhouse was adopted almost universally during the 1830s. It was cheaper and easier to administer, and the commissioners appear to have done nothing to discourage this development. Nearly all the 40,000 or 50,000 children in Poor Law institutions were thus educated in a wholly unsuitable environment. They could hardly be trained to virtuous habits in a workhouse geared to a regime of deterrence. They suffered the stigma of pauperism and felt demoralised. Contact with adult paupers was held to be morally harmful in itself, and likely to encourage habits of pauperism in the children. Any nominal industrial training was likely to be no more than a diluted version of the task work imposed on the adults.

Few workhouse schools could muster more than fifty pupils, in the age range of from 3 to 13 years or more. Few unions felt it necessary to seek exceptionally talented teachers for this handful of pauper children. Some were suspected of appointing very undistinguished teachers at very low salaries merely to keep them from pauperism, thus effecting a double saving to the ratepayers. The commissioners possessed no yard-stick for assessing the qualifications of teachers, but they argued in general that higher salaries for better qualified teachers would ultimately be justified by the reduction in future pauperism. Elective bodies rarely take so long a view, particularly where their constituents foot the bill.

By 1838 the Poor Law Commission had apparently found a way round these problems in a scheme enthusiastically endorsed by their Secretary, Edwin Chadwick, but devised principally by two assistant commissioners, James Kay (later and better known as Kay-Shuttleworth) and E. C. Tuffnell. Kay-Shuttleworth was to achieve greater eminence as secretary of the Committee of Council on Education from 1839 to 1849. Tufnell was one of the dissident allies of Chadwick among the assistant commissioners, until his transfer in 1846 to the newly established inspectorate of Poor Law schools. Kay and Tufnell realised that the amalgamation of parishes into Poor Law unions had not been enough to provide efficient schools in most cases. Groups of unions should therefore in turn amalgamate into school districts, to produce the schools of perhaps 500 pupils which they considered to be the most suitable in size. These district schools would be entirely separated from the main workhouse. Competent teachers could be appointed and a proper system of industrial training developed. The schools could be divided into viable classes, which was impossible in the average workhouse school. The commissioners hoped that all this could be achieved without any additional expense. Unfortunately they lacked statutory powers to create the new authorities which would be needed to run district schools.

In seeking the necessary powers the Poor Law Commission had the assistance of a working model, in which the administrative idea could be translated into an educational community. This was the contract school at Norwood used by a number of Poor Law authorities in London, and holding up to 1000 pupils. Although privately owned, Norwood was subsidised by the Commission, to enable it to recruit trained teachers from Scotland, and to supply books, materials and furnishings. Norwood became a school of method, in which improved techniques, particularly of industrial and moral training, could be developed. In this respect Norwood enjoyed a considerable success. A number of the larger schools in London adopted its system of industrial training. A few teachers from rural workhouse schools were sent there to imbibe its spirit. Its most spectacular imitators were the Poor Law schools of industry built by the Manchester and Liverpool authorities in the early 1840s at Swinton and Kirkdale respectively.

Norwood also had a significant impact on the wider development of elementary education in Britain. For a time it worked in close co-operation with the training college set up privately at Battersea in 1840 by Kay-Shuttleworth and Tufnell, primarily to train men to teach in district schools. It supplied Battersea with candidate-teachers who had already spent a number of years in preliminary teacher-training while still pupils at Norwood. This was the origin of the pupil-teacher system which was to become the main source of supply of elementary teachers for the rest of the century. But it was difficult to sustain Battersea's peculiar status until the district schools existed to employ its graduates. In 1843 Battersea was handed over to the National Society, the body which provided and assisted the Church of England's voluntary schools. Thereafter the college severed its special links with the Poor Law system.

The district school scheme suffered further setbacks in the 1840s. It had appeared at a politically unfortunate moment. The anti-Poor Law movement was only one of the burdens of the dying Whig government, and its Tory successor in 1841 was in no hurry to leap into the cauldron by provocatively indulging the Poor Law Commission's lust for further powers. When finally, under the Poor Law

Amendment act of 1844, the commissioners were enabled to establish school districts, the new powers were so circumscribed as to be inoperable.

No district was to exceed fifteen miles in over-all diameter. This effectively limited the new powers to the London area and a few other centres of population, since the combination of even two rural unions would in many cases exceed these dimensions. The commissioners have been blamed unjustly by most authorities for failing to press for effective powers with sufficient vigour, partly from, perhaps, undue sensitivity to the political climate, partly because hostility to their dissident Secretary, Chadwick, prejudiced them against any scheme with which he was associated.[2] However, their aim was to introduce district schools by successive stages, beginning in the major urban centres where opposition was likely to be slight. The success of this first stage, which was not prejudiced by the limit on size imposed in 1844, would be the most effective means of disarming criticism and would allow the subsequent extension of district schools.

When the assistant commissioner for the metropolitan area, Richard Hall, attempted to organise school districts in 1845 he confronted instead another insurmountable obstacle. The cost of building a district school was restricted to 20 per cent of the average annual poor relief expenditure of the unions involved. This proved quite unrealistic.[3] After the South Metropolitan school district was formed in 1849 it required six years, a legislative amendment raising the limit to 33 per cent, the addition of an extra union simply to swell the total sum available, and some considerable pruning of the architect's plans before a school could be built within the permitted expenditure. But if anyone is to be blamed for this miscalculation it must be, not the Poor Law Commission, but rather Kay-Shuttleworth and Tufnell, who too easily convinced themselves that district schools could be set up very cheaply by modifying former parish workhouses.

The easier political and economic climate which accompanied the fall of the Poor Law Commission in 1847 enabled its successor, the Poor Law Board, to secure the District Schools Act of 1848. The limits on size and cost were waived, provided the written consent of a majority of the board of guardians of each participating union was obtained. In the following months the first six school districts, comprising 20 unions, were formed, five under the terms of the new measure (the exception being the South Metropolitan district school). By 1849, however, the district school movement had lost some of its momentum, and only three more school districts were successfully established later in the century.

The formation of these six schools in 1849 in fact represents the abandonment of any systematic plan to establish a general and uniform pattern of district schools. Three of the six were formed in London, including Norwood, which was transformed into the Central London District School. Yet these three might well have impeded the future prospects of a more comprehensive pattern in London, in which the various unions might need to have been grouped rather differently. The other three schools each held only some 100 pupils. They were far too small to benefit from many of the advantages attributed to the district schools of 500 pupils originally envisaged. They resembled this pattern, and the three London schools, in little but name.

It became increasingly clear during the period when these six schools were taking shape that the advocates of district schools had overlooked some serious practical problems. That these problems had been overlooked or ignored is very much in character with the mood of Benthamite fervour which inspired both the New Poor Law and the manner of its administration in the early years. Officials seeking to promote the scheme appeared more preoccupied in refuting theoretical objections than in confronting practical ones. Many employers still feared that an elaborate education in a district school would unsettle the children, and make them dissatisfied with a life of labour. This point of view was proverbially identified with the farmers who often dominated boards of guardians in rural areas. They claimed to be supported by the poorer ratepayers who would find themselves subsidising (in district schools) a better education than they could hope to provide for their own children, who would therefore be disadvantaged in the labour market. More provocatively, opponents of district schools sometimes appealed directly to the principle of less-eligibility, and thus laid claim to Poor Law orthodoxy. Poor Law officials reiterated that less-eligibility applied to the able-bodied, but not to children. Defenders of district schools also insisted that able-bodied parents would not enter the workhouse in order to secure a better education for their children. The splitting-up of families on entry to the house was assumed to be a sufficient guarantee of this, whilst there was an implicit assumption that parents so conscious of the value of education were unlikely to be reduced to contemplate poor relief. In any case most pupils of district schools would be orphans. But most of the difficulties of the district school movement could not be resolved by theoreticians at Somerset House.

The economies of scale anticipated in the formation of district schools failed to materialise. The six set up in 1849 were more costly to administer than most workhouse schools, and the most expensive were the three in London, built to the prescribed scale. Although their over-all costs were inflated by capital repayments, their ordinary running costs, too, were high. This was due mainly to the large auxiliary staff employed in these schools, but overlooked in the plans of Kay-Shuttleworth and Tufnell. Their supporters were obliged to re-emphasise the long-term moral and reformatory value of district schools, which inspired enthusiasts, but won few converts.[4]

While the costs of district schools rose, the benefits began to appear more modest, in face of a number of practical problems of size and distance. A few local authorities, like Liverpool and Manchester, could furnish enough pupils to rank as school districts in their own right. At the other extreme, there were barely enough children in all the workhouses in Wales to provide two schools of 500 pupils. Such extensive districts would present monumental problems of administration. Kay-Shuttleworth and Tufnell had originally assumed that transient pupils, who entered the workhouse with their able-bodied parents, often repeatedly, for a few weeks or even days, would not be sent to the district school. It would then be free from the disruptive and unwholesome influence of these children, who were in constant touch with adult pauperism, and the school could, in theory, be any distance from the union workhouse. In practice, boards of guardians wished to dispatch all children to the school, rather than be saddled with providing parallel facilities at the workhouse. Once this problem had been identified, it was assumed that the geographical limits of any school district would be defined by the round trip which a pony and trap could make in a day. On this basis a maximum of fifteen miles from workhouse to school was, rather optimistically, considered viable. Some consideration was given to the railways as a means of transporting children over longer distances, but not even the Victorian railway mania could provide a line to link every workhouse to its district school! The existence of a railway appears to have played no actual part in the formation of school districts, although it did possibly influence the locations of the London district schools. Outside the major concentrations of population, the most hopeful prospects were for small combinations of unions to set up district schools which would resemble the original scheme in little but name. To judge from the three established on this pattern in 1849, even they would not be free from a discouraging number of administrative difficulties, involving transport, the hierarchy of authority within the school and the interrelations of boards of guardians and school managers.[5]

While the district schools were experiencing these practical difficulties, marked improvements were taking place in the organisation of many schools serving single unions. During the mid-Victorian years a growing number of unions followed the example of Liverpool and Manchester in setting up separate schools at a distance from the main workhouse. Other unions, whose school remained part of the main workhouse site, were paying greater attention to the importance of keeping the children apart from other inmates. A new term, 'detached schools', began to creep into official usage in the 1850s to describe the most comprehensive of these arrangements, in which the school was entirely self-contained, and walled off from the adult wards. Although most inspectors felt that detached schools still carried some of the stigma of the workhouse, the Poor Law Board normally classified them with district and separate schools as broadly satisfactory in terms of formal organisation. By 1870 every Poor Law authority in London maintained some kind of school away from the main workhouse. Outside London there were a further 49 separate and detached schools in 1870. This represented a little under 10 per cent of non-metropolitan unions, but included almost all the large urban authorities.[6]

Within the surviving majority of ordinary workhouse schools, too, improvements were taking place on a scale which had seemed unlikely in the first decade of the New Poor Law. This is largely attributable to the creation, in 1846, of a central fund to pay the salaries of teachers. The scheme involved the appointment of five inspectors of Poor Law schools, responsible to the Committee of Council on Education. Although broadly parallel to the general Education Minutes of 1846, which established the practice of state certification, this scheme was, within its field, more comprehensive. It covered all Poor Law schools, and in practice, though not in theory, the teacher's salary was directly determined by the certificate which he was awarded. The scheme was intended only as a palliative, pending the formation of district schools, but it inspired so much improvement in most of the workhouse schools, that the advantages of district schools soon appeared even less decisive.

After the new inspectorate had completed its preliminary survey, the Committee of Council on Education assessed the average ability of the teachers as roughly equivalent to that of a pupil-teacher in his first or second year, who would normally be a child of about 14.[7] Low salaries had been only one factor discouraging more competent teachers from taking up Poor Law appointments. There were no guaranteed holidays. Most teachers were required to live at the workhouse, and to perform a host of duties outside normal school hours, under the direction of the workhouse master or matron. Some of these duties could fairly be described as part of the general and moral education of the children, but often teachers were required to perform domestic duties, especially in small workhouses with few auxiliary officers. The better qualified elementary teachers were becoming understandably sensitive about the status, dignity and rights of what they, but few others, regarded as an emerging profession.

The impact, after 1846, of the new arrangements was dramatic. Certificates were awarded annually, though renewably, within four self-explanatory categories: 'efficiency', 'competency', 'probation' and 'permission'. The certificates awarded in 1849, the first year of comprehensive inspection, were overwhelmingly concentrated in the two lower, sub-competent classes. After this a mass evacuation appears to have occurred among those teachers who disliked the new system, or who despaired of their prospects of thriving under it. In general the new appointments were much better. Competent teachers were now assured of a reasonable salary, and the inspectorate afforded them at least some protection against intolerable conditions of service. Of the male teachers in service in 1849 only 137 obtained certificates of either 'efficiency' or 'competency', whilst 236 were awarded a certificate in one of the lower categories. By 1857 the proportions were reversed, the figures being 234 and 134, and of these only seven were certificates of 'permission', of which there had been 45 in 1849. A similar improvement occurred among women teachers, though their qualifications were on average lower, here as in other branches of elementary education. Comparable records of the certificate-awards have not survived for subsequent years, but it appears that the improved standards were at least maintained.[8]

The qualifications of the new teachers were still modest, since a sound elementary education and some minimal acquaintance with the principles of school-keeping were sufficient to cope with the written examination for a certificate of 'competency'. Few of the new teachers, except in the very large schools, would have been fully trained under the provisions of the general Minutes of 1846, though it must be remembered that a minority of day schools, too, were staffed by fully trained teachers in the mid-Victorian decades. Indirectly, though, the Minutes must have had some bearing. The inspectors suggested that pupil-teachers who were unable to complete their training at a college often served in Poor Law schools. If such was the case they would have been a marked improvement on most of their predecessors.

This improvement must have been reflected in the standard of the schooling. The annual reports of the inspectors, in their brief descriptions of the state of each individual school, tend to bear this out, although in their general comments they continued to emphasise the organisational defects of workhouse schools. The terms on which salaries were repaid, and the promptings of a professional and persuasive inspectorate, habituated the guardians progressively to the need for a more generous provision of books and materials. In theory the grant could be withheld if the guardians failed to carry out recommendations of this kind, or failed to adopt measures suggested by inspectors to improve the conditions under which the teachers worked. In practice this power was rarely employed. The President of the Poor Law Board warned the Education Department against attempting to 'hold the grant over their (i.e. the Guardians') heads by way of menace'.[9]

More spectacular advances, to which the inspectors' reports bore frequent testimony, occurred in the provision of industrial training, the branch to which workhouse schools had earlier been considered least adapted. In increasing numbers of rural workhouse schools in the 1850s, pointless task work, affording unlimited opportunities for harmful contact with adult paupers, was giving way to real industrial training. A serious attempt was made to give girls in these schools a genuine, if simple, training in domestic economy. Parcels of land were purchased, which the older boys were set to cultivate by spade. It was usually found possible to do this without jeopardising the arrangements for separating children from adults. Almost metaphysical qualitites were attributed to spade husbandry as a form of moral training. A more practical fringe benefit for the guardians was that these small 'farm schools' could often be made almost self-supporting. Even the farming community could see the advantages of this kind of education. Inspectors were relieved to find that it helped to allay hostility to the rest of the syllabus.

The cumulative effect of these improvements, together with the problems attending the formation of district schools, was to open up for the first time in the 1850s and 1860s a genuine debate among officials on the relative merits of district and workhouse schools. The lines of this debate were somewhat blurred, largely because the existing Poor Law schools did not fall neatly into two homogeneous and clearly defined categories. A more realistic, though still incomplete distinction would have been that between the large separate and district schools serving major urban areas, and the much smaller schools in rural areas, still in most cases integral parts of the workhouses, which were, in increasing numbers, being transformed into farm schools. The real question in dispute in the 1850s and 1860s was whether these smaller schools should be forced to amalgamate, to form district schools as large as circumstances would permit.

On the whole the Education Department pressed the case for district schools with greater vigour than the Poor Law Department. The schools inspectorate naturally clung more tenaciously to the original scheme of Kay-Shuttleworth, the former head of the Education Department, and Tufnell, who was himself the senior schools' inspector until his retirement in 1874. They may also have been more committed to the educational ideas enshrined in the original Norwood project, which could only be fully realised in large schools. In contrast, the Poor Law inspectors became increasingly convinced of the practical advantages of encouraging piecemeal improvements in the workhouse schools, and a few became genuine converts to the idea of small farm schools.

Shared values, and agreement over the aims of Poor Law education, usually ensured co-operation and friendship between individual inspectors of the two departments. But their responsibilities frequently overlapped, and a note of acrimony did sometimes intrude in relations between the two. Even in district and separate schools the Poor Law inspectors retained a general responsibility to ensure sound administration. They were generally more actively involved than the schools inspectors in attempts to form school districts, since vital questions of Poor Law administration and local politics were involved. A closer acquaintance with the obstacles encountered in these attempts tended in itself to make the Poor Law inspectors more cautious advocates of district schools. In other areas where the two responsibilities overlapped – for instance in the conditions of service and the accommodation offered to teachers, the provision of school books and materials, and relations between the teacher and the workhouse master – it required only that each inspector should follow faithfully the normal concerns of his own department for disputes to arise. The schools inspectors in general adopted a strong line on matters of educational principle. The Poor Law inspectors were more sensitive to the prejudices of guardians, less inclined to bully and threaten them and above all more alert to the dangers of upsetting the general balance of Poor Law administration. Occasionally the two offices were drawn into the disputes of their officials, though usually as conciliators.

The appearance in 1861 of the *Report* of the Newcastle Commission on elementary education provoked the final crisis of this uneasy relationship. The Commission, which had not sought evidence directly from the Poor Law Board, or its inspectors, had been 'fed' with witnesses by the Education Department. Predictably it condemned the prevailing system and called for the compulsory extension of district schools.[10] The effect was to provoke the Poor Law Board into a much less ambiguous defence of the workhouse schools, and a more formal renunciation of the idea of compulsory powers, although they continued to recommend the voluntary formation of district schools in more specific and limited circumstances. Four Poor Law inspectors, who between them boasted almost 100 years of service, were commissioned in 1862 to produce special reports to acknowledge their personal changes of heart. The problem of two departments in conflict over declared policy was resolved by dissociation in 1863, when the Education Department handed over its Poor Law responsibilities and inspectorate to the Poor Law Board.

The Poor Law Board's criticism of district schools was still, in the early 1860s, based on administrative rather than socio-educational grounds, but a new note is also apparent in the four inspectors' reports of 1862. Not only was complete separation from the adults possible in workhouse schools, but children from these schools rarely drifted into pauperism, vice and crime. This did not perhaps say very much, and it was based on evidence as fragmentary and selective as were the similar claims commonly made on behalf of district schools. But it challenged the district schools for the first time on their own strongest front. In one of these reports, Robert Weale argued that the comings and goings of the transient pupils were more harmful than the possibility of occasional contact with adult paupers. In another, W. H. T. Hawley, who had been like Weale one of the original pool of assistant commissioners, claimed that district schools would not spare children the supposedly demoralising notion that they were paupers. He added, somewhat retrogressively, that the children did not resent this.[11] But the views expressed by Hawley and Weale are precursors of a new current of thought which was meeting increasing sympathy from the Poor Law Board, and which saw genuine advantages in the small workhouse school, in contrast to the remoteness and institutionalisation of the great Poor Law schools.

This becomes clearer if their observations are set alongside the more sustained criticism of the district schools formulated by one of the schools inspectors, Thomas Browne. To the annoyance of his superiors at the Education Department, Browne decided during the 1850s that the celebrated Swinton and Kirkdale schools (see p. 70) were too large, and lacked the close contact and more sympathetic atmosphere which understanding teachers could create in the workhouse schools. A significant number of girls from Kirkdale drifted into prostitution. This was not the kind of independent service for which the school was intended to prepare them. Besides, it was assumed that prostitution inevitably led to pauperism. Browne concluded that the demoralisation of 'pauper associations' was more serious in district than in workhouse schools.[12]

This clearly heralds the attack on the 'barrack schools' which developed in earnest in the last decades of the nineteenth century, and which was strengthened by the recurrent outbreaks of eye infections which seemed to be characteristic of these schools. Its most persuasive advocate was Jane Senior, daughter-in-law of the co-author of the Poor Law *Report* of 1834. At the request of the Local Government Board, she presented in 1873 a woman's view of the education of girls in Poor Law schools which echoed many of the opinions expressed by Browne. Children from the large schools lacked vitality and practical awareness. Most of the girls sent out to service from the London schools in 1871 and 1872 had proved less than satisfactory in character, conduct and efficiency, even allowing for the unreliability as witnesses of some of their employers. The record of the district schools in this respect was significantly worse than that of the smaller London schools.[13]

Earlier critics of district schools had been obliged to defend the workhouse schools, or to canvass some minor variant, like the detached schools which Browne believed more successfully combined separation from adults with accessibility and a less impersonal atmosphere. Mrs Senior was able to recommend a number of more radical alternatives, most of which were introduced in some form during the last three decades of the nineteenth century. None of these fundamentally altered the aims expressed in the official requirement that the children should be trained 'to habits of usefulness, industry and virtue'. But the variety of new approaches to pauper education provided a welcome diversity of pattern, which was in practice encouraged by the cautious neutrality with which the Local Government Board normally greeted new ideas. The worst fault of the district school movement was that, in obedience to the spirit of 1834, it laid down a uniform and universal pattern for the upbringing of pauper children. It branded them as paupers precisely as it sought to free them from a self-identification with pauperism. To assemble the children into large Poor Law establishments as the prelude to ridding them of pauper habits and notions was bound to be self-contradictory at some level. In 1855 one of the schools inspectors, Jelinger Symons, argued that, although district schools must not be stigmatised as pauper schools, they should only admit pauper children, for whom a distinctive form of education was essential.[14] Not all the new expedients introduced in the last quarter of the century derived from a clear appreciation of the contradictions embedded in the district school idea; but at least in their very diversity they were bound to be beneficial.

The alternative which most directly gained prominence from Mrs Senior's recommendations involved dividing the larger schools into cottage homes, in which the children were to be housed in groups of perhaps thirty. This was sometimes described as the Mettray system, for significantly it drew inspiration from the French open-plan reformatory school of that name, a model of social control which had functioned smoothly through all the ravages of the French Revolution. The cottage-home pattern was adopted in a few unions, led by Neath in 1878 and Birmingham in 1879. The homes were located on a single site, and continued to function as a self-contained unit. Consequently they preserved many of the characteristics of the institutional Poor Law school. Although rarely proclaimed in these terms, cottage homes were an attempt to recreate in urban unions the best features of the small but well-conducted workhouse school.

The 'scattered homes' established by the guardians in Sheffield in 1893 were a more radical version of this scheme. These homes, too, accommodated groups of twenty to thirty children of different ages, but they were dispersed in different localities. The children attended local Board schools, within which it was intended that they should lose their distinctive identity among the mass of other pupils. In somewhat contrived conditions this was a more realistic attempt to recreate what the guardians assumed were the circumstances of a well-run working-class home. The most spectacular convert to this pattern was the Whitechapel Union, which withdrew its children from the Forest Gate district school in 1897.

Cottage and scattered homes provided for all the children who were under the institutional charge of the guardians. More piecemeal, but much more widely adopted, was the practice of boarding individual orphaned children in the homes of working-class foster parents, who recovered from the Poor Rates the cost of their maintenance. This practice, which removed the children almost entirely from a Poor Law environment, had been widely adopted in Scotland (see p. 188). It had no official status in England before 1869, when a number of unions, notably Bath, were permitted to operate the system experimentally. The Poor Law Board, and its successor the Local Government Board, viewed the idea with some suspicion, perhaps because during the 1860s they had become accustomed to defending the workhouse schools against all comers. More justifiably, they doubted the adequacy of provisions to ensure the respectability of the foster-parents and the satisfactory progress of the children. They feared that boarding-out could degenerate into unregulated outdoor relief. A growing number of unions outflanked these criticisms by appointing boarding-out committees, one of the earliest arenas of women's participation in local administration. In 1885 the Local Government Board capitulated sufficiently to appoint a female inspector to safeguard the welfare of children boarded out beyond their 'home union.' By 1877, 9248 children were in practice boarded out, though only 374 of these were under effective regulation by the Local Government Board, and in many cases boarding-out was probably little more than a disguised form of outdoor relief paid to relatives of the children.[15] After 1889 boarding-out was formally recognised and fully regulated by the Local Government Board, although the number of children involved remained fairly constant. The formal adoption of orphaned children occurred too infrequently to attract regulation, although guardians were instructed to satisfy themselves that adoption would benefit the child before giving their consent.[16]

After 1862 guardians were also permitted to send children to certified schools, which provided for special classes of children, usually either members of a particular religious persuasion, or victims of physical handicap. By the end of the nineteenth century certified schools freed a further 10,000 children from a distinctively Poor Law schooling.

A very much larger number of pauper children in 1900 received their education at an ordinary elementary school. A number of smaller unions sent their children to local day schools throughout the century. Before 1870 the practice was generally disapproved even by those inspectors most critical of workhouse schools. Day schools could not provide the industrial and moral training necessary for pauper children, and even the intellectual training was likely to be inferior to that of the average workhouse school, since the children were rarely sent to schools which were under government inspection and which employed certificated teachers. By 1870 only 64 English and 7 Welsh unions continued to use a local school, and almost all of these had only a handful of children. Thereafter the trend was reversed. By 1898, only 63 workhouse schools remained, whilst children normally attended a local day school in 493 unions. Clearly the 1870 Education Act, in ensuring the availability of reasonably well-conducted schools in all localities, played a crucial part in this transformation. But equally important were assumptions about the circumstances in which pauper children should be educated. Not least among the virtues of the workhouse schools was the fact that they were easily abandoned when these assumptions changed. The district and quasi-district schools were more likely to outlive their usefulness.

It was also the series of Education Acts beginning in 1870 which first brought regular schooling within the reach of most children on outdoor relief. Although guardians were empowered after 1855 to pay school fees for these children, few did so. By 1869 fees were paid from the rates for 22,033 children, still less than one in ten of the total number on outdoor relief.[17] Some advocates of district schools favoured admitting children on outdoor relief, but the idea was never adopted. The New Poor Law required that families be treated as units for purposes of poor relief. This meant that children of families on outdoor relief could, at most, attend on a non-residential basis, which would defeat many of the special aims of district schools; but, in any case, few children would have lived close enough to attend on a daily basis. Children on outdoor relief were admitted to the workhouse school at Brecon, as day-pupils, though the legality even of this seems questionable. In general Poor Law education was not available to these children. By 1870 most of them appear to have had some formal schooling but on a very irregular basis.

The transient children were similarly excluded from any continuous educational provision. The original district-school scheme was devised to exclude these pupils, who were the bane of Poor Law educationalists, but in practice they were normally sent to the district school for lack of any alternative. Mrs Senior recommended that these children might be compulsorily detained for the sake of their education, while their parents were sent to cultivate the Yorkshire Moors in order to pay off the cost of maintenance and schooling.[18] This was at least a more positive suggestion than most Poor Law reformers offered for the education of the 'in and outs'. Other enthusiasts wished to see the guardians assume parental powers over the children. The Webbs were clearly disappointed that legal powers of guardianship allowed to the Poor Law authorities were not applied in their case.[19] In the absence of such draconic solutions these children, too, were inevitably excluded from Poor Law schooling except for the brief periods when their family entered the house. Some of the most deprived of these children received a rudimentary industrial and general schooling in the 'ragged schools' which flourished in London and a few other centres from the 1840s, and which fostered the virtues of cleanliness, Godliness, duty and diligence amongst a segment of the dangerous classes. The rest awaited the gradual extension of effective compulsory schooling.

That these very large groups were necessarily excluded must be borne in mind in any assessment of the educational and social contribution of the systems of Poor Law schooling which developed in the 1830s and 1840s, flourished in the mid-Victorian years, and after 1870 merged progressively into the mainstream of elementary education. A succession of reports from the Poor Law and Education departments leave no doubt as to the explicit aims of pauper education, which were expressed most fully in the district school movement. It must not be overlooked that these reports were often addressed to a hostile or suspicious public. Inspectors who stressed repeatedly the suitability of the schooling for the children's station in life were usually seeking to widen rather than confine the syllabus. Arguments of social utility could be employed to justify an impressive range of subjects. Tufnell demonstrated how an errand-boy, in redirecting a parcel, made use of memory, general understanding, geography, etymology, arithmetic, secular reading, writing – and honesty in returning the change.[20] The recurrent emphasis, too, on sound practical education, general knowledge and an understanding of 'common things', must be understood in its proper context – an acute consciousness of the alarming practical ignorance of children who had lived out their childhood enclosed in a workhouse school. But the tenor of Poor Law schooling was genuinely and uniformly utilitarian, and rarely rose above the requirements of efficiency in preparing the children for independent service at an early age. It is a rare and refreshing contrast to encounter Thomas Browne's opinion that no child was properly educated who could not take up a book with pleasure, or his hope, echoed by Jane Senior, that pauper children might be introduced to poetry.[21] It is probably not coincidental that these were two of the earliest and most articulate opponents of 'barrack schools'.

The children were not, at least in theory, selected and reared for specific trades. This would be too great an interference in the labour market, and was out of keeping with the spirit of Victorian individualism. Their education was to fit them for their future station in life, but the station was a general one, in which the children must find their own level. In practice, some pupils were certainly marked out for particular careers, notably those appointed pupil-teachers, and the members of military bands formed in the larger schools and favoured by the recruiting officers of a number of regiments.

Boys were instructed in shoemaking or tailoring in many Poor Law schools. These were intended to provide not a future livelihood, but a general experience of work discipline in a skilled but demonstrable craft, in which output was clearly related to effort. It was also desirable that the children should learn to repair, and perhaps make, their own shoes and clothes. Perhaps even this small contribution damaged such over-stocked trades. Poor Law education could hardly fail to transgress the 1834 principle, that relief should not interfere with the labour market.

The great majority of boys became labourers, though in a wide variety of trades. Few of the girls escaped the alternatives of domestic service or marriage to a labourer. A few talented and fortunate individuals were able to rise in the world on the basis of their schooling, like the girl who, after justifying the teaching of geography by emigrating to Australia, was able to make a 'good' marriage. On her return to England she rode in a carriage to the workhouse to express her gratitude to her instructors.[22] A society fed liberally on Samuel Smiles did not resent such good fortune – though many below the middle class did not read Smiles. Most pupils were probably a little better equipped and better informed to cope with the economic and moral problems of a life of labour in a world of increasing industrialisation and literacy. Poor Law educationalists emphasised the individual as well as social benefits of this training. Those with allotments or gardens could turn their skill in spade husbandry to advantage. Here the possibilities for domestic and moral economy were boundless. The girl who had been instructed in plain cooking would be less extravagant. A grounding in arithmetic opened new horizons, enabling its beneficiaries to plan their humble finances and 'to check their score with the shopkeepers'.[23] Such prosaic blessings must be set alongside the more explicit goals of social control and work discipline, and balanced against the 'lowest view of the case' as presented by Tufnell: 'Imparting good education to the poorest classes is equivalent to an insurance on our property. . . . The cost of not doing so is a yearly expense exceeding two millions incurred for the repression of crime. . . . No money seems to return so good an interest as that which is laid out in securing the morals of the labouring classes.'[24]

Whether pauperism, crime, vice and political discontent were in fact reduced is not apparent. The evidence is too fragmentary to be conclusive for even the least subjective of these aspects.

For most children in Poor Law schools life must have been depressingly dull. Most of the teaching was unimaginative, to judge from inspectors' reports, though it was probably no better in most day schools. But for children in Poor Law schools there was no escape from their environment, with the exception of occasional outings for exercise or moral and intellectual improvement. The situation did improve during the century, as both the teaching and the administration became more imaginative. Increasingly the schools were better provided with books and materials. In the last two decades of the century such luxuries as balls, hoops and swings were often provided, and inspectors, fired by the spirit of muscular Christianity, were urging the importance of facilities for football and cricket. A few London schools even kept animals as pets for the children in the 1890s, and the guardians were permitted to award modest prizes to deserving pupils. Physical cruelty was always strongly discouraged; corporal punishment was forbidden for girls, and closely controlled for boys. But for parentless children who spent their childhood in Poor Law schools there must have been little substitute for parental affection, particularly in the largest schools.

Educational provision under the New Poor Law reflects both the strengths and weaknesses of Victorian administration. It possessed a clarity of aims which the twentieth century must envy. It pursued these with characteristic vigour, often against considerable local opposition. Victorian paternalism is shown at its best in the attention devoted to this submerged section of society, both in the scale of such ventures as the Swinton and Kirkdale schools, and also the Sheffield 'scattered homes', and in the spirit of missionary zeal with which most inspectors undertook their work of social regeneration. But the quasi-scientific clarity of these aims was based on grossly over-simplified assumptions which made too little allowance for the complexities of either human nature or political economy. Caught between the contradictory needs of deterrence and depauperisation, 80 per cent of pauper children were excluded altogether from Poor Law schooling, while the remainder were, for most of this period, immured in self-contained and ultimately self-defeating institutions.

Yet on balance it is impressive that Poor Law education achieved so much. A situation of chaos and neglect in 1834 had been transformed within 20 years. That the district school movement failed so completely is, among other things, testimony to the progress made in the mass of union schools. From the 1830s Poor Law schools had pioneered important developments in educational practice, often providing a lead to the state-aided elementary schools whose social and educational aims, though less pronounced, were similar. Prior to 1870 it was generally held that Poor Law schools provided a sounder basic education than comparable day schools, although they usually taught a narrower range of subjects. With the industrial training provided by Poor Law schools the day schools could never compare, and rarely sought to do so. In the closing decades of the century much had been done to break down the physical and psychological isolation in which pauper children were brought up. By 1900 events had moved substantially, though uncertainly, towards the destination anticipated in the Minority Report of 1909. Education under the Poor Law was entering the era of social services.

4. The Poor Law and Philanthropy

NORMAN McCORD

I F we are to understand the nature and the significance of the Poor Law we must always remember that in nineteenth-century society the state played a very different role from that which it plays today. Failure to place the study of the nineteenth-century Poor Law in its own proper setting has often been responsible for serious historical misunderstanding. Because of the importance which has often been attributed to the Poor Law as an illustration of the nature of nineteenth-century social relationships, a failure to understand its proper place in that society can lead to a defective understanding of the nature of that society.

The society which created the 1834 Poor Law Amendment Act was slowly and painfully learning to accommodate itself to an unprecedented accumulation of changes and strains brought about by the twin pressures of economic change and population explosion. The Industrial Revolution, and the parallel enormous increases of population, occurred in what was essentially a decentralised rural society, with very limited resources and techniques in the fields of government and official administration. The energies and achievements of that society were not primarily exercised in official forms, and it is scarcely surprising then that the response to social problems came for the most part not from the state but from the private and local energies which lay at the heart of Britain's development in the age of the Industrial Revolution.

One misunderstanding had better be cleared out of the way from the start. In *The Condition of the Working Class in England in 1844* Engels argued that the emergence of the new capitalist industrial society was accompanied by a marked deterioration in social relationships. He conceived of a pre-industrial eighteenth century marked by a high

For Notes to Chapter 4, see pp. 209–10; for Bibliography, see p. 199.

degree of freedom and comfort for the workers and their families; the coming of the factory system was marked instead by the ruthless exploitation of the workers and their families by dominant minorities exhibiting a degree of callousness from which the eighteenth century would have shrunk. This line of argument has been followed in various forms by Marxist historians studying modern British social history; something will be said later in this essay of some of the more modern versions of this interpretation. The picture drawn by Engels was, however, a very partial and over-drawn concept. It is not possible here to discuss this at length, but students of this period should read the passages in which Macaulay, in the celebrated third chapter of his *History of England* (written about 1840), discussed this romantic propensity of looking back to a mythical golden age.

Briefly, however, it may be stated that the romantic nostalgia for a pre-industrial past embodied in Engels and his successors is far too simple. Although our knowledge of eighteenth-century society is much less full than our evidence for the nineteenth century, it is abundantly plain that pre-industrial Britain saw much poverty and cruelty, and that the social problems of the eighteenth century were often viewed with a callous unconcern which the nineteenth century proved unwilling to emulate. Indeed, a major reason why we know so much more about the nineteenth century is that society then made a determined effort to find out what was wrong and to do something about it – traits which were not nearly so evident in the previous century.[1] The nineteenth century, and not any earlier period, saw the development of royal commissions and select committees of enquiry into social problems, the multiplication of surveys, investigations and tabulations, all of which provided the essential basis from which social reform could spring. Many of the social problems which faced the nineteenth century were not new, but represented a continuation, often an intensification, of social problems which were very old indeed; the new industrial society did not invent child labour or poor housing or bad sanitation or poor educational provision – it did, however, do distinctly more to remedy them than any previous generation had done.

It is by no means clear that the arrival of large-scale capitalist industry was accompanied by any major changes in social attitudes, and there are good grounds for supposing that the way in which poverty and its associated problems were approached was marked by continuity rather than transformation during the period of the Industrial Revolution. As we shall see it is very often impossible to distinguish between the philanthropic activities of members of the old landed aristocracy and those of successful industrial entrepreneurs, while the two basic approaches to amelioration – the official Poor Law machinery and unofficial philanthropy – do not seem to have been fundamentally affected by the circumstance that the country was undergoing a rapid process of industrialisation.

It would be very difficult indeed to establish the argument that the 1834 Poor Law Amendment Act was dictated by a desire to serve the needs of an industrial society. On the contrary, one of the major criticisms levelled against that Act has been its irrelevance to the then social needs of the growing industrial sector, and the Act was certainly passed by a legislature which was very far from being under the control of capitalist industrialists. On the other hand, a consideration of unofficial philanthropy in the eighteenth and nineteenth centuries will lead to the conclusion that, in general, the extended efforts of the nineteenth century represented essentially the continued expansion, intensification and elaboration of trends already present on a much smaller scale in the pre-industrial eighteenth century. It is with these concepts and methods that we are mainly concerned here, for without an understanding of nineteenth-century philanthropy in general it is impossible to have any clear notion of the significance of the Poor Law of the period.

We are well accustomed to the catalogues of suffering and oppression which have formed a prominent feature of much modern discussion of the social history of nineteenth-century Britain. It is no part of the argument here to deny that these elements existed, but rather to suggest that to over-emphasise one side of what was a complex and varied picture is to distort reality. Three reasons for caution should be adduced here. First, much of the evidence of that kind is derived from the investigations which nineteenth-century society made with the deliberate purpose of finding out what was wrong and trying to find means to improve matters. Secondly, we must bear in mind that the evidence as a whole has a considerable inherent bias. The continuation of relatively satisfactory normality is rarely represented prominently in the historical record, and instead evidence tends to accumulate most obviously when something has gone wrong; in many cases it is difficult to establish how typical these instances may be. Thirdly, the abundant evidence relating to another very important aspect of nineteenth-century social history – unofficial philanthropic exertions – has been unduly neglected in many of our contemporary accounts of that period.

This philanthropic activity can be conveniently discussed under three heads – organised societies, extraordinary charitable exertions to meet some temporary need, and the private charity extended by individual men and women. Most of my examples are drawn from my own home area, not only because it is the area I know best, but also in the hope that some readers may find the subject sufficiently interesting to carry out their own researches into the relevant material in their own districts, for that kind of local survey would be a useful contribution to knowledge.

The nineteenth century was probably the classical period of the work of organised charitable societies. The origins of such bodies plainly lie in pre-industrial society; before the Industrial Revolution and the factory system had spread widely the development of societies for the creation and maintenance of hospitals, dispensaries and a variety of other institutions for the benefit of the poor had made considerable progress. For the most part these bodies tended to be distinctly local organisations, a natural situation in a society which overwhelmingly lived in small locally orientated towns and villages. There was, however, a considerable degree of imitation and emulation between different places in the provision of such services. For example, the Newcastle Infirmary, founded in 1751, was modelled on a slightly earlier example at Northampton. Throughout the later eighteenth century and the whole of the nineteenth century, the creation of new voluntary societies for social purposes was a continuing and expanding process. A brief look at some of the activities of this nature in one town can illustrate the point.[2]

The Newcastle Infirmary, already mentioned, provided free medical treatment for the poor of the town, including a twenty-four-hour casualty service. It was staffed by the town's doctors and entirely supported by charitable subscriptions, donations and bequests. It was supplemented in 1778 by a dispensary, which provided free medicines for the poor of the town, as well as treatment for minor cases. The early nineteenth century saw the addition of similar institutions for maternity cases, an eye hospital and for the provision of help for prostitutes. The mid-nineteenth century saw the establishment by voluntary societies of specialised institutions for the blind and the deaf and dumb; the latter decades of the century saw similar societies engaged in providing treatment for tuberculosis and holidays for poor children. These are only a selection of the kinds of voluntary provision made for help to the poor, the sick and the aged in one town; there were in addition many other societies engaged in the provision of medical help, food and clothing, religious consolation, education, and so forth.

There was a great deal of common ground in the regulations which governed these charitable societies. It was normal for them to be controlled by those who provided the money which supported them, normal also for the rules to make it abundantly plain to beneficiaries that the help given was not a natural right but a valuable favour for which a becoming sense – and expression – of gratitude was an obvious duty. Often these regulations grate upon a twentieth-century ear, but we must beware of easy anachronism. There is no reason why we should believe that early nineteenth-century society should have been either democratic or egalitarian. Certainly no earlier period had possessed these qualities, and we may usefully remember the robust common sense of a recent dictum by one of our most competent Marxist historians, Professor Eric Hobsbawm: 'it is absurd to assume that socialism was a practical possibility in the Britain of Peel and Gladstone.'[3]

The second category of philanthropic activity, the *ad hoc* organisation of voluntary resources for temporary purposes, has been little discussed in recent writing on social history, but it deserves considerable attention, for it was important in a society which did not possess sophisticated state agencies to meet pressing temporary needs. Two distinct categories can be considered – the mobilisation of local resources to meet such adverse circumstances as trade depression and consequent unemployment, or some local catastrophe or tragedy, and, on the other hand, the mobilisation of these same resources to celebrate some cause of rejoicing which was held to involve the participation of the whole community.

It would take a very large book indeed to contain a discussion of the various ways in which the nineteenth century saw the voluntary mobilisation of subscriptions and organisations to meet a pressing local or regional need. Instances could vary from region to region, and from place to place and time to time within a region. Here are just a few specimens to illustrate the variety of these activities within one region.

In January 1805, five boats, carrying nineteen men, were lost in a storm off the Northumberland coast. A local collection for the benefit of the dependants of the drowned men raised £1701, mainly from propertied people on Tyneside.

The hard winter of 1816 saw public subscriptions in many places to provide employment for the poor – a normal reaction to hard times in the nineteenth century; for example, the Sunderland collection of 1816 raised £2437. Three years later the Home Secretary, Lord Sidmouth, wrote to express his warm approval of the efforts being made by public subscription 'for the purpose of finding Employment for poor Persons who have been deprived of it, in consequence of the peculiar Circumstances and Pressure of the Times.'⁴ Peterloo does not tell the whole story of social relationships in the Britain of 1819.

The cholera epidemic of 1853 saw extended official action by local and central authorities, but also notable unofficial subscriptions for the relief of victims and their dependants. The lists of subscriptions show sizeable, and often repeated, donations both from the region's old territorial aristocracy and from the newer wealth represented by industrialists.

In the following year a disastrous fire and explosion devastated large parts of the riverside areas of both Newcastle and Gateshead. At once a public subscription was set on foot to provide relief to those injured or rendered homeless, and to provide for the dependants of those killed. A total of well over £11,000 was raised, and again the list of subscribers is illuminating: on the one hand, the Queen gave £100, the Earl of Carlisle £200, the Bishop of Durham £150, the Duke of Northumberland £105, the Earl of Durham £50, Lord Ravensworth £25, and many other aristocrats contributed also; on the other hand, the Bank of England donated £105, Hawks Crawshay & Co. (iron works at Gateshead) £200, Robert Stephenson & Co. £105, Losh, Wilson & Bell (Tyneside iron works and chemical works) £100, W. G. Armstrong & Co. £25, Weardale Iron Co. £25, Backworth & West Cramlington Pit Owners £50, and there were many other donations from engineering, shipbuilding, chemical manufacturing, coal-owning and other elements from the newer industrial wealth. There is certainly no suggestion from many of these voluntary activities that capitalist industry was less willing to contribute to such causes than the older dominant minorities. The money raised on this occasion was used in various ways. In some cases grants were made to enable widows or disabled men to set up small businesses; some money was spent to relieve immediate necessity or to replace clothing and furniture lost; more than £3000 was set aside to provide long-term pensions for widows and allowances for bereaved children until they reached an age to support themselves.

In 1859 a building appeal for the Northern Counties Institution for the Deaf and Dumb quickly raised £3000. The industrialist Sir William Armstrong then offered to give £600 if an equivalent sum was raised from others in the next few weeks; this was managed without difficulty. Other donors included the Duke of Northumberland who gave £500, the Dowager Duchess of Northumberland £100 and the Duke of Cleveland £100. A concert by the Newcastle Amateur Musical Society provided the building fund with £120/17s.

One of the region's greatest mining disasters took place at Hartley in 1862. The public subscription for the benefit of dependants of the victims raised £81,838/19s./5d. The administering committee made grants for immediate needs, and worked out a long-term scheme of pensions and allowances which, for example, provided pensions ranging from 10s. 6d. per week for a widow with one child to 21s. 6d. for a widow with six children. These allowances were to cease on a widow's remarriage, but this was to be sweetened with a grant of £20 to each widow on remarriage. In this instance the sums collected exceeded planned expenditure by some £20,000; this surplus was divided between the country's mining areas, in proportion to the numbers of miners then employed, in order to provide a fund for future provision for those who suffered from mining accidents.

In 1865 a public memorial to the fourth Duke of Northumberland took the form of building a large convalescent home for the sick poor of the area. Armstrong gave £1000 and the lists of subscribers of £100 and above reads like a roll-call of the heads of the old aristocracy and the new industrial entrepreneurs.

Nor was it only the large-scale incidents which called forth this kind of local response. In 1868 an explosion of nitro-glycerine in Newcastle brought a public collection for the dependants of the four men killed; local banks, for example, each gave five guineas to this fund. In 1872 the same banks each contributed ten guineas to a collection for the benefit of the widow and children of Robert Arkley, a workman killed while trying to rescue the crew of a wrecked ship. In January 1889 more than £1000 was raised for the family of a Gateshead policeman killed while on duty.

In addition to cash donations, in time of local unemployment it was normal for firms to give substantial gifts in kind; collieries usually gave gifts of coal in hard winters for the benefit of the poor, while gifts of food would come from farming or fishing interests.

Nor was this kind of charitable activity confined to the relief of victims of catastrophe or sickness. Gifts in aid of communal celebrations were equally common. It was normal for collections to be made to provide comforts for the poor each Christmas Day, and when any occasions for national rejoicing occurred it was standard practice for them to be accompanied by local efforts to enable the poor to share in the celebrations. The New Poor Law was introduced into north-east England in the late 1830s; it is worth looking at some of the local activities which accompanied Queen Victoria's coronation on 28 June 1838. At Newcastle: 'The poor in the various workhouses, and even the prisoners in the gaol, had been provided with ample means of joining in the festivities of the occasion, and the inmates of the hospitals were presented with five shillings each, for the same purpose.'[5] At Gateshead:

> Upwards of 400 poor persons, of all ages and of both sexes, were afterwards entertained at dinner in a large tent, fixed in the yard of the Gateshead workhouse. The supply of roast beef and plum pudding, and ale, was most profuse; and the guests were waited on by the members of the town council and the board of guardians, the town clerk, the churchwardens and overseers, and other gentlemen; and highly delighted they were with the good fare set before them, and the courtesy which they experienced. An old lady – a venerable and mettlesome octogenarian – officiated as queen on the occasion, and was most stylishly attired for her high óffice. At the close of the feast, sixpence each was given to the company assembled.[6]

At North Shields there was a distribution of meat, bread and money to 2500 recipients, and a dinner for 900 old seamen. At Sunderland, among other activities, 1000 families were given three pounds of meat and three pounds of bread each. Similar arrangements for the distribution of money, food and drink to the poor were made in every centre within the region and, indeed, throughout the country. Royal marriages, successful wars, and a variety of other similar occasions brought out similar junketings throughout the century, with detailed provisions varying according to local preferences. If we are to arrive at a balanced conception of that society, we must remember that a community which could produce Peterloo, the Tolpuddle Martyrs and the Andover workhouse scandal could also produce a formidable catalogue of evidence of a very different kind, testifying to the presence of strong inclinations towards co-operation and sympathy between different elements in society.

The third category of philanthropic activity – the private charitable activities of individuals – is the most difficult to measure or evaluate. That it existed, and existed on a large scale, is sufficiently clear, but it is obviously impossible to calculate the amounts involved, or to evaluate the effects produced, because in the nature of things our evidence of such scattered personal activity must be hopelessly inadequate. This difficulty, however, should not induce us to forget the existence of this factor, and it may be worth considering again a few local examples. We may be tolerably sure that not many individuals in the propertied classes imitated the conduct of a late nineteenth-century Bishop of Durham, Westcott, who systematically set aside 25 per cent of his income for charitable purposes. Yet he was not alone in regarding charitable activity as a major preoccupation in his life.

At South Shields Dr Thomas Winterbottom devoted a great deal of his inherited fortune to the establishment of a whole series of local charities. In 1839 he set aside a fund of £2300 to provide pensions for retired master mariners, and subsequently fortified the endowment with a further sum of over £400 to maintain gardens for them. A further endowment of more than £5000 was set up for the benefit of seamen's widows; its trustees were to provide a number of annuities and the surplus was to be expended, at their discretion, in grants to such widows in need. A smaller Winterbottom enterprise was a fund of £150 set aside to provide presents on New Year's Day for loyal unmarried female servants – £2 for those with 7–10 years service, £3 for 10–13 years and £4 for those with more than 13 years service. Another fund of £403 provided annual gifts of £5 for retired scullermen from the Tyne's boats. Yet another was used to give prizes annually to the best ploughmen and ploughboys in north-east Durham. A sum of £200 was invested to provide free coal for the poor on Christmas Day. In 1837 Dr Winterbottom founded a marine school in South Shields, and he gave constant encouragement and some financial support to the seamen's union on the river, as well as sponsoring friendly societies and a savings bank.

Not many individuals were as bountiful, but many others showed themselves willing to help those less fortunate than themselves. Sometimes the help provided may appear trivial, yet it certainly indicates an attitude of mind. The brothers Robert and William Hawthorn were among the most important of Tyneside's engineering entrepreneurs. From small beginnings in 1817 they built up a large firm, employing nearly a thousand men by the late 1850s. They exhibited a continuing paternalism towards their workers, and one small instance may illustrate the kind of atmosphere in this important company which secured good industrial relations throughout the period in which the Hawthorn brothers directed its affairs. One day in the late 1850s William Hawthorn returned to his Forth Bank Engine Works in the afternoon to find the one-armed man who had been given a job as lodge-keeper 'decidedly intoxicated'. Hawthorn's reaction was to say to him, 'Here, Tommy my lad, is a fourpenny bit; go up to the public and finish thyself off.'[7]

Another example of industrial paternalism came from C. A. Parsons, inventor of the steam turbine, towards the end of the century. He once angrily discharged a workman who had not turned up on time for an important job. When, however, he was told that the man's absence was due to his wife's illness rather than to slacking, he sent for him, gave him a pay increase, and told him, 'Go home, and do not worry about anything, and only come back when your wife is well enough for you to do so.' Subsequently Parsons bought and personally delivered invalid foods and other presents for the invalid wife. Here we are faced with the same old problem of historical assessment; we can easily discover many examples of employers who seemed lacking in any sense of responsibility to those they employed, but it is also easy to find many examples of employers who took their social responsibilities very seriously indeed. It would be visionary to suppose that we could ever establish with any degree of certainty just what the proportions in each category were, but we would certainly be well astray if we pretended that all employers were on one side of the fence or the other. It remains undoubtedly true, however, that nineteenth-century society in general saw a great deal of voluntary charitable activity towards those in need, whether this help was tendered by friends, neighbours, employers or came from a wide variety of other sources.

It is difficult for the modern student to realise how much the relative importance of state intervention and unofficial philanthropy have changed in the course of the twentieth century. In the 1860s and

1870s London churches and chapels held annual collections on one Sunday in June for the benefit of local hospitals; this normally brought in some £30,000. This was only one small item in the voluntary philanthropic activity which in London alone was calculated in a contemporary survey in the early 1860s to amount to between £5·5 and £7 million annually.[9] Total Poor Law expenditure for England and Wales amounted to less than £6 million in 1861 and less than £8 million in 1871. When, therefore, we consider the Poor Law's operations we must remember that we are dealing, not with the sum total of that society's activities in the relief of poverty and suffering, but only with the lesser part of that activity which was carried out through that official agency. It is not possible to estimate with any accuracy the total sums of money expended on voluntary relief measures, still less possible to estimate the amount of time and energy so employed, but it is very clear that unofficial far outweighed official exertion.

It is worth considering one or two of the reasons underlying this disparity. In the first place the expansion of government, which was an important feature of nineteenth-century Britain, was a slow, painful and difficult process. It was not easy to persuade taxpayers and ratepayers that official administrative machinery could be relied upon to provide honest and efficient service. Nor was this merely the obscurantism of selfishness, for it was not difficult to find evidence to back this reluctance. Nineteenth-century government inherited a long tradition, often based on fact, of jobbery, nepotism and favouritism in appointment to official posts. The records of Poor Law unions after 1834 often show that the major disagreements were not about policy but about the conflicts between groups of guardians as to whose candidates were to receive the jobs within the system. It would be impossible to pretend that the officials of either the new or the old Poor Law presented an unspotted record to the public gaze. It is important to remember that, even if the general level of competence and integrity was reasonably satisfactory, wide ranges of public opinion could be seriously affected by a few well-publicised examples of official incompetence or dishonesty.

It was not an easy job to build up and maintain efficient and trustworthy staffs for the service of central and local government in a society which had relatively little experience of government intervention. For example, when the 1834 Poor Law Amendment Act came into force, there was only one main reservoir of experienced staff on which the new authorities could draw, and that was the existing staff who worked under the old legislation. This proved a resource of distinctly mixed quality, and did not always help to establish the public reputation of the new machinery. Again this can be illustrated by a few local examples, which could be readily paralleled in other areas. In 1836 William Pickering, relieving officer in the Castle Ward Union, was removed for drunkenness and neglect of duty, and in the South Shields Union Thomas Wilson was sacked in 1844 for embezzlement; both had long records of service as officials of the old Poor Law. The Sunderland Union inherited three relieving officers and three rate collectors from its predecessors. One of the three relieving officers died a few years later, and a check of his accounts showed that he had pocketed considerable sums of public money; another was dismissed in 1850 for drunkenness and other forms of misconduct. Of the three rate collectors, one was sacked in 1840 for embezzlement, another in 1850 for prolonged incompetence. Nor were higher Poor Law officials uniformly paragons of virtue. The first clerk to the Houghton-le-Spring Union served from that body's creation in 1836 until his death in 1853. In 1851 a meeting of the board of guardians had to be adjourned because the clerk was hopelessly drunk – the minutes of that meeting are a mere series of doodles. Despite a serious warning the same thing happened in the following year. It is difficult to differ from the considered judgement of the Poor Law Commission on another northern Poor Law official in 1844: 'The Commissioners desire to state that they think it extremely discreditable for a master of a workhouse to be wandering about in a state of drunkenness in the middle of the night so as to be robbed in a public highway by a prostitute.'[10]

These are only a few examples, and many others could be cited. It took only a few cases of this kind to make ratepayers suspicious of the calibre of officials, and increased their disinclination to sanction the payment of appropriate salaries – which for the poorer ratepayer might often mean the sanctioning of salaries higher than his own earnings. This produced a vicious circle which took many years to break through – low salaries could produce poor candidates and poor performance enhanced public criticism of officials and official salaries. It is understandable that in these relatively early days of the development of administrative services and techniques voluntary organisations and activity might seem more admirable methods of relief in contrast.

There were, moreover, serious deficiencies in the structure of the New Poor Law. Some of these will be discussed elsewhere in this book, but a few are particularly relevant here. The 1834 Act was in great measure a compromise between central supervision and the much cherished principle of local autonomy and responsibility. One feature of the compromise was the arrangement which left each local parish or township as a rating authority responsible for paying for the cost of its own poor (see pp. 40, 143). In Poor Law unions where the social problems were concentrated in one or two parishes with few wealthy ratepayers, this posed insoluble problems for the post-1834 Poor Law until the amending legislation of the 1860s. The history of the years after 1834 is punctuated with unions taking defaulting parishes to court, or agreeing after prolonged haggling to accept smaller payments from hard-hit parishes. In many unions where social problems were severe, this meant that the official agency simply did not possess the necessary resources for effective action, and this enhanced the need for the interposition of unofficial relief agencies.

The question of local autonomy was important in another way too. In a locally orientated society there was widespread hostility to the supervisory functions entrusted to a central authority under the post-1834 system, and this too enhanced the attractiveness of tackling local social problems through unofficial agencies immune from bureaucratic interference. Certainly the central authority and the individual Poor Law unions could often work together in tolerable harmony, but it is equally true that relations between central and local authority were frequently strained. Sometimes the central authority would try to make a local union act more vigorously and spend the ratepayers' money more generously on poor relief and sometimes the local board would steadfastly resist central attempts to cut out certain forms of relief in the interests of national uniformity. There always lingered a local resentment, which manifested itself in the refusal to admit that Whitehall could understand local problems better than the men on the spot (see p. 122). Work on the Sunderland Union has recently provided a splendid example of the depths to which local/central conflicts could sink. After a prolonged period of bickering about various matters the Poor Law Board in 1871 refused to sanction the Sunderland guardians' proposal to appoint an office boy until the guardians provided the central authority with a list of the duties which this important new official was to perform. With pardonable irritation – and no doubt enjoyment – the Sunderland guardians solemnly minuted: 'That the Poor Law Board be informed that the duties of the office boy will be such as are normally performed by boys in offices.'[11] Resentment at central interference in local affairs was another factor in making locally controlled voluntary efforts for the remedying of local problems more attractive. Communities which had always looked after their own affairs in the past did not take kindly or quickly to the embryonic centralising tendencies of the period.

Even the interference of recently created local elected authorities could be viewed with a considerable absence of enthusiasm by communities which were slow to accept that such official bodies were necessarily competent, impartial or unaffected by the private vested interests of their members.

It would, however, give a misleading picture to suppose that the official Poor Law machinery and unofficial philanthropy existed in two different spheres in the nineteenth century. Throughout the period British society was niether democratic nor egalitarian, and in practice official and unofficial activity for the care of the poor were controlled by much the same people. Those who sat as Poor Law guardians would very often be the same people who sat on the committees which controlled schools, hospitals and dispensaries, and the other varied forms of charitable organisations; they would also often be among those who took the lead in sponsoring local voluntary efforts in times of disaster or communal celebration.

Active co-operation between official and unofficial agencies was a frequent occurrence in these circumstances. During the periods of industrial depression in the 1820s and again in the 1840s this kind of co-operation was exhibited on a national scale, in the very close contacts maintained between the central government and an ostensibly voluntary charitable organisation known generally as 'The City of London Tavern Committee', a committee of leading citizens who disposed of very considerable sums collected by subscription in all parts of the country.[12] Education too presented a picture of close co-operation between official and unofficial agencies. The building of schools for poorer children was largely carried out by voluntary bodies, aided from 1833 by a grant from public funds. This grant gradually grew, accompanied by the greater degree of state inspection and regulation derived from the principle of accountability for public funds, but the Education Act of 1870 was avowedly action by the state to supplement rather than replace voluntary efforts.

On a local basis this kind of co-operation was common. When a public subscription was set up to help victims of an epidemic or a local disaster, Poor Law officials were often used to make case studies of those concerned in order to measure their need for help from the voluntary fund. It was common in British towns in the late nineteenth century for police forces to play an important part in distributing among the very poor clothing and footwear provided by voluntary subscription. It was often the holder of an official position who took the lead in initiating voluntary relief activity. Mayors appealed for donations for relief work either in hard times or to meet local catastrophes such as large fires or mining accidents. At the end of the century the compendious information gathered from all parts of the country by the Select Committee on Distress from Want of Employment in 1895 clearly demonstrated not only the crucial importance of the work carried out by voluntary agencies in times of heavy unemployment, but also the way in which these activities were carried out in close co-operation with the official agencies of local government. This kind of co-operation was not, however, confined to emergencies; it was common for local authorities, such as town councils and boards of guardians, to make regular donations from public funds, both in the nineteenth and twentieth centuries, to charitable organisations which took part in the relief of poverty in their districts. Sometimes the co-operation between official and unofficial machinery for relief could be very close. Some of the best examples of this come from the work of the charity organisation societies in the late nineteenth century, for these unofficial organisations sought to establish a close working relationship with Poor Law authorities within the areas with which they were concerned. This co-operation was often based on the belief that unofficial philanthropy, based on a close examination of the needs of individual cases, was the best method of providing help to those who were in need through no fault of their own, leaving the official machinery to cope with those whose wants arose from circumstances for which they themselves were largely responsible.

From this point of view the work of charitable organisations and the Poor Law machinery was essentially complementary. For example, the Vice-Chairman of the St Marylebone board of guardians fully accepted this division of function, 'maintaining by every possible means the principle that deserving cases should be liberally and judiciously dealt with by charity, while idle, thriftless and dissolute characters should be left entirely to the Poor Law. . . . It is in the agreement between the Poor Law authorities and representatives of charity how each case should be treated, that co-operation is chiefly needed.'[13]

The same source produced another instance of how official and unofficial activity could be closely linked in practice. Some of the members of this same London board of guardians had chafed under the restricted categories of relief which they were able to provide under the official rules, which sometimes prevented them from giving the kind of specific help which might be most useful in individual cases; the kind of help which they had in mind included 'purchasing or taking tools out of pawn to give a fresh start' and 'migration cases where work can readily be obtained elsewhere'. To obtain a flexibility of treatment impossible from the Poor Law's own funds it was necessary to go beyond official resources. A leading and much respected member of the St Marylebone board accordingly launched a public appeal for this kind of discretionary fund, and the resultant money 'was separately administered by a certain number of Guardians in a private capacity'.

One aspect of co-operation between official and unofficial agencies deserves special mention because it played an important part in the development which led eventually to the creation of the twentieth-century welfare state. As voluntary initiative led to the creation of special institutions for various special categories of those in need, it became common for Poor Law authorities to place in these institutions paupers within the special category concerned, paying the necessary charges out of the poor rates. This development appeared early, for instance, in the case of mental illness; as increasing numbers of private lunatic asylums were founded, it became an increasingly regular practice for Poor Law authorities to send the lunatic poor to those asylums at public cost, and the increasing prevalence of this custom was a natural precursor to the establishment of an official system of publicly provided lunatic asylums. Private initiative provided the institutions in the first place, and then increasing public participation in the institution's activity paved the way for the provision of a public system.

By the early twentieth century this kind of co-operation had reached very large proportions, and paved the way for much more extensive state provision. Official placing of people in care within private or charitable institutions meant more than a trivial contact, for the spending of public money meant some form of public supervision, and it was normal practice for boards of guardians to keep a close eye on the activities of institutions to which they were paying fees of this kind. Guardians were regularly commissioned to visit and inspect such places, and these duties were normally taken seriously; it was not uncommon for surprise visits to be arranged, and normal for visits to be thorough and followed up by full reports to the parent authority. It is startling to realise how extensive these contacts could be. In 1913 deputations from the South Shields board of guardians visited the following institutions in which poor people for whom they were responsible had been placed: Wigton Convent of Mercy, Carlisle; St Joseph's Home, Darlington; Lancaster Asylum; Border Counties Home, Carlisle; Carlisle Asylum; St Peter's Home, Gainford; St Mary's Home, Tudhoe; Hospital of St John, Scarton; Storthes Hall Asylum, Huddersfield; Edgeworth Children's Home, Bolton; Sunderland Boys Industrial School; Wellesley Training Ship; Green's Home for Boys; Shotley Bridge Training Home for Girls; Deaf and Dumb Institution, Newcastle; Blind Institution, Newcastle; York City Asylum; Beverley Asylum, Doncaster; Balby Home, Doncaster; Dr Barnado's Home, Ilford; Field Heath House, Middlesex; Leatherhead School for the Blind; Stoke Park Colony, Bristol; Midland Counties Institution, Chesterfield; Middlesbrough Asylum; Sedgefield Asylum. This one union was connected with a large number of specialised institutions, some of them public in nature by then, but many of them still operated by voluntary societies. Well before the end of the nineteenth century it was common for boards of guardians to support such groups as the blind and the deaf and dumb in special institutions operated by unofficial agencies. The twentieth century has seen much of this co-operation between official and unofficial agencies translated into the much more widespread creation of full public provision.

It was not only in these organised forms that co-operation between official Poor Law machinery and unofficial philanthropy developed. Especially in the latter part of the nineteenth century it became common for charitable individuals, or groups of individuals, to provide amenities of various kinds for the inhabitants of Poor Law workhouses. These could include gifts of pictures, books, musical instruments or, for instance, a barrel of beer at Christmas time. The workhouse children were often taken to shows of various kinds, or for a visit to the seaside. Let one example illustrate this growing custom. The South Shields board of guardians received this letter after a visit by the workhouse children to the Newcastle Jubilee Exhibition of 1887:

Dear Guardians,

We are glad to let you know that through your kindness we were taken to the Exhibition at Newcastle on Monday. the Guardians who met us at the Tyne Dock Station, wer Mr thornton Mr Proud and Mr. Oldroyd. We spent such a jolly afternoon and saw lots of things. We always thought to go down a black hole, the pit we were in, we walked straight in. We asked the gentleman if he wanted any putters he said he was full up. He took us through. By! what a black hole, some of us got lost in the pit at last Mr Thornton and Mr Proud came to seek us to get some cocoa as it was so cold. By! what a canny man Mr Proud is. And by 5 o'clock we had such a good tea far more than we could eat we had to get paper bags to put some in. we went where we had a mind. the people at the Exhibition did not think we came from a Workhouse they said we had such good clothes on and looked so well, and we were so glad for the master said that we had all behaved well. We do not know the Ladies and Gentlemen that gave the money for our treat but you might tell the Newspaperman to thank them for us. A Gentleman some said his name was Mr Marshall and the Guardians that was with us bought two much big footballs and penholders one each and we spent an afternoon not soon to be forgotten we must not forget the kind officers who are over us.

We are your children

Christopher Thompson   Annie Spittlehouse
John Glancy   Margaret J. Gorman
John Findlay   Margaret Parkin
Thomas Peel   Minnie Hoey.[14]

One interesting development in the late nineteenth century was the arrival of small groups of working men among those who directed the local agencies of both official and unofficial relief activities. In the voluntary agencies with which we are primarily concerned here this change resulted for the most part from changes in their financial support. The growth of industry saw the creation of a growing number of arrangements whereby in exchange for access to the facilities of a voluntary charitable foundation – especially in the case of medical facilities – the workers of a given firm agreed to pay regular small subscriptions to the institution's funds. By the 1870s, especially in industrialised and urban areas, many local voluntary hospitals were heavily dependent upon this resource, and its existence brought about two important changes in the government of many of these institutions. With the increasing importance of widespread small subscriptions the old common system of admitting patients by letters of introduction died out while, at the same time, working men were admitted to governing bodies to represent the interests of these new groups of mass subscribers. In both official and unofficial sectors of relief work, however, it would be too simple to suppose that the arrival of small numbers of workers in positions of genuine influence necessarily meant the arrival on the scene of more generous attitudes towards the very poor. The kind of worker who arrived among the Poor Law guardians might very well be a houseowner and ratepayer himself, and the addresses of worker governors of hospitals usually suggest that they were drawn overwhelmingly from the more prosperous workers in the firms whose subscribers they represented. The idea that the workers in general have always been among the champions of the very poor may be an attractive one but it scarcely accords with the facts. In practice the champions of the very poor were recognisable minorities drawn from a wide range of social groupings. It is not possible to understand the story of nineteenth-century philanthropy in stark terms of class analysis. The men and women who fought for social reform, and who created, supported and administered voluntary agencies for relief – as well as those who opposed or ignored them – are not to be found in any one class, nor can the process of social amelioration be ascribed romantically to the efforts of 'the people' or 'the workers'.

It is very tempting to see social relationships in the nineteenth century in simple terms, but the temptation must be resisted, for the reality was complex and variable. The motives which lay behind philanthropic activities could in themselves be mixed. In some cases ostentatious charitable activity might be a means to social distinction, or to a form of social rivalry between members of the propertied groups. Involvement in ameliorative activities could be derived from more subtle motives, such as a desire to buy off potential unrest and disaffection. It was perfectly possible for a genuine desire to help those in need to be combined with an appreciation that such work could have distinctly useful effects in extending sympathies between different groups in society. For example, the 1849 *Report* of the Newcastle Ragged School – one of many such schools provided by voluntary organisations in British towns for the benefit of the children of the very poor – included this revealing passage:

> The Committee take this opportunity to express their grateful sense of the kindness of the Worshipful the Mayor, and the other gentlemen, in providing the children with a handsome dinner of roast beef and plum pudding, on Easter Monday . . . and they are of opinion that the social mingling of the rich and poor on such occasions, and the personal interest thus exhibited in the enjoyments of the humbler classes, are well adapted to strengthen and consolidate the bonds of civil society.[15]

While admitting that the motives which induced men and women to involve themselves in charitable work could be varied, it remains true that much of it was inspired by nothing more sophisticated than a generous desire to help those in need. Far from exhibiting a degree of callousness unknown in earlier periods, British society in the nineteenth century evinced a degree of genuine benevolence which transcended the efforts of any previous period.

It is worth stressing this point because some of the most influential modern books on the social history of late eighteenth- and early nineteenth-century Britain have given us a very strained and lop-sided account of the social relationships within British society. One of the elements within this distorted picture is a wholly inadequate appreciation of the voluntary activity in relief measures during that period. Brian Inglis, in his *Poverty and the Industrial Revolution,* presents a very one-sided picture. The stress is very much on oppression and cruelty, exploitation and suffering, without sufficient comprehension of the evidence which shows that there were other sides to that society. The whole book is suffused with a spirit of righteous indignation; admirable though that sentiment may be, it is not always a passport to balanced historical judgement.

In E. P. Thompson's *The Making of the English Working Class,* we are dealing with a higher standard of historical craftsmanship, but the same basic weaknesses are present, though the treatment is much more subtle and sophisticated. This immensely readable book contains a great wealth of detailed evidence, testifying to the author's very wide researches, but the evidence presented is chosen too selectively, and does not present an adequate demonstration of the social relationships within British society, which it is the aim of the book to analyse. There is always a great temptation when a writer is trying to make a case to miss out evidence which might impair the simplicity and symmetry of the favoured interpretation. Thompson's treatment of charitable activity admirably illustrates this danger, for the existence of any substantial efforts by the propertied classes to help the poor could only cloud a picture of oppression and conflict. Two examples may illustrate this point.[16] In Thompson's analysis of the cotton industry there is a passing reference to the existence by the 1830s of various new forms of paternalistic charity within this key industry, but there is no suggestion that this was a common feature of contemporary British society and had shown a continuous development from pre-industrial origins. At another point we are told that, in the 1830s, many paternalistic Tories drew back from further co-operation with militant radicals – surely a comprehensible development – and that instead 'The majority . . . contented themselves with schemes for humanitarian amelioration of different kinds.' This, however, is put forward as a form of back-sliding to be deplored, and there is no discussion of the possibility that schemes for humanitarian amelioration might have had useful effects in mitigating social evils, might indeed have had some interesting influences on the social relationships between the different groups involved.

To some historians, and to some students, much of the paternalistic philanthropy of the nineteenth century is abhorrent because of the elements of condescension and superiority which were so clearly part of the story, but we must not think back twentieth-century assumptions into a very different context. A useful general principle to bear in mind is this: that which happened in the past was, in the circumstances of that time, the most probable thing to have happened, and the principal task of the student of history is to understand just what those circumstances were. The kind of history which springs from the assumption that something else should have happened instead is generally bad history.

These matters are invested with a greater importance than most academic differences on historical interpretation, for one peculiar feature of our society is that it tends to be obsessed by its modern social history to an inordinate degree. The approaches to present and prospective problems by very many people – probably most – are highly coloured by their impressions of how our society has evolved in relatively recent periods of history, and it is important that all of us involved in this kind of study should do our best to arrive at a balanced understanding. It is very easy indeed, in view of the wealth of evidence available, to produce a distorted picture by the simple expedient of selecting the evidence which will help to make a particular case, and ignoring evidence which points to a more complex reality. This danger of prejudice and undue selectivity is not, of course, confined to one side of the modern ideological spectrum, and it would be patently wrong to suggest that nineteenth-century philanthropy provided a panacea for society's ailments. Its coverage, since it was largely based on a wide variety of local interests and activities, was undoubtedly patchy and heterogeneous. In many cases well-meaning projects in this field, as in many fields of human effort, produced a mixture of good and bad effects. The efforts of the charity organisation societies of the late nineteenth century are a case in point. Certainly their attempt to bring order into overlapping voluntary activity, and their strong pressure for better facilities for some categories of those in need, produced some beneficial effects; their continued distinction between the 'deserving' and 'undeserving' poor undoubtedly resulted in a sterner approach to the relief of suffering in other cases.[17] There is in addition a further dimension of charitable activity within nineteenth-century society which must be brought into account, even though again it is impossible to measure its significance with any precision. That is the very great amount of philanthropic help existing within the poorer groups themselves. In the third chapter of his classic *Poverty, A Study of Town Life*, Seebohm Rowntree paid tribute to the importance of this factor in mitigating poverty and distress at a time when state welfare agencies were relatively primitive:

> Families which are, from any cause, in particularly hard straits, are often helped by those in circumstances but little better than their own. There is much of this mutual helpfulness among the very poor. In cases of illness neighbours will almost always come in and render assistance, by cleaning the house, nursing, and often bringing some little delicacy which they think the patient would 'fancy'.

In some districts also it is a common practice, on the death of a child, for one of the neighbours to go round the neighbourhood to collect coppers towards defraying the cost of the funeral.[18]

Needless to say this is one aspect of voluntary charitable activity which the expansion of the state's resources has only very partially replaced. Over all, however, it can be stipulated that the continuous expansion of voluntary philanthropic activity is an important factor to be taken into account in any evaluation of British society in the nineteenth century.

Perhaps the most profitable way to look at the relationships between the Poor Law and philanthropy is to see them as a microcosm of more fundamental developments affecting the evolution of modern British society. In the early nineteenth century Britain was a little-governed society based essentially on small, local inward-looking communities, in which it was very natural for the relief of poverty, like other communal activities, to be primarily organised as local measures to tackle local problems. In practice, those who needed help were to be relieved at the cost of those among whom they lived, though this more intimate knowledge was not always a recipe for greater generosity to the poor. The development of the much more populous industrialised society intensified social problems, but provided enhanced resources with which to combat them. Underlying the major changes which occurred during the nineteenth century was a basic shift in the nature of social interdependence. Instead of a situation in which, for the most part, the great majority of people depended only upon those with whom they lived and worked, a much more complex pattern of interdependence evolved. To take one very obvious example, the development of systems of public utilities – an undoubted boon – produced important new patterns of dependence, in which large numbers of people depended, for the supply of water for example, on small groups of other people who had no immediate contact with those who depended on them in this way. In the much more complicated and sophisticated society emerging before the end of the nineteenth century local autonomy and local responsibility were ceasing to be appropriate vehicles for the conduct of social policies, and the role of the state inexorably advanced. This process was to be marked by the eventual swallowing up by public services of many welfare activities created in piecemeal fashion in an earlier, less-governed society by voluntary philanthropic agencies. Yet during the vital and difficult period of transition, when the state disposed of neither the resources nor the expertise to fulfil its later role, a key contribution to social progress was made by these voluntary efforts. This is not to say that voluntary charitable activity has died with the expansion of the state's welfare function; however it is undeniable that its relative importance has declined.

It is not possible to claim more than that nineteenth-century philanthropy provided increasing resources and extended machinery with which to diminish the undesirable effects of that period's social problems. Charity did not solve those problems completely by any means. However, the work of nineteenth-century philanthropy, and its pioneering activities in advance of major state intervention, provided one of the main foundations on which the twentieth-century welfare state has been built. The relationship of nineteenth-century society to poverty cannot be understood without an appreciation of the contribution made by those men and women who worked to help the poor from outside the ambit of the official Poor Law machinery.

5. The Poor Law as a Political Institution

DEREK FRASER

HISTORICAL studies of the nineteenth century have committed the
Poor Law to a non-political limbo. Political historians have assumed
that politics was primarily concerned with parliamentary elections
and have shown little interest in Poor Law affairs, except perhaps
when they impinged on the wider political stage. Social historians interested in poor relief have concentrated heavily upon social administration and have ignored political dimensions. Yet the Poor
Law was a vital political institution, granting to those who directed
affairs in their own community great powers and much patronage.
The office of guardian was an elective one and it was therefore a
potential source of political conflict. Poor Law policy was frequently
controversial and was therefore a potential source of political contention. To fail to appreciate the political aspect of poor relief is to
misunderstand the role of the Poor Law in Victorian society.

In defining the political role of the Poor Law this chapter will
elucidate the three ways in which the Poor Law operated as a political
institution. First, it was politicised by the local political structure
itself, becoming a vehicle for political conflicts which were resolved
within a wider political context. A struggle for power within the Poor
Law was often part of a much broader contest for total local control.
Secondly, Poor Law policy could be highly controversial and this
generated political tension over how Poor Law power should be exercised. In such disputes the political feeling often cut across normal
party lines. Thirdly the Poor Law was legally involved with the whole
franchise system. Parliamentary, municipal and even parochial
voting depended upon payment of poor rates and for this reason
control over the Poor Law could yield electoral advantage.

For Notes to Chapter 5, see pp. 210–11; for Bibliography; see pp. 199–200.

I

Leeds provides a good example of a fierce local party battle politicising poor relief. The struggle for power between rival elites within the
urban middle class of Leeds made it impossible to insulate the Poor
Law from local political controversy. As assistant commissioner Mott
explained: 'political party feeling prevails to a mischievous extent at
Leeds – the parties are nearly balanced and it is scarcely possible to
take any step in Leeds township without exciting strong party
feeling.'[1] In the 1830s, when the Liberal versus Tory battle for local
control infected every local institution, the Leeds Poor Law operated
on a traditional system comprising churchwardens, overseers and
trustees. The overseers, appointed by the magistrates, were Tory,
while the wardens and trustees, elected by the vestry, were Liberal.
The position was well explained by the Leeds doctor and Poor Law
migration agent, Robert Baker: 'The Boardroom has long been a
sort of arena for party politics on a small scale . . . of late politics have
run high with us . . . and to such a pitch has this feeling been
carried that public poor law business has been very much neglected
and very bad feeling has existed.'[2] The short-term solution to con-
firm the overseers in sole control was a pyrrhic Tory victory, for in
1836 municipal reform led to a creation of Liberal magistrates, who
in turn appointed Liberal overseers. Blatant partisanship was dis-
played in sacking the Tory clerk and replacing him at twice the salary
by a Liberal activist and by using the new offices of registrar of births,
marriages and deaths as spoils for Liberals, one of whom was a paid
agent of the Anti-Corn Law League.

Leeds was given an opportunity in 1837 to put partisanship behind
it and operate the Poor Law by merit rather than party. An attempt
to impose the New Poor Law upon Leeds tested the sincerity of those
who had argued that politics should play no part in the Poor Law
elections. The local political battle prevented non-political intentions
bearing fruit and the Tory defence of a party list of candidates for
guardians explained why: 'It is at all times desirable that party
politics should be excluded from matters connected with parochial
affairs but the grasping spirit of our political opponents has turned
the election of every petty parish officer into a question of party.'[3]
The resort to party in self-defence was characteristic of Leeds politics
and the Tory list produced a Liberal response. Edward Baines,
Liberal M.P. for Leeds, urged speed on the local party agent 'so that

we may at all costs have a liberal Guardianship . . . The Tories are working hard. . . . I trust that our friends will not be less zealous nor less early in their movements.' The dejected assistant commissioner reported that the Leeds election 'has been made entirely a party question . . . and all the excitement and mutual jealousies of parties have been entertained here in a very strong degree'.[4] Defective election machinery made the declaration of a result impossible and the attempt to form a union was abandoned.

When the attempt was renewed in 1844 the same pious hopes were frustrated as the election was made a party contest and the anti-Poor Law, anti-workhouse Tories gained an easy victory. By this time Leeds Liberals were in full control of the corporation and were not unduly concerned that Tories should monopolise this area of local administration. When, however, the new regime resulted in increased poor rates, the Liberals became extremely concerned, but found that, though they could win elections for other positions, they were powerless in Poor Law contests. It did not take long to deduce that all was not above board as far as the conduct of elections was concerned. The system of election, by which voting papers were delivered to homes and later collected, was open to abuse by the clerk (the returning officer), especially when, as in Leeds, his was a political appointment. As a respected Liberal solicitor explained, the collectors of voting papers 'will always in contested elections be chosen if possible for their adhesion to the party views of the clerk especially when his own happens to be the reflex of those of the Board in possession, willing and perhaps anxious to retain office'.[5] The only Liberal option was to call for a Poor Law enquiry which was conducted in 1852 by a shocked inspector who concluded: 'I have seen a great many electioneering proceedings but I never saw anything as gross as this.' Voting papers had been selectively distributed and collected; they had been altered; they had been burned; they had been filled up by Tory agents. Poor Law elections in Leeds were shown to be not the expression of the will of the electorate but of an 'unexampled mass of frauds, forgeries, tricks and knaveries'.[6]

The clerk was severely censured and in 1853 two collectors were imprisoned for electoral abuse. No doubt things improved for a short while but the system was such that it provided opportunities for electoral advantages which party workers could hardly ignore in times of close contests. When a second Poor Law enquiry was held in 1870 it was revealed that the abuses of 1852 still persisted, notwithstanding new regulations introduced by the Poor Law Board in 1867 designed to prevent 'accidents and malpractices'.[7] For a second time it was revealed that people had been disfranchised by non-delivery or non-collection of voting papers; that blank papers had been filled up by party agents; that illiterates had been defrauded by their verbal preferences being reversed on the paper; and that papers had been altered and destroyed. These all flowed from the appointment of known party workers as collectors of voting papers; but, as the clerk complained, he needed a hundred men and in Leeds 'where am I as returning officer to get 100 men altogether free from political bias?'[8] Allowing for this difficulty, it may be thought that to appoint as collector a candidate's son-in-law and the chairman of the Tory ward committee was somewhat contentious. The operation of the system was clearly revealed when the inspector, Henry Longley, asked one of the election officials, in connection with the Tory candidate, 'How came it that you, a distributor and collector, considered yourself one of Mr Woodhead's party? . . . . I considered I was justified by the manner in which he (the liberal collector) was annoying voters saying "vote for these three men" and in self defence I said "vote for the other three".'[9] As ever in Leeds, politics in self-defence was the cry and the Poor Law as an integral part of the local political structure was deemed an appropriate avenue for political advancement.

In Leeds the politicising of the Poor Law was a characteristic feature of the fifty years from 1830. In Salford, the flame of politics burned brightly during the 1830s and 1840s and was then dimmed. During those decades Salford affairs were directed by a Liberal oligarchy of manufacturers and merchants, the most prominent of whom was William Lockett, a silk mercer, who launched a distinguished political career from a parochial apprenticeship. Lockett first emerged as an overseer in the early 1830s and by the mid-1840s was Salford's first mayor and chairman of the board of guardians, thus straddling the two most powerful administrative institutions of the town.[10]

The parliamentary election of 1832 organised Liberal/Radical forces and led to the election of a Radical select vestry in 1833. As in Leeds, the mid-1830s were characterised by a fierce struggle for local control in which the contest for power over Salford's Poor Law figured prominently. In 1835, when Tories used the Salford Operative Conservative Society to seek control of the vestry, a Liberal leader urged ratepayers 'not to be diverted from their points by any tory tricks whatever to regain power'.[11] The phrase is significant. In Salford real local power was at stake in a Poor Law contest. Subsequent vestry elections were fiercely fought, and the Poor Law was the main issue in the parliamentary election of 1837 when the Tory candidate pledged himself against the introduction of the New Poor Law into Salford. Ironically, as it turned out, it was a Tory select vestry which introduced the Poor Law in 1838. In that year the Liberals had lost control of the select vestry because of 'the extraordinary activity of the tories who canvassed as for an election, carried up their voters in coaches and ... paid the rates of a very considerable number of the poorer voters'.[12] However, the Tories did not capture the office of overseer and so there was a deadlock in Poor Law affairs with poor relief clamped between opposing political forces. The New Poor Law resolved the deadlock and a Tory victory in the first election mellowed the party's attitudes to the 1834 system.

One of the first acts of the Tory guardians was to dismiss a Liberal assistant overseer and replace him with one of their own party faithful, Francis Wrigley. The Wrigley case is a fine example of the political-spoils system at work within the Poor Law and encapsulates in one fascinating episode the politicising of Salford's Poor Law. Wrigley enjoyed his office for only a short time, for when the Liberals under Lockett won the 1840 election they sought to dismiss him for participating in electoral misdemeanours. Charles Mott, the assistant commissioner, had no doubts that this was 'a political party question' and he explained the background to the Commission:

> The dispute has existed from the commencement of the union. The late assistant overseer Mr Wakefield was displaced by the first Board of Guardians, composed principally of Conservatives, chiefly on the ground of his being a partizan of the Reformers or Whigs. The changes are now made against Mr Wrigley because he is a partizan of the Conservatives and the interests of the union are lost sight of and the Guardians of the other Townships [Broughton, Pendlebury and Pendleton] kept in a continued state of excitement by the political disputes of the Township of Salford.[13]

Wrigley certainly found himself on a political see-saw – his elevation accompanied the Tory victory of 1838 and his fall followed the Liberal victory of 1840.

The charges against Wrigley were brought by Smith P. Robinson, a fierce Liberal activist, and Wrigley explained ruefully how he was caught in a network of political intrigue:

> I am sure it will not be overlooked that these charges are preferred by Mr Robinson – a most active and enthusiastic partisan – transmitted by him to Overseers who employed the Secretary of the Reform Association in arranging the lists of claims and objections to the franchise — forwarded by them to the Board of Guardians; approved there by a majority every member of which was a Gentleman professing Liberal politics ... and that they were so approved upon the evidence of persons two of whom are in the pay of the Reform Association ... it is obvious that the whole of these proceedings have been got up by the Reform Association.[14]

That Lockett's enquiry would find Wrigley guilty was predictable and the Poor Law Commission, on appeal, ordered its own enquiry. Mott reported sadly that the Commission could not win since, where politics were so involved, any judgement would give satisfaction to only one side. Mott's recommendation that Wrigley be merely censured was overruled, and Wrigley – a pawn in a political game whose field of play stretched right across Salford's institutions – was sacrificed in the interests of local power-politics. Lockett continued to use the Poor Law for external political purposes (see below p. 125) and at least until his withdrawal in 1848 politics were the main factor in Salford's administration of poor relief. As Mott expressed it, in Salford the Poor Law was 'used as a political engine by the majority of the Guardians'.[15]

Leeds and Salford are only two examples of towns where the Poor Law was highly politicised. Party contests and a political-spoils system are also to be found elsewhere including Leicester, Nottingham, Bradford, Gateshead and Birmingham. In the last-named town a Tory victory at a guardians' election in 1840, following a decade of Liberal success in town politics, was hailed as something of general significance: 'the people are growing tired of the reign of Radicalism, with the terrorism and all the other *isms* with which it has been accompanied ... Birmingham has achieved a glorious victory ... has set an example to the nation by declaring for Conservatism.'[16] In the partisan political atmosphere of early Victorian Birmingham the Poor Law provided but one more context in which political victories could be registered. The crucial factor in politicising the Poor Law was the local political system, and where there was intense political rivalry then it was likely that the guardians would become involved. Since politics were more keenly contested in urban than in rural areas, a political administration of the Poor Law was more likely in towns than in the countryside. In England and Wales as a whole most guardians' elections were uncontested and even in large towns political interest frequently waned. Yet if only intermittent, the political involvement was often intense, as rivals settled political scores whose origin lay outside the Poor Law itself.

II

In other circumstances the political interest could be generated from within, when disputes arose over the proper exercise of the intrinsic powers of the Poor Law. The best known example of this *genre* of political activity is that provided by the anti-Poor Law movement. This was not a straight party-political conflict but a cross-party alliance against specific methods of poor relief and against a certain form of administration. As explained in the Introduction (p. 11 above), anti-Poor Law feeling could be Tory in one place (for example in Salford) and Whig in another (for example in Banbury). Fear of the workhouse and dislike of centralisation were the two main planks on which the movement was built and it emerged that neither the workhouse test nor centralisation were quite as immutable as had been feared. Conflict over such issues continued inside the Poor Law as opponents discovered that the best battle ground was the board of guardians rather than the public meeting. Of the many issues which continued to stimulate political interest in the Poor Law from within, none was more emotive than the question of new workhouses. Often with the best of intentions, the Commission and its officials sought to provide a comprehensive system of 'well-regulated workhouses', only to find themselves engaged in a major political row.

When a workhouse dispute occurred soon after the imposition of the New Poor Law, it tended to merge with the anti-Poor Law movement. This was the case in Nottingham. The board of guardians there was an important focus of political interest in the town and it became central in town politics when in 1840 it decided to build a new workhouse. The clerk Absolem Barnett worked in close liaison with the assistant commissioner and his superiors, and he pushed the scheme very hard indeed. Town meetings and press criticism could not deflect the small majority of guardians in favour of the new workhouse and a Tory/Radical alliance was created on an anti-Poor

Law platform. This was well reflected in the disposition of the Nottingham press, with Richard Sutton's Radical *Review* and John Hicklin's Tory *Journal* against the new workhouse and Thomas Wakefield's Whig *Mercury* in favour of it.[17] The refusal of the guardians to abandon the project made the workhouse question the key political issue in Nottingham politics in the winter of 1840–1, and a political dispute within the Poor Law spilled over into other areas of the local political system.

Anti-workhouse feeling expressed itself in three separate Nottingham elections. (1) The municipal election of November 1840 was contested in many wards on the workhouse question even though poor relief had nothing to do with the town council. Richard Sutton concluded simply 'we were not wrong in describing the feeling of a majority of the ratepayers to be in opposition to the erection of a new workhouse', while a Whig defender of the scheme forecasted optimistically that 'next year the high state of feeling among the townspeople will have passed away when they see the benefits that will be conferred upon the deserving poor by the new building and the discouragement that will be given to vice and immorality and they will again rally round their party'.[18] Such a return of the faithful would be needed since the Tories captured four council seats from the Liberals in 1840 on this workhouse question. (2) Predictably the spring election for Poor Law guardians in 1841 also went against the workhouse party when Hicklin, the anti-workhouse Tory editor, came top of the poll in one parish. (3) The workhouse dispute coincided with a parliamentary by-election and this Poor Law issue provided 'a centre of union around which those, whose opinions upon other subjects are widely different, may harmoniously rally'.[19] John Walter, proprietor of *The Times*, registered a spectacular victory in April 1841 on the strength of the Nottingham workhouse question. It was this which rallied to his side men of all political persuasions and it was noticed during the election that 'his colour *blue* is worn by the very children in the streets not as a tory but as an enemy of the new Poor Law'.[20] Thus the contentious issue of the Nottingham workhouse altered the composition of the board of guardians, sacrificed four Liberal seats on the municipal council and finally enabled the local Tories to return their candidate as the first Tory M.P. for Nottingham since 1807. Such were the ramifications of an apparently non-political decision to build a new workhouse.

It is sometimes argued that, in time, feelings mellowed on the

workhouse issue. Yet, in Sheffield over twenty years after the birth of
the New Poor Law, a dispute arose of intense acrimony in which the
workhouse became 'very properly the all engrossing subject for the
Sheffield public; ratepayers, shopkeepers, tradesmen and
mechanics'.[21] The story in outline is as follows. A new clerk to the
guardians, Thomas Spencer (who was to occupy the post for over
forty years), and a new chairman, Robert Younge (a self-made silver
plater and prominent philanthropist), decided in consultation with
the master of the workhouse and the Poor Law inspector that Sheffield needed a new workhouse. In October 1855 Younge launched
the plan, which was received with public hostility. The familiar
pattern of newspaper editorials, deputations and public meetings did
not weaken Younge's resolve and the board of guardians approved
the scheme with the lowest possible majority: eight out of fifteen. In
the early months of 1856 a site was chosen and a deposit paid, for
Younge wished to commit Sheffield to build a workhouse whatever
his own future might be. As expected the 1856 election swept the pro-
workhouse guardians from office and the new board, pledged to
reverse the scheme, shelved the workhouse question for a year. In
1857–8 the guardians were pressed to complete the purchase of the
site and for the second time the inspector confirmed that the town
must have a new workhouse. Relations worsened when the Poor Law
Board closed part of the Sheffield workhouse as unfit for use. Reluctantly the guardians agreed to alter the workhouse in 1859, but
Younge's cherished new workhouse was not erected until the 1870s.

A review of the Sheffield workhouse question reveals some familiar
themes. There was, understandably, great concern over cost – it was
estimated that the town would be saddled with a debt of £60,000 –
and union economy was always popular. There were interesting class
dimensions to the dispute. Many observers remarked on the wealth
and respectability of the pro-workhouse party and few would have
quarrelled with the inspector's view that 'the more respectable and
higher rated inhabitants of the union are generally in favour of a new
workhouse'.[22] These two issues were never really central. Financial
concern was an underlying worry rather than a prime mover and the
class explanation was always undermined by the fact that Younge's
main opponent who succeeded him as chairman, Alderman J. E.
Mycock, was as wealthy and respectable as any. Mycock, for twenty
years the chairman of Sheffield's watch committee, was hardly a *sans
culottes*. These and other issues resolved themselves into disputes on

three grounds; the question of authority, the role of the workhouse and the issue of centralisation.

Inevitably in the Sheffield of the 1850s the workhouse question raised the fundamental issue of whether final authority in local affairs was vested in the guardians or in the ratepayers. Sheffield politics had been democratised by Isaac Ironside, a disciple of Joshua Toulmin Smith who wished to create a real participatory ratepayer democracy.[23] All local institutions in Sheffield in the 1850s were subject to control and veto by Ironside's 'Ward-motes'. It was natural, therefore, that the inalienable rights of the citizen should be cited against Younge's apparent despotism. Ironside's case was that the guardians had no authority to act against the general will, particularly as taxation was to be levied without consent. Younge would have nothing to do with such notions and, in a distant echo of Burke's famous debate over delegates and representatives, pronounced that 'he for one should exercise the discretion which God had blessed him with and he would not be a delegate'. He certainly made it clear that as chairman he would respond to no pressure on the guardians from without: 'No public meeting in Sheffield should deter him from his duty, which he would perform respectfully but firmly. . . . He looked upon the present movement as nothing more than an attempt to influence the actions of the board of guardians. . . . If there were any guardians there . . . who would have their judgment put in swaddling clothes by a public meeting they were proper men to be re-elected to the next board, always to sit as the delegates of others and decide upon their opinions and not their own.'[24] The 1856 election confirmed greater support in Sheffield for Ironside's rather than Younge's view on representation.

Younge and his supporters believed a workhouse to be necessary in order to help the deserving poor and in the interests of classification. There was a general belief in the workhouse party that indiscriminate relief was undermining self-help and preventing adequate care for the sick and old. As one of their handbills explained, most paupers were

> persons who have never been in any club, have made no provision against 'the rainy day' and who, on the first appearance of difficulty, apply for relief at the workhouse, where on the hard earned money of the Poor Ratepayers they live month after month without making the slightest effort to get their own living. . . .

Pauperism is eating its deadly way into the vitals of your prosperity, its blighting influence is rapidly increasing. The idle and dissolute crowd your workhouse. The Asylum is too small; the infirmary is too small, the Infection wards are too small; and as an inevitable result – the bad corrupt the good.... Let Us Have A New Workhouse.[25]

This propaganda has a Chadwickian air and the anti-workhouse lobby also revived the language of the 1830s. Ironside denounced the whole 'blasphemous atheistic and materialistic' New Poor Law, with its 'unheard of cruelties and tortures such as never disgraced even the Spanish Inquisition'. The workhouse was seen as a cruel bastille, in which the unfortunate poor were to be incarcerated.

Two real issues underlay the flamboyant language of the anti-workhouse party. First, there was a genuine disagreement over the cause of pauperism. Where Younge's friends saw voluntary paupers having an easy ride on the backs of the industrious poor, Ironside's men ascribed destitution to factors beyond personal control. Sheffield was in the midst of a trade depression and in such times a deterrent punitive Poor Law was 'as unjust as it is tyrannical. They propose to punish a man who unfortunately requires parish relief, from bad trade or other circumstances by putting him and his family into the workhouse. They want to treat him as a criminal and make his poverty a crime.'[26] The second fear was that the workhouse was to be used to manipulate the labour market. Younge's superb description of the reformatory aims of the workhouse has been quoted earlier (see p. 13), but his views were drowned by a chorus of abuse about the workhouse grinding the poor down. They might say they wished to secure the comfort of the poor but, as one speaker proclaimed, their intention was otherwise: 'a model prison they wanted to build in order to get the working classes under the finger and thumb of the arbitrary and avaricious manufacturers: and then they would be obliged to work for what the masters chose to give, or go into the model prison.'[27] Here the class dimensions were clear. The rich wished to reduce poor rates, increased as they were by fraudulent abuse of poor relief; the poor were anxious about employment in a fluctuating labour market. The Sheffield workhouse dispute was certainly extrapolated into a wider political world.

Younge had always been regarded as a mere tool of the Poor Law Board and once an anti-workhouse majority had been secured on the board of guardians the dispute became a simple centralisation battle. Ironside, perceptively as always, placed the dispute in its centralisation context. When the 1856 board received a reprimand from London he wrote,

> The busybodies of the Poor Law Board have shown their official insolence this week by sending a letter to the Sheffield Guardians, telling them to get on with their work and send it up for examination... The Guardians know that no workhouse is necessary, and 8000 ratepayers have voted them into office on that knowledge. The Poor Law Board know all this and the more they are told to mind their own business the better for those who have to pay their salaries. We can manage our business in Sheffield without their insolent dictation and we mean to do so.[28]

This was as live an issue as it had been in Yorkshire and Lancashire in the 1830s and, when the Sheffield guardians stone-walled, relations with the Poor Law bureaucracy deteriorated alarmingly. The Sheffield guardians resolved in 1857 to have no correspondence with London on the workhouse and to do nothing about it. In 1858 the anti-centralisation bitterness was as intense as ever as shown by this editorial: 'What is the use of the ratepayers electing every year a Board of Guardians to manage the administration of relief to the poor in the Sheffield union if they are constantly to be controlled, thwarted, overruled, instructed, directed, ordered and coerced by the Poor Law Board in London?... The tone they have adopted has gradually become more and more imperative until it is now insulting and dictatorial.'[29] Despite the tone, Sheffield did not give way to central direction and the workhouse was not built.

We see here that a determined board with popular support could successfully resist the Poor Law Board, whose resolve would eventually weaken. The central authority in the last resort could not compel the building of a workhouse since 'they are well aware that their authority lies in words and threats rather than in deeds'.[30] In this essentially political dispute over the exercise of power within the Poor Law executive discretion remained in local hands.

III

Those who controlled the Poor Law had other important discretionary powers that were remote from issues of poor relief. Voting in Victorian England depended upon the payment of poor rates. This simple fact endowed the Poor Law with a great potential for the party in power to derive significant political advantage. Until 1872 there was no secret ballot and so individual political preference could be easily identified. In the revision courts which produced the official list of electors, party agents could challenge the names of opponents and sustain the claims of supporters. This party warfare was much aided by the provision of information that could only come from a Poor Law source. This included the precise rateable value of property, the actual rates paid, whether the rates were paid personally by the occupant or by the landlord and, crucially, whether any payments had been missed. These minor details were in the province of the overseers who collected the rates, produced rate books and drew up the provisional list of voters for submission to the revision court. If a party controlled the overseers they had access to vital information and, furthermore, had opportunities to manipulate the system in a partisan way. Above all they could be alerted to the names of supporters who were in arrears as the qualification date approached. Party funds could then be used to pay the arrears and so keep sympathetic voters on the list.

In the nature of the case these devious doings were hidden from the public eye and so accusations of abuse were more frequent than proven cases. Historians sometimes have to use inferential evidence to deduce that election malpractices were occurring. Where there were widespread charges that abuse existed and these were followed by a deliberate attempt to neutralise the overseers by power sharing, then we may assume that something underhand was going on. Herein was an implicit admission of abuse with an assertion that the political advantage should not lie exclusively on one side. Leeds and Liverpool provide examples of this sort.

In Leeds there was some cooling of party feeling in the early 1840s, and the appointment by the Peel government of nine Tory magistrates gave the Leeds bench a more balanced political composition. It was the magistrates who appointed overseers, and Baines senior attempted to extend the sharing of spoils to these Poor Law posts. He argued somewhat uncharacteristically that 'the sooner they got rid of party the better and the more they attended to the fitness of men for parochial duties and the less they attended to the particular colour men might wear the more fitly they would discharge their duties'.[31] Gradually the plan was adopted to appoint an equal number of overseers from each party, a compromise welcomed by the Tory *Intelligencer*, which remarked 'party has, after many years of injustice been at length put on such an equilibrium as must to all reasonable ratepayers give satisfaction'.[32] In Leeds the electoral advantage was neutralised by power sharing and the overseers became a haven of non-political administration in a highly political Victorian city. By 1859 this had become a firm tradition, as the overseers explained: 'to preserve unity of feeling and to avoid any political bias the magistrates have elected an equal number of persons professing opposite political sentiments and the harmony which has existed among the overseers has never been broken.'[33]

In Liverpool the Poor Law never became as politically controversial as in Leeds but in the mid-1840s electoral abuse by the select vestry became so contentious that the aggrieved party felt bound to act. In 1845 the *Liverpool Mercury* began a campaign for reform of the select vestry and this created public interest. Superimposed on this public concern was the registration activity of the Liverpool Liberals. The Anti-Monopoly Association, the Liverpool branch of the Anti-Corn Law League, had been entrusted with Liberal registration of voters and the society decided to take a stand against abuses by which Tory overseers drew up partisan registers in the Tory interest. The 1845 select vestry election was politically contested in order to neutralise a party which had 'used its power for the purpose of tampering with the registry'. The assistant overseer, the official responsible for the lists, had supplied the Tory party with the names of those in arrears and the party paid up. Liberals, denied access to rate books, could not compete. In 1845 the Liberals won a number of seats and in 1846 they gained parity with the Tories, so producing an 'annihilation of party in one of our great local bodies'.[34] Power sharing had again neutralised the political advantage implicit in control of the Poor Law.

The Leeds and Liverpool cases were inferential: Salford and Preston were much more conclusive in the illumination of the dark deeds that were perpetrated in the name of poor relief. We have already seen how highly politicised the Poor Law was in Salford and the precise charges in the Wrigley case, discussed earlier, involved perverting his office to political purposes. Wrigley freely admitted supplying information to the Tory party for the payment of rate arrears because this was practised by both sides in Salford and he did not think he could be convicted for irregularities which Liberal guardians condoned. Wrigley had been under severe pressure because, as the Commission admitted, 'a strong contest was going on of a political character in which the payment of rates constituted the qualification of the voters'. Wrigley was finally brought low because of an abuse not open to Liberal outsiders, the pre-dating of receipts for rates. If rates were still in arrears by the qualification date the voters were thereby disqualified but it was a simple matter to pre-date arrears so that the payment appeared within the qualification period. Though the Commission was prepared to condone the leak of information, they could not ignore fabrication which 'effected a fraud upon the franchise of the duly qualified ratepayers'.[35]

The Liberals professed moral outrage at Wrigley's actions yet when the Lockett clique was in control it committed similar abuses. Fortunately for us, the clerk to the guardians privately reported to Charles Mott what was going on and so we get a rare peep into this dark sewer. It sounded innocent enough when the Salford board requested that rate collectors be in control of the overseers rather than the guardians yet Mott immediately smelt a political rat. The clerk had exposed the real purpose of the exercise: 'If the true reason was known for wishing to have the collectors the immediate servants of the Overseers, I fear it would expose some abuse of the official position of those Gentlemen, and that of a Political Nature; they cannot, whilst they are under the protection of the P. L. Commissioners use them for their own special purposes as they could wish. . . . A number of the Guardians are much chafed at the interference of the Commissioners and our chairman [Lockett] does not hesitate to say in the Board that he will have no communication with the Commissioners that he can possibly avoid.'[36] In other words Lockett wished to insulate the collectors from the control of the Commission so that they could be free to commit the offences for which Wrigley was dismissed.

Lockett was not prepared to forgo any political advantage that could be gleaned from the Poor Law and in 1842 and 1847 he deliberately delayed the levy of a poor rate for fear of disfranchising Liberal voters. Non-payment of rates was most likely in times of economic depression and in both years it was expected that many householders would default on their rates. So Lockett deferred the rate beyond the qualification date so that the franchise would be protected. In 1842 the guardians had to obtain a bank overdraft to finance poor relief rather than levy the rate. This delay was not only at the suggestion of the guardians, for the clerk 'discovered that the

Overseers themselves were equally anxious to delay the rate for the same reason'.[37] We see how much Poor Law policy could be distorted in the interests of politics. Yet since this occurred in secret the most serious public charge laid at the door of Lockett was that he had his garden tended by paupers.

In turning from Salford in the 1840s to Preston in the 1860s we are again fortunate in detecting the chance factor which exposes Poor Law malpractice. George Melly, a wealthy Liverpool merchant with parliamentary aspirations, was a Liberal candidate for Preston in the early 1860s. In nursing the constituency he became friendly with a Preston guardian and party agent, Edward Ambler. Ambler kept Melly informed on the progress of his candidature and from Ambler's letters (which survived in the Melly correspondence) we get first-hand evidence of electoral manipulation. Being a guardian enabled Ambler to know who was on poor relief and this was important in Preston where there were still old franchise holders qualified to vote as freemen. He suspected in 1863 that 'there is a large number of old franchise recipients of relief on the other side; if so they must go.'[38] Ambler could use receipt of relief as grounds for objecting to Tory votes in the revision court.

However, Ambler's most vital work was done before the revision court, for, as in Salford and Liverpool, arrears of rates were made up by the politicians. He reported to Melly on those who were in arrears in July 1863: 'Our opponents of course have been permitted to drop off, and are done with for this year. In the cases of well known and thoroughly reliable *friends* . . . I have been advised of all cases on our side and have in a number of instances guaranteed payment of rates, by this means retaining their names unopposed on the list of voters.'[39] Melly was footing the bill so that he was financing the manipulation of the list of voters through control of the Poor Law. Implicit in Ambler's arrangements must have been the pre-dating practised at Salford.

In the following year Ambler again obtained the requisite information and suggested to Melly that he follow the same practice: 'A friend of ours in the overseer's office has informed me that a considerable number on both sides are in arrears for Poor Rates and has promised me a list of our friends in that position. Don't you think I had better do as I did last year . . . to pay the rates to keep *good men* on the books for votes. . . . We shall have this advantage, that the other side will not have a similar chance of saving this class of voters.'[40]

Ambler, as a real professional, knew how vital the Poor Law was in fighting parliamentary elections. Given the technicalities of the mid-Victorian franchise system there could be no doubt that power over the Poor Law could yield impressive electoral dividends.

The aim of this chapter has been to illustrate the ways in which the Poor Law operated as a political institution. Sometimes the Poor Law was part of a local party battle in which forces were pitted against each other and in which the extra dimension of Poor Law politics assumed significance, either as a means of registering victories, or as a source of irregular advantage. Sometimes the party labels were blurred, and this was often the case within the Poor Law itself. Here we have noticed workhouse disputes; in the same category were conflicts between overseers, guardians and magistrates, between the central authority and the local board and between different parishes or townships within the same union. In these and others there was an implicit acknowledgement that the Poor Law involved the exercise of power. As a protagonist in the Sheffield dispute complained to his opponents, 'you are in a majority and are all powerful', thus echoing a Manchester observer who pronounced 'the Guardians can do as they please, they have complete and despotic power'.[41] We may safely conclude that bodies which exercised such power were intrinsically political.

6.   The Urban Poor Law

DAVID ASHFORTH

THE nineteenth century witnessed an urban as well as an industrial revolution, in which expanding towns grappled with the problems created by rapid economic and social change. For several important provincial centres, however, such as Exeter, Bath, Norwich and Shrewsbury, it was a period, not of unparalleled growth, but of stagnation. Their experience serves as a reminder of the variety of urban history; under the New Poor Law, as under the old, diversity was often the system's most conspicuous characteristic.

The Poor Law Amendment Act inaugurated an administrative revolution, but it was a slow and incomplete transformation. The Act made no adequate provision for the dissolution of parishes, unions or incorporations operating either under local acts, or under Gilbert's Act of 1782 (22 Geo. III cap. 83) and, after 1834, these bodies therefore remained in existence, immune, in varying degrees, from the central authority's control. Bristol, Chester, Exeter, Hull, Norwich, Plymouth, Southampton, and some of the large London parishes all fell into this category; as late as 1856 twelve of the fifty most populous parishes and unions in England and Wales were administered under local acts.[1] Not until 1848 was Chester's work-house regularly inspected by an assistant Commissioner; and as late as 1857 the Poor Law Board had to take legal action before the Directors of the Poor of the parish of St Marylebone would admit an inspector to their meetings.

Over the years the central authority gradually chiselled away at these semi-autonomous enclaves. During the 1850s the incor-porations of Southampton, Bristol and Exeter submitted to the Poor Law Board's control; during the early 1860s Chester and Norwich followed suit; and in 1867 the Metropolitan Poor Act (30 Vic. cap. 6) paved the way for the remaining London parishes to be brought under the Poor Law Amendment Act.

For Notes to Chapter 6, see pp. 211–12; for Bibliography, see pp. 200–1.

Despite this variety it is possible to identify what may be regarded as characteristic urban problems and responses. The Royal Commission of 1832–4 directed attention towards the problem of unemployed and underemployed adult able-bodied paupers. The 1834 *Report* assumed that, with the possible exception of a small minority, all able-bodied males could find employment in a free labour market. Able-bodied pauperism was seen as the result of the irregular administration of relief, combined with individual indolence and improvidence. The remedy was to force the unemployed back on to the labour market. This could be achieved by enforcing the principle of less-eligibility, by means of a deterrent workhouse test.

The commissioners' analysis, based on evidence drawn largely from the rural south, was irrelevant to the experience of many industrial areas. The massive temporary unemployment encountered in the textile manufacturing districts of Lancashire, the West Riding of Yorkshire and the East Midlands was not the result of an epidemic of generosity, indolence or improvidence, but of fluctuations in the trade cycle; and the chronic poverty of the handloom weavers, hand combers, framework knitters and lace makers was recognised as being the inevitable consequence of mechanisation and of a lack of alternative employment opportunities.

Northern opponents of the New Poor Law were repelled by the prospect of the workhouse being used as the universal test of relief for all able-bodied applicants. Peter Bussey, the Radical leader of Bradford's anti-Poor Law campaign, asked, 'did the new law draw a line of demarcation between the good and the evil? No. In the bastille they found the most virtuous people crowded with the most vicious people on earth, and the treatment of one the same as the treatment of the other, and both worse than the common felon.'[2] Prospective workhouse inmates were left in no doubt as to the horrific conditions and treatment they could expect to meet, and the proposed system of workhouse classification attracted particular criticism being seen as a threat to family unity and to the sacred institution of marriage. Critics agued that the workhouse test would depress wages and force the poor to emigrate, for self-respecting labourers would accept starvation wages, or go to the 'fine countries', rather than submit to imprisonment in the bastille. The commissioners' ill-timed migration scheme (1835 to 1837) was seen as confirmation of the conspiracy to reduce wages.

Apprehension for the treatment of the industrious able-bodied man was a less formidable source of opposition than the intense dislike of centralisation. This was the great common denominator amongst opponents of the New Poor Law, and many who were otherwise prepared to accept the new system could not stomach the thought of being ruled by 'three Big Wigs in London'. Interference with the exercise of local discretionary powers was always unwelcome, whatever the purpose, and many northern townships, having already carried out a series of administrative reforms, felt that no further changes were necessary, and no improvements possible.

Contrary to the expectations of sections of the northern press, relative administrative efficiency and economy did not qualify the area for exemption from the central authority's interference, and during the winter of 1836–7 the commissioners turned their attention northwards. The 1834 *Report* appeared to provide a remorselessly purposeful basis for future action, but, in fact, the central authority had no clear relief policy. The Poor Law commissioners relied heavily on their assistants, and these overworked field officers, often with little time to familiarise themselves with their districts, approached their tasks with different preconceptions. Alfred Power, the first assistant commissioner for Lancashire and the West Riding, claimed to have found 'abuses in the administration of relief', including the payment of relief in aid of wages, 'parallel to those which, under more disadvantageous circumstances, had produced so much evil in the southern counties of England.' However, his successor, Charles Mott, reported that many of the abuses found in the south, and more especially the payment of relief in aid of wages, did not exist.[3] On the other hand, while Power was favourably impressed with the qualities of the working classes, Mott claimed that their habits were 'so ruinous in their consequences as to justify an interference with their domestic and social arrangements'.[4]

The truth was that Power had no consistent views as to how relief should be administered. He appreciated that, during trade depressions, there would be insufficient workhouse accommodation to cater for all able-bodied applicants, and he advised against the issuing of an order prohibiting outdoor relief. At the same time, he emphasised that the danger of imposition was at its height during a depression, and therefore considered it essential that, in doubtful cases and in those involving single men or men without large families, the workhouse test should continue to be applied. In a remarkable statement the first assistant commissioner argued that in his district the workhouse test was needed most for the aged and in-firm 'on account of the dissimulation and fraud constantly practised by the relatives of the paupers at the expense of the poor rates'. This was something the 1834 *Report* had not contemplated, and Mott later made a point of criticising the way in which, as he alleged, stringent rules designed for able-bodied paupers had been applied to the aged poor.[5]

In the event, early decisions affecting the shape of relief policy in Lancashire and the West Riding were forced on the commissioners by the activities of the anti-Poor Law movement. Faced with mob violence in Bradford, a total boycott of the board of guardians election in Oldham, and a resolutely anti-Poor Law board in Huddersfield, the commissioners were forced to adopt a concili-atory approach. Early reassurances as to the guardians' powers were confirmed in the Order issued during the course of 1837 and 1838 to boards in Lancashire and the West Riding. The circular letter which accompanied the Order emphasised that, with the exception of cer-tain limited powers, to be vested in the hands of the overseers and J.P.s, 'the board of guardians will have the entire and absolute authority of deciding whether any person should receive out-door relief, or should be relieved by admission to any of the poorhouses or workhouses of the union'.[6] Power remained optimistic that the prin-ciples of 1834, including the application of a well-regulated workhouse system, would 'be without hesitation adopted',[7] but the constant early theme of reassurance and concession set a pattern which the commissioners were to find hard to change.

Northern hostility to the New Poor Law was not a monolithic reac-tion. In Manchester, and in the nearby Chorlton union, there was little anti-Poor Law activity, and the same was true of Doncaster, Selby and Goole. Variations in the structure of unions, in the relationship between political groups and in the influence of domi-nant local personalities, ensured that no two unions reacted in exactly the same way.

In other industrial areas the commissioners encountered far less initial resistance. The hosiery manufacturing centres of Nottingham and Leicester had already accepted the New Poor Law with apparent equanimity. Derby followed suit, and on Tyneside too there was a minimum of active opposition. There were several reasons for this. The depression which hit the textile industry in 1837 barely touched the north-east's mixed economy. There was no large body of poverty-stricken handworkers and, from the start, the relief authorities were concerned, not with the problems of able-bodied pauperism, but with the aged, the sick, and illegitimate children, who comprised the bulk of relief recipients. The assistant commissioner for the area, Sir John Walsham, was quick to adopt the view that the first object of the workhouse was 'to afford an asylum for the aged and infirm',[8] a view which was not acted upon in other districts for many years. Walsham had strong personal ties with the area and his flexible approach was an important factor in the smooth transition to the new system. The easy relationship that Walsham enjoyed with the local boards of guardians contrasted sharply with the experience of his counterparts in the north-west. Charles Mott, in particular, had a remarkable capacity for arousing the guardians' hostility, often quite unnecessarily, and in Bradford and Liverpool at least, he and the board of guardians viewed each other with intense mutual contempt.

The popular Anti-Poor Law Movement was soon absorbed into Chartism. The boards of guardians, however, quickly assumed the mantle of resistance. Under the provisions of the Poor Law Amendment Act, the consent of a majority of the guardians was required before the Poor Law Commission could order the erection of a new workhouse. Acting alone, the commissioners could only compel a union to spend a sum not exceeding £50 or one-tenth of the average annual poor rate on alterations to existing buildings. Without the guardians' co-operation, therefore, the commissioners had no effective control over the provision of workhouse accommodation. The guardians feared that, if they agreed to expand their workhouse facilities, the commissioners would enforce the workhouse test, to the detriment not only of the deserving poor but also of the ratepayers' pockets. Apart from the cost of a new workhouse, indoor paupers were more expensive to maintain. During the 1850s it was estimated that the average annual cost of relieving each workhouse inmate in Lancashire and the West Riding was £5 10s., while relief to an out-door pauper cost only £3 11s. As was so often the case, the dictates of humanity happily coincided with those of economy.

During the late 1830s and 1840s the commissioners were in no position to pressurise boards into building new workhouses. In several unions, notably Oldham, Rochdale and Ashton, the commissioners had only the most precarious foothold, and in many others any attempt to bring forward the workhouse question would have caused an immediate outcry. The best the commissioners could hope for was that the example set by model unions, such as Chorlton and Stockport, would be so successful that other unions would be encouraged to imitate them.

The commissioners were to be disappointed. No workhouses were built in the West Riding during the 1840s (though Leeds built an industrial school); in Lancashire (though Manchester authorised the building of a new workhouse and Liverpool spent £22,500 on the enlargement of its existing buildings) the general response was equally poor. The central authority's decision to concentrate on classification within one general mixed workhouse actually encouraged the reduction of available workhouse accommodation. Unions were frequently authorised to abandon small, unsuitable township poorhouses and transfer their inmates to the larger remaining buildings; Blackburn closed four of its five poorhouses, Bradford four of its six. In Todmorden the guardians sold all the workhouses and managed without. Ironically, during the early years of the Poor Law Commission, northern unions were far busier closing old workhouses than opening new ones.

The capacity of workhouses usually represented a tiny fraction of the total population. As late as 1854 only nine of the West Riding's twenty-seven unions could provide one workhouse place for every one-hundred inhabitants. In Lancashire the Ashton-under-Lyne union, with an 1841 population of 102,000, provided accommodation for only 145 indoor paupers, or 0.14 per cent of the population. During trade depressions the number of applicants far exceeded workhouse capacity. The Bradford union could cater for 260 indoor paupers, yet on 1 July 1848 the union was relieving 13,521 people; 1397 of these were adult able-bodied men, only one of whom was *not* in receipt of outdoor relief.

The early successes achieved in other areas rarely survived the economic crises of the late 1830s and 1840s. In Nottingham, the guardians' initial support had enabled the commissioners to issue the Outdoor Relief Prohibitory Order. Almost immediately the onset of a trade depression put the workhouse system under severe pressure. In April 1837 the board of guardians resolved 'that in the present state of trade in Nottingham it is inexpedient and impracticable to carry out the full regulations of the Poor Law as to outdoor relief',[9] and in August the commissioners were obliged to suspend the Prohibitory Order and allow the outdoor labour test to be used as a supplement to the workhouse. In December 1839 the Order was again suspended, and though the commissioners succeeded in persuading the board to erect a new workhouse, it was a pyrrhic victory, gained at the expense of alienating both public opinion and subsequent boards of guardians.

Like Nottingham, Leicester was regarded as one of the commissioners' showpieces. Its new workhouse was completed in 1838, but by 1840 the assistant commissioner, Edward Senior, was reporting that relief had been given 'almost indiscriminately to all who have applied, without requiring any labour, or in any way making the condition of the recipient of relief less desirable than that of the industrious labourer'.[10] The workhouse system was simply not capable of coping with the massive temporary unemployment experienced in textile centres. The Leicester workhouse could hold 500 paupers, but during the winter of 1847–8 the number receiving relief exceeded 17,000, or between one-quarter and one-third of the population.

In Durham, under Walsham's benevolent eye, workhouse construction proceeded smoothly, though it is noticeable that the sums spent on workhouses were relatively small. Darlington spent only £280 on modifications to its existing buildings, and none of the new workhouses in the Durham, South Shields or Teesdale Unions cost more than £3000. Some Durham boards reacted to the economic depression of the early 1840s by adopting a stricter relief policy and making more use of the workhouse as a test for able-bodied applicants. In South Shields a report issued by the guardians in 1839 referred to 'the wholesome principles of the new act', and emphasised that the workhouse was 'intended as *a test* of the necessities of the applicants for relief, and not as an *asylum* where the inmates may live better than the independent labourers in their own houses'.[11] In 1843 the South Shields board decided that single able-bodied men and men with one child should be relieved in the workhouse; and in Durham as a whole the proportion of workhouse inmates who were able-bodied rose from 19 per cent in 1840 to a peak of 39·7 per cent in 1844. These figures need to be looked at in perspective. Even in 1844 only 8·2 per cent of all paupers and 10·1 per cent of all able-bodied paupers were being relieved in the workhouse. The system's most striking feature continued to be the small proportion of paupers, including the able-bodied, who received indoor relief.

This was to be the general pattern in urban areas, where only a small minority of paupers were relieved in the workhouse. In the West Riding during the first quarter of 1842 the figure was 7 per cent; in 1845 it was 8 per cent. On 1 January 1872, in the eight north-eastern unions of Newcastle, Tynemouth, Darlington, Gateshead, Hartlepool, South Shields, Stockton and Sunderland, the number of indoor paupers represented 12·6 per cent of the pauper host. Similarly, most able-bodied paupers continued to receive outdoor relief. In the West Riding, on 1 January 1855, only about 4 per cent of all able-bodied paupers were in receipt of indoor relief. In the Bradford union, between 1858 and 1871, never less than 85 per cent of all able-bodied paupers were in receipt of outdoor relief; in all but two of these years the able-bodied workhouse inmates were exclusively women. Furthermore, the able-bodied were a minority of the pauper host. In Durham between 1840 and 1845 the mean percentage of paupers who were able-bodied was 29·05 per cent. In Bradford between 1858 and 1871, the figure was 17·2 per cent, and the vast majority of these paupers were women. It follows that most indoor paupers were not able-bodied. In 1854 it was estimated that in Lancashire and the West Riding 12 per cent of workhouse inmates were able-bodied, 47·2 per cent were non-able-bodied adults, and 40·8 per cent were children. In the Basford union, Nottinghamshire, between 1846 and 1870, a mean percentage of 7 per cent of the workhouse inmates were able-bodied, 46 per cent were aged, infirm, sick or disabled, 37 per cent children, and 10 per cent mentally ill. In most years, in most urban unions, somewhere between 6 and 15 per cent of all those who were receiving relief, were receiving it in the workhouse. As a rule, the only able-bodied applicants sent to the workhouse were those considered to be idle, troublesome, morally unsound or Irish. The general attitude was expressed by the chairman of the Burnley board, when he stated that 'the house was not a workhouse, it was a poor house. It was for the old and infirm and the destitute poor. It was never intended for able-bodied, hard working, honest men.'[12]

Forced to come to terms with a continuation of outdoor relief to the able-bodied, the central authority fell back on the expedient of regulating the conditions under which such relief could be administered. During the early 1840s the Outdoor Labour Test Order was issued to a group of industrial unions, as an inferior substitute for the more stringent Outdoor Relief Prohibitory Order. In several unions, including South Shields, Stockton and Basford, the commissioners were forced to sanction so many exceptions to the Prohibitory Order that the Labour Test Order was also introduced. Finally, in 1852, the Outdoor Relief Regulation Order was issued to all those unions not yet subject to the Prohibitory Order.

Both the Labour Test Order and the amended 1852 Order required that, when outdoor relief was given to able-bodied males, the recipient should be set to work on a prescribed labour test, that no relief should be given in aid of earnings or in the form of rent payments, and that half of the relief awarded should be given in kind. Both these Orders, together with the Prohibitory Order, contained loopholes which have been fittingly described as 'wide enough to drive a coach-and-four through',[13] though the liberal provision of escape clauses did not extend to the payment of rents or to the purchasing of furniture or tools for pauper applicants.

Northern boards of guardians disliked the outdoor labour test almost as violently as the indoor one, and for much the same reasons. For those whose poverty and inability to find work were obvious, the test was still essentially a punishment and nothing more. Honest men would be contaminated and demoralised by being brought into contact with undeserving idlers; and a whole range of workers, from the furnacemen of Merthyr Tydfil to the silk weavers of Macclesfield, were alleged to be unsuited to outdoor labour, which would ruin their hands and render them unfit to return to their own trades. The test was unproductive and expensive, and the guardians did everything in their power to hamper its enforcement. In Warrington the test was not in operation until more than two years after the Order was first issued; in Easington, Durham, the guardians refused to appoint the necessary superintendent of outdoor labour; and in Sunderland it was nearly a year before the appointment was made. Obstruction was supplemented by a frequent resort to the escape clauses. In Bolton in 1855, and in Rochdale in 1862, the guardians were allowed merely to report the number of exceptions to the 1852 Order, without giving details of individual cases. In a single letter to the Rochdale guardians, the Poor Law Board sanctioned outdoor relief without labour for 174 families.

There was always a limit to the concessions the central authority were prepared to make and, even during the cotton famine, the Poor Law Board resisted demands for the Order to be suspended completely. Nor was the workhouse test entirely a dead letter. During the depression of 1857-8 the Poor Law Board reported that the Leicester guardians had chosen to apply the workhouse test to as many able-bodied applicants as possible. In two weeks during January 1858, 183 applicants had been offered the workhouse, but only 21 had accepted. The union clerk triumphantly concluded that 'the great problem, whether in a large and populous manufacturing town the workhouse test can be maintained in times of great commercial depression, has been solved in the affirmative, and an example has been given of how easily this may be done, (even in a manufacturing town, wherein the rate of wages is uniformly low), when the guardians act unitedly and resolutely in carrying out the law'.[14] During the winter of 1860–1 the same policy was pursued and Robert Weale, the Poor Law inspector, was able to report that the majority of able-bodied applicants were being tested, not with outdoor labour, but by the offer of the workhouse.[15]

Leicester was not the only union to have absorbed the principles of 1834. During the Lancashire cotton famine the Manchester board of guardians proved more dogmatic than the commissioners themselves. Under the provisions of the 1863 Public Works Act (26 & 27 Vic. cap. 70), unemployed operatives working on improvement schemes organised under the Act could be paid wages, over and above their relief. The Manchester board would have nothing to do with such schemes, arguing 'that the payment by boards of guardians of wages in return for labour to poor persons chargeable or seeking to become chargeable upon the rates . . . is opposed to the whole spirit and intent of the Poor Law, and it is inexpedient both upon social and economic grounds'.[16] The scheme was tantamount to paying relief in aid of earnings, a major target of the 1834 *Report*, but a form of relief which had always been the acknowledged method of dealing with the problems of short-time working and the low-wage structure of domestic industry. In Lancashire, during the quarter ended 25 March 1839, as many as 78 per cent of the able-bodied men on outdoor relief were being relieved on account of insufficient wages. Guardians could see no sense in forcing underpaid handworkers and underemployed operatives to give up their inadequate incomes altogether, merely in order to be maintained entirely at the ratepayers' expense.

In issuing the amended Outdoor Relief Regulation Order in December 1852, the Poor Law Board was obliged to reassure the guardians that Article 5, prohibiting relief in aid to able-bodied males, was only intended to prevent 'the giving relief at the same identical time as that at which the person receiving it is in actual employment, and in the receipt of wages . . . and that relief given in any other case, as, for instance, in that of a man working for wages on one day, and being without work the next, or working half the week and being unemployed during the remainder, and being then in need of relief, is not prohibited by this Article'.[17] Though the guardians were given considerable room for manoeuvre, the impact of the Order is not altogether clear. There were certainly many cases where relief in aid to able-bodied paupers continued. Until 1858, Blackburn ignored the Order altogether; and in Burnley, between 28 November 1857 and 28 August 1858, a weekly average of 113 able-bodied paupers were receiving relief in aid of wages. On the other hand, the able-bodied category included the temporarily sick to whom Article 5 did not apply, and a great deal of the relief distributed in aid of earnings is known to have gone to women, who were not subject to the Labour Test or Outdoor Relief Regulation Orders. The gradual extinction of the textile handworkers probably reduced the need for wage subsidies and the Poor Law Board also put pressure on boards of guardians to keep relief in aid to a minimum. In the North Bierley union, throughout the 1850s and 1860s, most of the cases submitted as exceptions were, in fact, precisely that. Almost invariably, relief was proposed in order to enable widowers with young children to employ a nurse while the father was out to work. In one or two cases, where the applicant's earnings were considered sufficient to cover the extra expense, sanction was refused. Very often further details of the case were required, together with periodic reports on any changes in the paupers' circumstances; where relief was approved, such approval was limited to a fixed period, usually three months. During the early 1870s, the Local Government Board's campaign for a stricter control of outdoor relief may have further reduced the frequency of relief in aid to able-bodied men. In the Bradford union, during the week ended 12 November 1878, as many as 39·4 per cent of all outdoor relief cases were receiving relief in aid of earnings, but only 5·7 per cent of the single men aged 60 or under, and 10·8 per cent of the single women, were receiving relief of this kind.

Popular revulsion against the workhouse test meant that the guardians were able to pose as the defenders of the rights of the poor, and of the ratepayers, against the designs of an interfering and unfeeling body of commissioners. There was nothing particularly enlightened or humane, however, about the system of relief defended by the guardians. The cash doles distributed to outdoor paupers were barely adequate supplements to any other income applicants may have received. In Lancashire and the West Riding, few boards of guardians drew up a fixed scale of relief, but income was generally made up to somewhere between 1s. 6d. and 2s. 6d. per head, with single paupers, and the aged and infirm, perhaps receiving slightly more.

Indoor paupers fared no better, and though boards of guardians waxed indignant at any suggestion that they should force paupers into a workhouse 'bastille', conditions in the old workhouses often bore comparison with the worst nightmares of anti-Poor Law spokesmen. The widespread evasion of the regulations governing workhouse uniforms, dietaries and visiting hours was poor compensation for other deficiencies. Many of the township poorhouses were merely converted farmhouses or cottages, in which every variety of pauper was thrown together in a squalid jumble. An investigation into the state of the Bolton workhouse in 1843 discovered 'the aged and the young covered with vermin; infants, patients suffering from scarlet fever, or scaldhead, and children free from disease, all cooped up in the confined rooms of a series of cottages.'[18] During the 1848 typhus epidemic, children in Huddersfield's poorhouse were sleeping up to ten in a bed, five more than their counterparts in Blackburn. At the other end of the country, in Southampton, a Poor Law inspector reported 'the mixing together of all classes, including old, infirm, and idiots, in rooms in which it was almost impossible for human beings to live'.[19]

These workhouses, and many others like them, were unclassified, overcrowded and unhealthy. Yet boards of guardians persistently refused to build new ones, or even substantially to enlarge or improve existing buildings. The guardians' reluctance was not based solely on opposition to the workhouse test. Some guardians subscribed to a crude interpretation of the principle of less-eligibility to defend workhouse deficiencies. One of Bradford's guardians said that 'they might talk of finer rooms, and this, that, and the other, but they should go and examine . . . the vile, wretched hovels and the dismal cellars in which the poor abide, and they would find that there was not one in a hundred so comfortable as the poor were in their workhouse'.[20] This was a common attitude. In 1842, when it was reported that the inmates of the Bolton workhouse averaged more than three to a bed, some guardians asked, 'whether or not, in the houses of the poor, they did not average more than three in a bed?'[21] Poverty outside the workhouse might still dictate discomfort within, even where the guardians were keen opponents of the New Poor Law. It was clear that, if the poor were to be cared for adequately, their treatment could not be dictated by reference to the principle of less-eligibility.

A more important consideration was that of economy. Guardians were reluctant to spend large sums on workhouse improvements if it meant having to maintain more indoor paupers and paying higher establishment charges. Their parsimony was pervasive. Amongst other sins, boards of guardians were consistently guilty of employing too few relieving and medical officers, and of paying them inadequate salaries. In Bradford, during the late 1830s and early 1840s, one relief district contained over 65,000 people; another was eight miles in length, covered almost 16,000 acres, contained 35,000 people, and had as its relieving officer a man with one leg who could walk only with the aid of crutches. Districts which were large in normal years, were unmanageable during trade depressions. In December 1847 Bradford's relieving officer was having to deal with as many as 178 new applicants every day. The clerk reported 'that the paupers assembled in the passage at two o'clock in the morning, fighting for their turns', the relieving officer began distributing relief at 3 or 4 a.m., and was still being called on at midnight.[22]

Medical officers received much the same treatment, despite the standards which the General Medical Order of 1842 sought to impose. Each of Liverpool's medical officers were responsible for approximately 37,000 people. In Leeds a population of over 88,000 was shared between two officers. In Bolton and Bury aspiring medical officers were required to agree not to claim any of the extra fees prescribed in the 1842 Order, and though the central authority declared the Bolton agreements void, they were replaced by an unwritten agreement which, until 1857, effectively saved the union from further claims.

There was more to the guardians' penny-pinching than mere tight-fistedness. Sudden outbreaks of unemployment, the influx of destitute Irish and the repercussions of the cotton famine put union finances under a tremendous strain. In Liverpool relief expenditure rose from £57,000 in the year ended March 1847 to nearly £117,000 the year after; while in Sheffield expenditure rose from £20,728 in the year 1841–2 to £42,577 in the year 1842–3. The unions' financial structure was ill-equipped to deal with pressure of this kind. Broadly speaking expenditure could be divided into two categories. The individual townships or parishes in each union paid for the relief afforded to paupers chargeable to them, while the establishment charges (such as the cost of running the workhouse) were paid out of the common or union fund, which was divided between the townships on the basis of their 'averages' or the average annual expenditure for the relief of each township's poor. The system had several defects. Above all, it meant that the most heavily pauperised townships were required to provide most of the funds – where poverty was greatest, rate demands were highest. In addition, the system of apportioning the common charges on the basis of past 'averages' meant that, during periods when expenditure was rising rapidly, the demands made on individual townships were based on an obsolete pattern of relief. Townships whose own relief expenditure had not risen were unwilling to provide funds to meet rising relief costs in other townships.

The actual collection of poor rates presented a string of problems. In many unions the assistant overseers were appointed by the magistrates or parish vestry; and even where the guardians elected the officers themselves, their control over them was imperfect. The assistant overseer was responsible not only to the guardians, but also to the unpaid annual overseers of each township within his district. Each overseer, paid and unpaid alike, shared equal power and equal responsibility, so that the annual overseers had a considerable hold on union purse strings.

Occasionally the township overseers refused to allow the paid assistant to play any part in the assessing and collecting of the poor rates. In 1848 the annual overseers of Hunsworth, in the North Bierley union, withheld the rate books and for the next twenty years carried out the assistant overseer's duties themselves. More often the annual overseers would refuse to allow a rate sufficient to meet the guardians' demands, a refusal which merely added insult to injury since the laying of an adequate rate was no guarantee that it could be collected.

Rates based on obsolete or inequitable valuations might be challenged and the whole rate threatened. In many urban unions a high proportion of the rate assessments related to property with a low rateable value. A return for the Bradford union covering rates laid towards the end of 1849, showed that 70·4 per cent of all assessments were made on property of annual value of less than £5. During economic crises large numbers of these small ratepayers were unable to pay and had their rates excused. Empty property caused further rate leakages. In 1841 almost one in every ten houses in the Bradford union were reported to be empty; in December of the same year, in Dewsbury, 28 per cent of the rate was either excused or in arrears. In Leeds, in 1842, the leakage was nearly 19 per cent and, in 1848, was over 20 per cent.

The problem was exacerbated by the unreliability of the assistant overseers themselves. Defaulting rate collectors were two-a-penny. In Lambeth the collector extracted £1200 from the poor rates of 1847–8; and in the Edmonton union the collector for Hampstead resigned after an examination of his books revealed arrears of £2900. In Bradford between 1838 and 1848 no less than seven of the union's twenty-three appointees were dismissed or encouraged to resign because of substantial arrears or embezzlement.

The net result was that townships became chronically in arrears with the calls made on them and, during the 1840s, one union after another reported its account overdrawn. In 1842 the Nottingham union was £3400 in the red, the Merthyr Tydfil union £1200 overdrawn, and the treasurer of the Chester-le-Street union had resigned in protest at the state of the union's account. Bradford became overdrawn in 1842, 1846, 1848 and 1854; Wakefield was reported insolvent in 1847, and Merthyr Tydfil was again in the red in 1849. These were not the sort of statistics from which expansive policies, or new workhouses, were likely to emerge, and the guardians' concern for economy was to some extent an inevitable consequence of their inadequate financial resources.

During the 1850s and 1860s increases in rateable values enlarged the unions' potential financial resources. Between 1861 and 1867 the annual rateable value of property assessed to the poor rate in the Bradford union increased by 54·5 per cent whereas between 1841 and 1847, when the population was expanding at a faster rate, the increase was only 24 per cent. Changes in the rating system meant that larger potential resources could be tapped more effectively. The Small Tenements Rating Act of 1850 (13 & 14 Vic. cap. 99) allowed parishes to assess the owners, instead of the occupiers, of all tenements with a yearly rateable value not exceeding £6. It was hoped that this would eliminate the need to excuse the poor their rates, but the Act was permissive and by 1858 less than one-in-five West Riding parishes had adopted it. During the early 1860s, partly in response to the financial strains placed on unions by the cotton famine, a series of important reforms were introduced. The Irremovable Poor Act of 1861 (24 & 25 Vic. cap. 55) decreed that the contributions of parishes to the common fund of the union should in future be calculated according to annual rateable value, and not relief expenditure. The Union Relief Aid Act of 1862 (25 & 26 Vic. cap. 110), aimed specifically at unions in the Lancashire cotton belt, made provision for a hard-pressed parish to be assisted by rates in aid from other parishes within the union and, if necessary, by loans from the Poor Law Board and contributions from other unions in the same county. The Union Assessment Committee Act of 1862 (25 & 26 Vic. cap. 103) gave the boards of guardians greater control over the valuation of parishes, with the object of securing uniformity, and in 1865 the Union Chargeability Act (28 & 29 Vic. cap. 79) completed the transformation by making the union, instead of the parish, the area for rating purposes.

Before these reforms there had often been considerable tension between townships within the same union. Unions like Salford, Leeds and Sheffield were compact and almost exclusively urban in character, but other developing towns, such as Cardiff and Huddersfield, were merely the focal point of unions containing a large number of small semi-rural parishes. In unions of this kind conflicts tended to develop between the central, urban townships and the out-townships. At the heart of these controversies were the common, or union, charges: those which were apportioned on the basis of each township's past relief expenditure.

The out-townships' chief complaint was that the union charges covered expenditure of a kind which benefited only the larger urban townships. A disproportionate number of workhouse inmates, for instance, were drawn from the manufacturing districts, yet townships with few indoor paupers still had to contribute towards the salaries of workhouse officers. In the Bolton union, Great Bolton, with one-third of the union's population, usually provided two-thirds of the workhouse inmates. In Bradford, in one quarter of 1847, six of the union's twenty townships provided two or less of the 419 workhouse occupants; Bradford itself, with less than 30 per cent of the union's population, was responsible for more than half of the indoor paupers.

The situation was greatly exacerbated by Bodkin's Act of 1847 (10 & 11 Vic. cap. 110) which made the relief afforded to those paupers who had become irremovable by means of a five-years residence, under the Poor Removal Act of 1846 (9 & 10 Vic. cap. 66), a union charge. Since the large industrial towns had many more irremovable paupers than the rural out-townships, country guardians felt that they were being forced to subsidise the rates of their wealthier neighbours. Small townships, with few indoor or irremovable paupers, might find themselves spending as much on union charges as on relief to their own poor. The result was that the out-townships tended to resist all proposals involving an increase in union charges, and, since these townships were invariably overrepresented, their opposition often amounted to a power of veto. During the late 1840s Bradford, Bolton, Huddersfield and Wakefield proposed schemes for workhouse improvements, for providing vagrant or fever wards, or for increasing the salaries of workhouse staff – all such schemes were sabotaged by the out-township guardians. In Merthyr Tydfil in 1848 the voting on the motion for a new union workhouse was also along strict urban–rural lines, and it was only because the two industrial parishes of Merthyr Tydfil and Aberdare returned a majority of the board that the motion was passed.[23] For the country guardians the question was not how much would it cost, but who would have to pay?

The financial framework was a crucial determinant of policy. In Bradford in 1848 and Manchester in 1850 friction between the central and out-townships reached such a pitch that the unions were divided. These were both towns which devoted a great deal of atten-tion to the law of settlement, a subject which has been unjustifiably neglected (cf. Chapter 1). It has been said that in Bristol no social problem caused the relief authorities more time and trouble than the settlement laws,[24] and the same could be said of other urban authorities. Ports and developing industrial towns attracted large numbers of migrant workers, people who usually had no legal settle-ment in the parish in which they resided. In 1851, 43 per cent of Derby's inhabitants had been born outside Derbyshire, and 53 per cent of Liverpool's outside Lancashire. This situation was reflected in the relief statistics; as early as 1837 one-fifth of Sheffield's paupers and almost one-half of Nottingham's were non-settled.

The most conspicuous migrants were the Irish. In the 1830s towns like Manchester and Cardiff already contained a substantial number of Irish-born inhabitants, but it was during the late 1840s that the Irish influx reached its peak. During a period of less than four months at the beginning of 1847 more than 144,000 immigrants arrived at Liverpool from Ireland. The Irish impact was intensified by their relative poverty. In Bradford during the week ended 7 March 1855, 38·3 per cent of the union's paupers were Irish, though only about 8 per cent of the union's population were born in Ireland. In Manchester in one week in 1854, 42 per cent of the outdoor paupers were Irish, and in Liverpool during the year ended March 1848 the figure was 43·1 per cent. As early as 1834 the parish of St Andrew, Holborn, had complained that 'at least ½ of the expense of the poor rates might be traced in some way or another to the Irish',[25] and in 1854 it was claimed that in ten years the Irish poor had cost Liverpool £124,000.

Non-settled residents who became chargeable were liable to be removed back to their parish of settlement and, consequently, Irish paupers could be passed back to Ireland. In general, however, the number of non-settled paupers who were dealt with in this way was a small proportion of the total number applying for relief. Removal was an extremely uncertain process and parishes who resorted to it indiscriminately were likely to incur expense without achieving their object. Instead, most unions preferred to rely on the non-resident relief system, whereby the pauper's parish of settlement agreed to reimburse his parish of residence for any relief afforded to him; though it ought to be said that this system, too, was very uncertain in its operation. Large-scale removals during an economic depression might have led to a shortage of labour when trade recovered, and it is significant that in both Bradford and Bolton, during the depression of 1839–40, public-relief subscriptions were raised with the specific object of relieving non-settled and Irish applicants.

Removal may have been uncertain, unjust and relatively little used, but it was a weapon which urban relief authorities were loath to relinquish. Removal was the sanction which induced other unions to authorise non-resident relief. The threat of removal, as the Poor Law Commission recognised, was also a 'far more stringent' test of destitution 'than any offer of the workhouse',[26] and one which some unions had little hesitation in using. Two Poor Law inspectors, Alfred Austin and Harry Farnall, told the 1854–5 Select Committee on Poor Removal that a vast number of the Irish poor in Manchester and Liverpool were deterred from applying for relief by the fear of removal, and the vice-chairman of the Manchester board of guardians admitted that this was considered to be one of their best tests. In Manchester, out of 5111 people for whose removal steps had been taken, 3858 had been struck off the relief lists rather than be removed. When Bradford's clerk was asked why the number of removals was such a small proportion of the total number of Irish poor, he replied that not more than one-third of those ordered to be removed were, in fact, removed. Most chose to be taken off the relief lists, though the clerk was unable to say how they managed to eke out a living.[27] For many paupers, there was more to be feared from the threat of removal than from the well-publicised workhouse test.

The Poor Law Removal Act of 1846 (9 & 10 Vic. cap. 66) was a serious blow to industrial townships. The rendering of certain classes of pauper irremovable, notably those who had lived in a parish for five years, meant that, in their case, non-resident relief would no longer be given. Townships with a large migrant population were the financial losers. Norwich was said to have been faced with an extra relief bill of £5000 a year, and in Leicester it was alleged that the Act had caused the poor rates to double. Certainly, in some large urban unions, relief to the irremovable poor accounted for a large proportion of relief expenditure. In the Bradford union, between 1857 and 1861, the annual cost of relief to the irremovable poor never fell below a sum representing 57·7 per cent of the total cost of relief. The corresponding figure for Manchester was 57·1 per cent, for Sheffield 36·8 per cent and for Liverpool 33·3 per cent.

A few unions, including the Strand and Bradford, took the view that the 1846 Act did not apply to Irish paupers, and that they could be removed regardless of how long they had been resident in the parish. In 1848 Bradford's clerk told the commissioners 'that orders of removal for Irish paupers have been obtained irrespective of their five years industrial residence', and, four years later, his successor reported that the guardians had 'latterly removed nearly all Irish paupers applying for relief without inquiring the length of time they have resided in the respective townships of the union'.[28] Irish paupers were protected by the clerk to the justices, who took the conventional view that the Act did apply to the Irish, but the correspondence on the issue raises a strong suspicion that irremovable Irish paupers were induced to swear that they had not lived in the parish for five years, by warning them that, if they were not passed, they would be refused relief.

After the issuing of the amended Outdoor Relief Regulation Order in December 1852, a *modus vivendi* may be said to have been reached over the treatment of able-bodied paupers. In 1855 the Poor Law inspector for Lancashire and the West Riding stated that it was 'quite impossible' to obtain the additional workhouse accommodation needed for a system based exclusively on indoor relief. The Prohibitory Order could not be introduced into the manufacturing districts, 'because the stoppage of a few mills in any one town would render it absolutely necessary to give out-door relief'. Another inspector, Alfred Austin, likewise did 'not think that out-door relief could be abolished or much diminished in England'.[29]

The spate of workhouse building activity which took place during the early 1850s was only partly a response to reassurances about the workhouse test. Harry Farnall told the North Bierley board that an efficient workhouse would be a help in dealing with 'that mischievous and dangerous class, the tramps',[30] an argument which had already been successfully employed at Merthyr Tydfil and Wakefield. The workhouse would enable the idle to be tested, the old to live comfortably, the children to be educated, the sick to be treated properly and, in the long run, money to be saved.

With the heat taken out of the able-bodied debate, and workhouse construction under way, there was a noticeable improvement in the relations between boards of guardians and the central authority (but note the Sheffield dispute in Chapter 5). Boards which had previously treated assistant commissioners as unwelcome intruders were to be found thanking them for their 'valuable services', and transmitting resolutions of regret when they left the district.

Once the great obstacle of a union workhouse had been surmounted, boards of guardians were less reluctant to spend money on further enlargements and improvements. In 1870 the Poor Law Board reported that 'the extreme parsimony displayed by boards of guardians of the older school has, in some of the larger unions, given way to a desire to conduct all the duties devolving upon the guardians upon a somewhat grand and liberal scale'. In one Lancashire union a greenhouse was being erected to supply the workhouse infirmary with flowers and the Poor Law Board reported that, in many cases, they were 'now compelled to intervene in order to check the outlay which the guardians would be willing to incur in the more ornamental part of the various structures which they propose to erect'.[31]

Some unions continued to hold out against a new workhouse. In Rochdale the compulsory closing of two township poorhouses failed to produce the desired effect, and it was not until 1871 that the guardians finally agreed to a new building. Southampton's new workhouse was not started until 1866 and Chester's was delayed until after 1870.

By this time, the intended function of workhouses had undergone a radical change. In 1854 the master of the South Shields workhouse had complained that he was 'superintendent of a general hospital as well as master of the workhouse',[32] and by 1870 the Poor Law Board could casually record that 'workhouses, originally designed mainly as a test for the able-bodied, have, especially in the large towns, been of necessity transformed into infirmaries for the sick'.[33] The central authority had stopped viewing poor relief exclusively through the window of the Poor Law Amendment Act. Their acceptance of the fact that guardians would not use workhouses as a test for the majority of able-bodied applicants had been matched by an increased concern for the treatment of non-able-bodied indoor paupers; and in 1867 the seminal Metropolitan Poor Act (30 Vic. cap. 6) acknowledged that the sick were not suitable objects for a deterrent system of workhouse management and were entitled to receive special treatment in separate institutions (see p. 64).

The passing of the Metropolitan Poor Act owed a great deal to the activities of outside pressure groups, but it would be wrong to underestimate the extent to which the Poor Law Board itself acted as a progressive force. Throughout the 1850s and 1860s improvements in workhouse facilities for the sick, the mentally ill and for deserted and orphan children were largely the result of constant prodding by the Poor Law inspectors, the inspectors of schools and the visiting commissioners in lunacy. Together they provided a framework for progress based on inspection, recommendation and eventual action. The Poor Law Board may have lacked the Poor Law Commission's early crusading spirit, but the commissioners' abrasive approach had often limited their effectiveness. In many ways, the Poor Law Commission's rough passage paved the way for substantial, if less noisy, progress under the Poor Law Board. Organised bureaucracy often succeeded where dogmatic zeal had failed.

7. The Rural Poor Law

ANNE DIGBY

O N L Y five years after the Poor Law Amendment Act of 1834, the Poor Law Commission announced proudly that the allowance system was 'almost totally extinguished' in the rural areas of southern England and Wales.[1] Historians have tended to accept this judgement and have concentrated on the more obvious and continued difficulties experienced by the administrators of the New Poor Law in urban, industrial areas. The Royal Commission on the Poor Laws of 1832–4, by focusing on the abuse of outdoor allowances to the able-bodied poor in the countryside, seemed to have provided remedies for the problems of rural poverty and these were adopted in the 1834 Act. That the New Poor Law in rural areas was apparently successful was shown by the swift formation of new unions, the erection of workhouses and the implementation of reformed relief policies to which there was no concerted local opposition. The central Poor Law authority found it easy to make effective propaganda based on these early achievements, but gave minimal publicity to the later failures of the 1834 Act in rural England and Wales. By 1840 the provisions of the Poor Law Amendment Act had been implemented effectively in many rural areas, but in the ensuing decade local administrators discovered that in practice they had substantial autonomy over relief policies. For the rest of the century many rural boards of guardians adopted a system of poor relief which they considered to be more appropriate for the socio-economic conditions of the countryside.

Before this system is analysed it is helpful to assess the importance of the rural unions in the history of the New Poor Law. The Poor Law Commission gave their ideal Poor Law union as 'a circle, taking a market town as a centre, and comprehending those surrounding parishes whose inhabitants are accustomed to resort to the same market'.[2] From the beginning most rural unions therefore included an urban element, and with the growth of population in industrial areas during the nineteenth century there was often urban overspill into surrounding rural areas. By the early twentieth century 528 out of a total of 645 Poor Law unions, or four out of every five unions, had a rural or semi-rural character.[3] However, the large number of rural unions may obscure the fact that rural relief administration affected a declining proportion of the population. In 1841 more than one out of two, but in 1901 fewer than one in four, people lived in a rural area.

The administrative impact of the 1834 Act in combining over 15,000 parishes into some 600 Poor Law unions was marked in rural areas where the existing local governmental units of hundred and county were frequently ignored in favour of a new and artificial grouping. The assistant Poor Law commissioners, who were the agents of the central Poor Law administration in this complex task, paid more attention to convenience of formation and operation than to the Benthamite principle of uniformity of size, and used their discretionary authority to accommodate social, political and economic interests in the countryside. They called meetings of local owners and occupiers of land to persuade them of the value of the New Poor Law and at the same time gained a valuable insight into the life of the locality.

In practice the approach of individual commissioners varied, as can be seen in the different experience of union formation in Northamptonshire and Norfolk. In Northamptonshire, where there were unusual numbers of peers and great landowners, Richard Earle had to give paramount importance to the views of the landed magnates, and Poor Law unions in this area were therefore designed to accommodate the structure of land ownership and to reflect the related systems of social and political deference to the gentry.[4] Sir Edward Parry and Dr James Kay, the assistant commissioners who worked in Norfolk, which was a county with fewer magnates, took sufficient account of the interests of the landed gentry to get their support for the New Poor Law, but viewed this as being of only secondary importance. Their first priority was to take account of the insititutional restrictions which the local relief administration of the old Poor Law imposed upon them. Before 1834 Norfolk had one-third of its parishes either in incorporations for the relief of the poor under local act, or in unions under Gilbert's Act. The assistant commissioners needed to gain the consent of two-thirds of the guardians or directors of each union or incorporation before these could be dissolved and new Poor Law unions created. The boundaries of these new unions were then influenced by the existence of plentiful workhouse accommodation in the form of incorporated houses of industry and Gilbert union poorhouses which could be used as union workhouses under the New Poor Law.[5] Union formation therefore varied according to local constraints, but assistant commissioners in Wales and southern England had sufficient time to work pragmatically and with a careful attention to local interests so that a stable system of rural unions was established. This contrasted with their hasty work in the north of England which could produce unions which were too big and in which there were conflicts of interest within boards of guardians.

Poor Law unions in southern England were formed between February 1835 and May 1837, and once this essential geography of the New Poor Law had been established the elected guardians and their officers began to implement the revised relief policies of the Poor Law Commission. The rural poor reacted to these changes belatedly and ineffectually. Hostility was not shown when the unions were first declared because this did not impinge on the life of the labourer. However, when these administrative changes produced new methods of relief, there were disturbances. Opposition came when outdoor relief to the poor was changed from payment entirely in money to part relief in flour or bread. An early incident of this kind of protest occurred in the spring of 1835 in the Milton union in Kent when both relieving officers and guardians were assaulted. A second occasion for opposition to the New Poor Law was the opening of a newly built union workhouse for the reception of paupers. That in the Amersham union in Buckinghamshire in May 1835 was a typical example of rural protest against the New Poor Law: it was spontaneous, lacked leadership and organisation, and produced no permanent changes in the local administration of relief. In this case a crowd surrounded a cart taking paupers from the parish workhouse at Chesham to the new union workhouse at Amersham. The horses pulling the cart laboured slowly up a steep hill and the crowd had ample opportunity to remove the paupers so that long before it reached its destination the cart was empty. The liberated paupers had no alternative to workhouse accommodation and merely returned to the Chesham workhouse from which they were later removed under guard, and without further major incident, to Amersham. A third cause of opposition to the New Poor Law was the adoption in the union workhouse of the Poor Law Commission's regulations which classified members of families in different parts of the building and which was occasionally the pretext for incendiarism. Considerable damage in 1836 and 1837 was caused to the Heckingham and Rollesby workhouses in Norfolk by incendiarists protesting against the introduction of workhouse classification. These acts of protest grew from a sustaining undergrowth of rumour which increased fear and suspicion about the new law among credulous villagers. In most areas there were tales of starvation and cruelty to indoor paupers 'imprisoned' in the union workhouses, while apprehension about the fate of those accepting outdoor relief ranged from a belief in north Devon that the bread distributed by the relieving officer was poisoned, to a fear in south Norfolk that the relieving officer would physically brand paupers in order to display their dependent status.[6]

The Poor Law Commission's strategy of piecemeal changes in the administration of relief which was introduced union by union, and within each union, parish by parish, prevented a concerted opposition from developing in the south of England. There was no anti-Poor Law movement, as there was later to be in the urban and industrialised north of England, to provide leaders who would organise resistance, while the less densely populated countryside made it harder to concentrate action effectively. The spontaneous and dispersed character of rural protest against the New Poor Law meant that it attracted little national publicity. The researches of local historians working on eastern England suggest that the incidence and persistence of rural protest against the 1834 Act was perhaps greater than had hitherto been assumed in general studies.[7] That the rural labourers' hostility to the New Poor Law continued was shown by the Courtenay rising in Kent in 1838, by rural Chartism in Suffolk in 1837–8, and by incendiarism in East Anglia in 1843–4.[8]

The attitude of the rural labourer was influenced by the speed and vigour with which local guardians adopted the policies of the Poor Law Commission, and this in turn was affected by the social composition of boards of guardians. In the counties the 1834 Act permitted J.P.s to act as *ex officio* guardians administering relief side by side with elected guardians. This perpetuated the influence of the landed gentry, although there is disagreement among historians on whether the 1834 Act increased their power. Instead of exercising the indirect supervision over the provision of poor relief which they had done as magistrates previously, they could now share in the direct administration of the New Poor Law as *ex officio* guardians. The involvement of the landed gentry in this new capacity varied considerably among different rural areas in the first year in which the New Poor Law was in practical operation. In Northamptonshire the landed magnates took an unusually active role as chairmen of the new Poor Law unions, and the *ex officios* went to half the guardians' meetings; an attendance which was as good as that of the elected guardians. In Norfolk, on the other hand, the two landed magnates who were chairman of boards of guardians were largely absentees, and *ex officio* guardians averaged only one in three board meetings which compared unfavourably with the one in two attendances of the elected guardians. Generally the landed gentry appear to have taken an active interest in the New Poor Law only when the initial, important decisions were being taken. With some exceptions the gentry threw the weight of their influence behind the new system and hoped that the Poor Law Commission would acknowledge their support by giving a sympathetic consideration to their own local interests in the drawing up of union boundaries and the siting of workhouses. Once the routine and trivial business of relief administration replaced important decision-making, their active involvement as *ex officio* guardians in the local administration of the Poor Law tended to diminish.[9]

The influence of the landed gentry over the New Poor Law was exercised increasingly by indirect means through the presence of their agent or their tenants on the boards of guardians. Control of local relief policy in the countryside frequently passed to the elected guardians, and in rural areas three-quarters of these were farmers so that boards of guardians virtually became farmers' associations. Continuity in rural relief administration, pre- and post-1834, was very strong; not only were the farmers ascendant in the guardians' boardroom as they had been before 1834 in the parish vestry, but they were also confronting the same economic problems. The crucial difficulty in many rural areas of southern England continued to be that of surplus labour.

This problem of the seasonal underemployment of able-bodied labourers had been a central preoccupation of the Royal Commission on the Poor Laws of 1832–4. It had concluded optimistically 'that even in the parishes where the greatest surplus above the actual demand exists, it would be rapidly reduced and ultimately disappear' if relief was administered properly under a workhouse system.[10] In order to reduce the suffering of the labouring class in the interim period of transition, the 1834 *Report* recommended that money from the parish poor rates could be assigned to finance emigration, and this provision for assisted emigration to British colonies was included in the Poor Law Amendment Act of 1834. Between 1835 and 1837, 6403 people from twenty counties in southern England were assisted by their parishes to emigrate, mainly to Canada. Nearly two-thirds of the emigrants came from East Anglia alone; there were 1083 emigrants from Suffolk and 3354 from Norfolk, where the desire to emigrate became a kind of contagious fever. Anxiety about the amount of surplus labour in Norfolk and the increased cost of relieving it by the expensive indoor relief laid down by the 1834 Act meant that local property-owners were prepared to finance emigration.[11] The underemployed Norfolk poor disliked the grim prospect of being relieved in the new workhouses and a group from Attleborough wrote that 'the miseries of starvation and poverty makes us quite tired of our native land for we know that we cannot be worse off than we are at all events'.[12] Although the Poor Law Commission's emigration scheme operated until 1870, numbers of participants declined markedly after these first years. This was not because surplus labour had disappeared, as had been envisaged by the Royal Commission, but because local relief administrators began to appreciate that, in practice, they had a greater freedom to accommodate surplus labour in a more convenient and economical way than was laid down under the relief provisions of the central board.

Where 'vicious modes of administration had become the most deeply rooted, and where the pauperized classes were the most demoralized, and the burthens of the rate-payers were the heaviest' and in short where there were the worst problems of surplus labour, the Poor Law Commission thought that there was the greatest urgency in implementing the provisions of the New Poor Law.[13] It was for the benefit of these places in the south of England that the central board thought it helpful to start a migration scheme in 1835 which would be complementary to the emigration scheme and which would assist unemployed but industrious labourers to find work in the north of England. The administration of the migration scheme was centred on two agents in Leeds and Manchester, who attempted to co-ordinate the requirements of northern factory-owners who were short of labour in a boom period with those of southern boards of guardians who wanted to reduce the number of dependent, able-bodied paupers. The first migrants in 1835 came from Bledlow in Buckinghamshire, a village with only 1135 inhabitants but whose poor rates had averaged £1857 for the previous three years. Here a vicious circle of rising poor rates (paid by farmers as the principal ratepayers) with falling employment and wages (offered by farmers as employers) had resulted in a large number of underemployed labourers. The Poor Law Commission arranged for three-year contracts of employment for 83 Bledlow inhabitants who were persuaded to leave their homes and journey north with the help of the parish officers. The family of John Stevens typified the changed economic situation of these migrants. His Bledlow earnings of ten shillings a week compared unfavourably with the average of twenty-six shillings he and his four children earned while employed in a Cheshire textile factory. He was reported as saying that 'all the horses in Buckinghamshire should not draw him back again'.[14]

The exact dimensions of the Poor Law Commission's migration scheme are unknown partly because of the later destruction of much central documentation made by the migration agents, and partly because of the frequent association of independent with assisted migration which makes enumeration from local sources difficult. For these reasons the standard figure given of slightly under 5000 migrants probably understates the total.[15] The migrants came from seventeen southern English counties and most went to Lancashire, the West Riding of Yorkshire, Cheshire and Derbyshire. Single men were assisted to find work on railway construction projects. Families had work found for the children in factories while the father was given a labouring job. In theory the surplus labour in the rural south and the shortage of hands in the industrial north complemented each other; but, in practice, the southern parishes wished to rid themselves of unemployed men (and preferably the lazy or poor workers) while the northern factory-owners preferred the recruitment of children as a cheap and docile labour force. As a result the migration agents were unable to keep pace with the requests of southern boards of guardians and grumbled at the indifferent quality of the people who applied to migrate. These economic difficulties were compounded by the social problems of rural migrants who had to adjust to life in a manufacturing area; some found the effort too great and returned home. Nearly half the total migrants came from Suffolk, and two out of every five of these had returned home before August 1837. This suggests that the number of migrants who returned home was greater than the 5 per cent failure rate admitted publicly by the Poor Law Commission. With the deepening industrial depression during 1837–8, disgruntled Poor Law guardians in the south of England found that they were having to send relief to destitute migrants whose contracts of employment provided, in practice, no guarantee of permanent work.[16]

Surplus labour had been absorbed 'by the joint efforts of the labourers to obtain, and the agriculturists to supply them with employment' wrote the assistant commissioner, W. T. Hawley, about Sussex in June 1836.[17] This comment was typical of the biased reports of the assistant commissioners to the Poor Law Commission in 1835 and 1836 in reaching satisfying orthodox conclusions about the apparent disappearance or diminution of surplus labour in the rural south of England. The assistant commissioners reported that farmers were providing more regular employment because, if they did not, they were now liable as substantial ratepayers to finance expensive indoor relief in the union workhouses to the unemployed labourer under the relief regulations of the Poor Law Commission. The labourer was described by the assistant commissioners as being more anxious to obtain work and more industrious when employed. This was because his alternative source of income, that is poor relief, was no longer in the form of fairly nominal employment under the parish overseer or surveyor as it had been before 1834, but was now indoor relief in the uncongenial conditions of the workhouse. But the reports of Alfred Power on Hertfordshire, Cambridgeshire and Essex, and Colonel Ash A'Court on Wiltshire differed from those of their colleagues. They wrote about what they saw to be the economic realities of the countryside rather than transmitting the complacent conclusions which they knew the Poor Law Commission wished to receive about the beneficial effects of the New Poor Law in the rural south of England. They stressed the difficulty of deciding whether there was a surplus of rural population in certain areas because for two-thirds of the year irregular employment in agriculture produced fluctuating amounts of pauperism but during the four months of haymaking and harvest the labour market was so tight that there might even be a shortage of labour.

This underemployment in arable and mixed farming areas did not disappear with the implementation of the 1834 Act in the countryside. Its significance went unacknowledged by the central Poor Law authority but its continued existence was a key factor in determining the relief policies of local boards of guardians which came to diverge from the relief regulations of the Poor Law Commission. By 1842 most unions in rural areas in England had been issued with a prohibitory order which forbade outdoor relief to the able-bodied although it specified certain exceptions to the rule. In 1844 a general order called the Outdoor Relief Prohibitory Order was issued to unions in less-populated areas as the culmination of years of piecemeal introduction of the order to individual unions. The central board was unable in practice to ensure that individual unions made their relief policy conform to the spirit, as well as to the letter, of this Prohibitory Order because the numbers of assistant commissioners or inspectors was reduced from twenty-one in 1837 to nine between 1842 and 1846. The increasing size of their districts meant that a perfunctory twice-yearly visit by the inspector to each union effectively delivered the detailed administration of relief into the hands of rural guardians who were able to systematically exploit the exceptions in the Prohibitory Order and so give outdoor relief to the able-bodied labourer in employment.

The Poor Law inspector for Buckinghamshire and Oxfordshire commented as early as 1841 that the relief regulations gave guardians in his district large discretionary powers which in practice 'admit of the granting of outdoor relief under almost every contingency that can befal a man or his family'.[18] Two years earlier it had become apparent that in unions in the east and south-east of England, in the south and west Midlands, as well as in most areas of Wales, rural guardians had begun to give outdoor relief to able-bodied men who were temporarily unemployed.[19] They were able to justify it to the Poor Law Commission as relief on the ostensible grounds of sickness in the family. This was an exception in the central board's order prohibiting outdoor relief to the able-bodied, and as such it was permissible. Their reason for granting outdoor rather than indoor relief was that it was a cheaper method of dealing with underemployed or surplus labour. The farmers who dominated rural boards of guardians were therefore able in their relief policies to resolve the conflict of economic interest which they faced in their other roles as the principal employing and ratepaying class in the countryside. As employers, they wanted a plentiful supply of labourers available to meet their peak requirements for labour at haymaking and harvest time, but they did not want to give regular employment during the slack periods of the farming year to this reserve labour force. In contrast, as ratepayers, they were reluctant to meet the high cost of relieving unemployed labourers and their families in the workhouse during the winter months, which such an employment policy would have produced. But as Poor Law guardians they could make the central board's relief regulations an instrument of social policy subordinate to their own economic interests. They did so by giving cheap outdoor relief to the able-bodied labourer under the sickness exception clause in the Prohibitory Order. An alternative policy, which had been adopted earlier in several areas, was to circumvent the New Poor Law entirely. This could be done by using money from the highway rates or from private subscriptions to relieve able-bodied men with large families because this was cheaper than sending them to the workhouse at the cost of the poor rates.[20]

The Poor Law Commission stated in 1846 that its policy was restricted to eliminating outdoor relief to the able-bodied in rural areas. Its failure to do so was underlined forcibly the following year by Edwin Chadwick, the Commission's Secretary, who stated that in many areas of eastern England the abuses in the administration of poor relief were as great as they had been before the Poor Law Amendment Act of 1834.[21] The administrative change from Poor Law Commission to Poor Law Board in 1847 did nothing to check the trend in rural unions towards giving most able-bodied applicants for relief an outdoor allowance. In 1871 a survey of outdoor relief suggested that its use was still widespread in the east and south-east of England. Fifteen years earlier the Poor Law inspector for this area, Sir John Walsham, had pinpointed the reason for this when he suggested that rural boards of guardians regarded their relief administration 'from a rate-paying and a wage-paying point of view'.[22] The Local Government Board's crusade to restrict outdoor relief to the able-bodied was largely ineffective in rural areas and the proportion of the total money spent on poor relief which went on outdoor allowances continued to be particularly high in the central, east and south-east parts of England. In 1881 the Local Government Board admitted that because 'the dole to the out-door pauper slightly exceeds 3d per day ... the old abuse of relief in aid of wages must largely prevail in some form or other'.[23] That the New Poor Law was merely a continuation of the old was undoubtedly true of many parts of southern rural England, but it was most glaringly obvious in the Welsh countryside.

An experienced Poor Law inspector, Colonel Wade, complained in

1846 that Welsh unions formed 'as difficult a district to deal with as ever existed' and he expected to make little progress in implementing the Poor Law Amendment Act in Wales. By 1842 most rural areas in England had accepted the order prohibiting outdoor relief to the able-bodied but many Welsh unions still had not adopted it. In Welsh unions where it did operate Wade commented that it 'is hardly worth the paper it is written upon' because it was systematically evaded with the connivance of the guardians. Indeed, according to Wade's disillusioned predecessor, Mr William Day, an able-bodied man in employment could usually expect to get relief by means of a medical certificate issued because 'his son had a whitlow on his finger, or his daughter a hangnail'.[24] Although the New Poor Law in Wales could be vindicated on humanitarian grounds because it improved the treatment of the sick, the aged, and those relieved in workhouses, it was nevertheless unpopular with many Welsh people. In the impoverished countryside of the late 1830s and 1840s Welsh ratepayers found it difficult to meet the cost of relief and there was an increasing reluctance to pay poor rates to meet the expense of union administration. Whereas in England initial support had been given to the local rural administration of the New Poor Law by resident gentry and magistrates, the different social structure of the Welsh countryside resulted in a minimal participation of these social groups. Small farmers, with low social status, were elected as Welsh guardians. These farmer guardians were representative of the main class of ratepayers and, like their English counterparts, they opposed the expensive policies of the Poor Law Commission. They wanted to reduce the salaries of Poor Law officials, felt that the workhouse diet was too generous, and economised on capital expenditure so that many Welsh unions had small workhouses; indeed, seven Welsh unions had no workhouse accommodation at all.

The nervous over-reaction of the Home Secretary, Sir James Graham, to the Rebecca Riots is understandable when this experience of trying to implement an unpopular law through hostile Welsh administrators is remembered. He regarded the administration of the New Poor Law as a prominent cause of these rural disturbances in Pembrokeshire, Carmarthenshire and Cardiganshire in 1842–3. There appeared to be good supporting evidence for this point of view as the New Poor Law was frequently discussed at secret protest meetings, memorials were sent from the disturbed districts to the Queen and the Home Secretary asking for the Poor Law to be changed, threats were made against workhouses in Carmarthenshire and Pembrokeshire, and in June 1843 the Carmarthen workhouse was attacked and ransacked. But in fact the Poor Law was only one of many socio-economic grievances in the poverty-stricken countryside of west Wales which sparked off this revolt by small farmers.[25] It was this class which continued to serve as Welsh guardians in rural areas and viewed the New Poor Law as an alien, Saxon device which was to be subverted rather than administered. Over sixty years of English frustration in failing to impose the principles of the 1834 Act was summed up in the comment of the Poor Law inspector, Mr F. T. Bircham, in 1896, that Wales was a district 'where out-door relief has always been the rule and not the exception'.[26] At the end of the nineteenth century the average proportion of relief expenditure which went on outdoor allowances was slightly more than one-half in England and Wales as a whole, but in Wales more than four-fifths of the money went on outdoor relief.

The defective operation of the New Poor law in its early years in Wales and elsewhere was well publicised by *The Times*, whose proprietor, John Walter, was a vigorous opponent of the Poor Law Amendment Act. The investigating skills of a young legal journalist, John Campbell Foster, who had reported on the Rebecca Riots for the newspapers were soon employed in a series of articles in June and July 1844 on incendiarism in East Anglia, which again linked rural disturbances with the operation of the New Poor Law. A system of labour allocation called the 'ticket' system was operated in some East Anglian Poor Law unions by which an unemployed man who applied for poor relief was given a ticket by the relieving officer. This was taken round the employers in the parish who were reminded in this way of the cost to the parish poor rates of relieving an unemployed labourer and who might therefore offer low-paid work to the labourer. Alternatively they signed a statement to say that they could not employ the man, and only after this had been done would the guardians offer relief. Foster argued that the East Anglian labourer had acquired a great hatred for the workhouse when the workhouse test had been enforced rigorously during the first years of the New Poor Law. The labourers' distrust of the reformed relief system meant that he would now take work at minimal wages rather than apply for poor relief. Foster thought that the ticket system had intensified the process and that this abuse in the operation of the New Poor Law had created an engine to depress agricultural wages. He was correct in thinking that farm wages in the area were low but omitted to consider that the continued existence of surplus labour in East Anglia meant that labour supply was greater than demand for much of the year and that market forces alone would have operated to keep wages low. The supporters of the 1834 Act had argued earlier that the imposition of a reformed system of poor relief would raise wages so that the continuation of low agricultural wages gave ammunition to the opponents of the New Poor Law who, like Foster, argued that it had depressed them. This same allegation that the New Poor Law had lowered wages was made about the Andover Union during the next highly publicised incident in the history of the rural Poor Law.

The Andover affair began, as the Home Secretary rashly remarked, as 'a workhouse squabble in the south of England' but widened into a Select Committee of Inquiry in 1846 and a virtual trial of the administration of the Poor Law Commission which contributed to its downfall in 1847. The scandal broke with the disclosure that the rigorously economical administration of the Rev. Christopher Dodson and his board of guardians in this Hampshire Union, compounded by the peculation of the workhouse master, Colin M'Dougal, had produced an inadequate workhouse dietary. Hungry able-bodied paupers employed in crushing bones for manure had been sufficiently ravenous to gnaw the marrow out of putrid bones.[27]

The drama and publicity which surrounded the cruel administration of the Andover workhouse has had the effect of giving it a disproportionate importance in any evaluation of life in the rural union workhouse. Many country workhouses were indeed run on relatively humane lines, and many of the contemporary stories of workhouse cruelty published in *The Times* and elsewhere have been shown to be hostile propaganda which was unsubstantiated by factual evidence. Material conditions in most rural workhouses were not particularly harsh. The reports of Poor Law inspectors who collected information from relieving officers, guardians and clergymen about the household budgets of the poor in the 1830s and 1840s suggested that the workhouse diet was better than that of the independent agricultural labourer's family in much of the rural south of England. This superiority was not found in every union at this time, and by the 1860s the pioneering inquiry of Dr E. Smith into the food of the agricultural labourer, indicated that it was now generally better than that in the standard Poor Law dietaries.[28] Country workhouses usually had smaller newer buildings with a better standard of accommodation than those in large towns or cities which had often had to utilise old, substandard workhouses built under the old Poor Law. But the virtual absence of any system of indoor relief for the able-bodied in many country areas before 1834 meant that the union workhouses of the New Poor Law came as a dreadful shock to the rural labourer. He tended to regard indoor relief under the New Poor Law as a prison sentence, and the union workhouse as a prison in which he would have to wear a degrading uniform and be separated from other members of his family. It was this psychologically repugnant aspect of the rural workhouse, rather than any actual physical cruelty or material deprivation in it, which deterred any but the really destitute able-bodied poor from entering the union house in the countryside.

The reluctance of the able-bodied to enter the workhouse was reinforced by the farmer guardians' disinclination to pay for expensive indoor relief when they could give cheaper outdoor relief on the ostensible ground of sickness. The consequence was that there were relatively few adult able-bodied inmates in rural workhouses. The county of Norfolk, with its predominantly rural population, provided a good illustration of this pattern of poor relief (see Table VII).

The Poor Law Commission was successful initially in implementing the New Poor Law in Norfolk by reducing outdoor allowances, and by 1843 only 64 per cent of the adult able-bodied poor in the county were receiving outdoor relief. But in the 1840s

TABLE VII

Proportion of adult able-bodied paupers receiving outdoor relief in Norfolk

A	Per cent*	B	Per cent†
1840	75·5		
1841	72·4	1850s	82·1
1842	67·8	1860s	83·8
1843	64·0	1870s	86·4
1844	66·2	1880s	75·9
1845	66·9	1890s	76·2
1846	66·7		

* Figures based on returns for the quarters ending 25 March in each year in the *Reports* of the P.L.C.

† Figures based on returns for 1 January and 1 July in each year in the *Reports* of the P.L.B. and L.G.B.

the reduction in the number of Poor Law inspectors and the political weakness of the Poor Law Commission transformed the balance of power between the central board and local guardians, with the result that rural boards of guardians had practical freedom in their administration of relief. Exact comparisons between the pattern of Poor Law relief in the 1840s and that in later decades is not possible because of the different basis for the statistical returns. However, the upward trend in the proportion of outdoor-relief cases among the adult able-bodied poor is clear and by the 1870s 86·4 per cent were relieved in this way. It was not until the Local Government Board declared war on outdoor allowances that there was again, in the 1880s and 1890s, a restriction on relief outside the workhouse to this category of pauper. The failure of the central board to eliminate the administration of outdoor relief to the able-bodied poor meant that Norfolk union workhouses which had been built primarily for the reception of this category of pauper were seldom more than one-third full. Mr Lockwood, the Poor Law inspector for the area, commented in 1892 that 'during the last 20 years the rural workhouse has become almost exclusively an asylum for the sick, the aged, and children'.[29]

Children made up a significant proportion of those receiving indoor relief but their actual numbers in any one workhouse school were quite small and, because of this, rural guardians were reluctant to provide sufficiently good educational facilities and salaries to recruit well-qualified teachers. Many boards of guardians were also hostile to the idea of giving the children of the labouring class the instruction in reading and writing which the central board's regulations required and they allowed the workhouse master and matron to take children away from their lessons to help with household duties. Educational progress was therefore slow in most areas in the early years of the New Poor Law. But, in East Anglia, good workhouse schools were set up because of the driving enthusiasm of Dr J. P. Kay, the assistant Poor Law commissioner for the area, who was later to play such a notable part in the development of national elementary education. A more general improvement in pauper education in country areas came after 1846 when central government grants for workhouse teachers were given on condition that proficient teachers were employed and reasonable educational facilities were provided by the guardians (see p. 74). These were evaluated by the inspectors for workhouse schools who were appointed in 1847. As a result of this many rural workhouse schools in the 1850s and 1860s had a liberal academic curriculum and a programme of industrial training for girls as domestic servants and for boys in a variety of trades. As such they provided an education for pauper children which was superior to that in neighbouring elementary schools, but the institution of many good Board schools after 1870 meant that a better education could now be obtained outside the workhouse. An increasing number of rural boards of guardians seized this opportunity to free themselves from the trouble and expense of running a small workhouse school and sent the workhouse children to the Board school.

A brake was placed on the full development of Poor Law educational and medical services in the countryside both by the restricted financial resources of rural unions and by the small numbers of workhouse inmates present at any moment in time. At first, the narrowly circumscribed medical services provided within the deterrent framework of the New Poor Law meant that there could be little difference between those of rural and urban areas, but with the triumph of the curative principle in Poor Law medicine after the 1860s rural unions lagged behind urban areas in the expansion of medical facilities. In rural Wales the provision of Poor Law medical services was on an even more restricted scale than in the English countryside. By the end of the nineteenth century the majority of rural unions in England and Wales still had not built separate workhouse infirmaries but had preferred to expand the provision of sick wards within the main workhouse buildings. This was possible because rural workhouses had surplus capacity arising from the small numbers of able-bodied inmates. The main requirement in country workhouses was to provide for the large numbers of the aged and infirm rather than the few paupers who were seriously ill. Sick wards in country workhouses were typically light, airy and spacious rooms which were rather short of furniture and medical appliances. They were also deficient in trained nurses and rarely had night nurses so that serious cases of physical illness were generally sent for treatment to provincial hospitals. The mentally ill were, in practice, divided into the two broad categories of 'the harmless idiots' or feebleminded who were housed in the same accommodation as the sane in the workhouse, and the troublesome or insane lunatics who were removed to county lunatic asylums. The quality of Poor Law medical services to the outdoor poor was, despite frequent complaints of

alleged neglect, much better than could reasonably have been expected, given the low salaries and large medical districts of the rural
medical officers (cf. Chapter 2).

Social policy in the form of a narrow-minded administration of
rural poor relief was a response to the economic conditions of the
countryside. In 1851 James Caird analysed the state of the labour
market and its consequences for social policy thus

> We may draw a line across the map of England: all to the south of
> that line we have high poor rates and low wages, and all to the
> north of it high wages and low poor rates – on one side an en-
> forced excess of labour, impoverishing and bearing down the
> working man, and, by consequence, rates pressing on property
> with undue severity; on the other a comparative deficiency of
> labour, raising its price to an unequal average, and operating un-
> fairly on the cost of production.[30]

In the north of England the existence of industry on a large scale
attracted workers from rural areas and farmers had to raise
agricultural wages in order to retain labour. The absence of a surplus-
labour problem meant a minimal amount of able-bodied pauperism,
low poor rates and a relative lack of concern and therefore of information about the administration of the New Poor Law in the
northern countryside. In contrast, the condition of the agricultural
labourer was at its nadir in the southern counties of Wiltshire, Dorset,
Somerset and Devon. The level-headed E. C. Tufnell, the Poor Law
inspector for the area, wrote in May 1845 that 'wages are so low, that
they cannot fall. . . . Their *normal* state is one of the deepest privation
to lower which would be to depopulate the land.' He was asked to
make a fuller inquiry and reported that wages for the agricultural
labourer were seven to nine shillings a week. The labourer's diet con-
sisted principally of bread (sometimes barley bread) and potatoes so
that the diet of the pauper in a local workhouse was superior to it,
and not less-eligible, as the reformers of 1834 had intended.[31] A few
years later the Hampshire clergyman, Charles Kingsley, gave an imaginative insight into the life of the southern rural labourer in his
novels. In *Alton Locke* published in 1850, an agricultural labourer
cursed the New Poor Law because 'it ate up the poor, flesh and
bone', and at a protest meeting the poor complained about the lack
of farm work and the penny-pinching relief policies of the rural
guardians. In *Yeast*, brought out a year later, Kingsley pointed to the

restricted rural labour market which resulted in able-bodied men being consigned periodically to the workhouse, and to the pauperisation of the labourer because low wages meant that he was as well off with the parish as he was in independent work.

'By penning the labourers, each strictly in the parish of his settlement, skill and industry on his part are valueless to him as they would be to the serf or to the slave' wrote John Revans, the Poor Law inspector for Dorset, Hampshire and Somerset.[32] The failure of the 1834 Act to change the parish as the unit of settlement meant a continuation of a narrow, parochial labour market until the creation of union settlement in 1865 (cf. Chapter 1). Farmers were still faced with the alternative of employing or relieving the labourers with Poor Law settlements and therefore a right to poor relief from the parish. They preferred to maximise the number they employed even if this necessarily meant that they paid low wages because the alternative was unremunerative expenditure on the high poor rates which would be the consequence of higher levels of unemployment. In 25 per cent of the Poor Law unions between the Thames and the Wash this situation had led to a labour-allocation policy in the form of the ticket system which has already been described (pp. 160–1). A similar method of apportioning labourers among occupiers had been found in individual parishes which had operated the labour-rate and roundsmen schemes under the pre-1834 Poor Law. With a parochial labour market farmers felt that they were compelled to employ the settled labourers in the parish while the latter knew that the resulting low wages meant that their skills went unrewarded. As a consequence of this situation social relationships between master and men deteriorated and economic efficiency on the farm was lowered.

The pattern of employment on the farm was influenced substantially after 1834 by the varied cost of poor relief to different categories of people. The labourer with a Poor Law settlement in the village had a better chance of work than one without, because the former, if unemployed, could claim relief. The married labourer with a family was employed in preference to the single man because the cost of relieving him and his dependants was much greater. The single man was most likely to be consigned to the workhouse, when destitute because of lack of work, as the cost to the parish was relatively negligible, while the family man, if occasionally forced to go to the guardians for help, would be likely to be given temporary relief outside the workhouse on the ostensible grounds of sickness in the family. After the Poor Law Amendment Act had restricted the liberality of outdoor allowances to families, their independent income was brought up to subsistence level, but not by an increase in ordinary wages being given to the head of the family as the 1834 reformers had predicted. Instead, the married man was given a good opportunity to raise his earnings by increased amounts of piece work, and his wife and children were also increasingly employed in the field work associated with the improved farm cultivation of the mid-nineteenth century.[33] In arable farming areas in eastern England the increased employment of children on farms was particularly noticeable after the 1834 Act and their organisation in agricultural gangs in the 1840s and 1850s was criticised because of the bad effect it had on their conduct and because it interfered with their schooling.

It is important to appreciate the extent of the variation in local experience when discussing the rural administration of the New Poor Law. This was particularly noticeable in the differentiation of villages into 'close' and 'open' parishes (see Chapter 1). The artificial restriction of the supply of cottages for labourers in close parishes, in order to reduce the number of settled poor with a claim to relief and so to keep poor rates low, meant that a correspondingly greater number were forced to live in open parishes where accommodation was available and settlements more easily gained. It was the open parishes which confronted the worst problems of surplus labour and, associated with this, high levels of pauperism. The close parishes, where a small number of landowners had succeeded over a long period of time in reducing the number of resident labourers below that necessary for the cultivation of local farms, relied on a mobile labour force coming in from these surrounding open villages. Inquiries by Poor Law inspectors published in 1850 highlighted the depreciation in the value of labour caused by this situation in many parts of the Midlands, and the south and east of England where a badly housed labourer living in an open village or town might walk four or five miles to and from employment in a close village.

The Poor Law Board's *Report* of 1850 was prompted by the controversial changes in the settlement laws of 1846–8 and because of this it over-emphasised the impact which the settlement laws had made on the labour market and the supply of housing in the countryside. The cottage destruction which was alleged to have taken place in agricultural clearances in many places as a result of the settlement laws was of far less significance in the over-all shortage of rural housing than the uneconomic nature of investment in cottage building. Minimal returns could be expected by landlords from the low rents which were all that could be charged a badly paid agricultural labourer. In the East Riding of Yorkshire, in Lincolnshire and in Nottinghamshire not only the settlement laws but the improved cultivation of land were important factors in settlement distribution and labour mobility.[34]

By the third quarter of the nineteenth century developing labour shortages in rural areas were changing attitudes towards the settlement laws and the related question of chargeability to the poor rates. On the state of the labour market Caird perceptively remarked that 'The over supply is . . . apt to be exaggerated. As labourers begin to withdraw, employers will soon discover, under the pressure of higher wages, that the surplus was not so great as they led themselves to believe.'[35] Four years earlier in 1847, the Docking Union in Norfolk had been the first Poor Law union in the country to utilise the clause in the Poor Law Amendment Act of 1834 which allowed the guardians to declare the union, instead of its constituent parishes, as the unit of settlement and rating. This effectively made the union rather than the parish the local labour market and eased the scarcity of labour in an area where one-third of the villages were close parishes. The labour shortage had become serious as a result of migration from the west of Norfolk which reduced the supply of labour at a time when improved farm cultivation had increased the demand for workers.[36] By the 1850s and 1860s there was a more widespread anxiety about the alleged effect of the settlement laws in reducing the quantity and quality of rural housing and therefore in increasing migration to the towns. The changes in the law of settlement and rating in the early 1860s culminated in the Union Chargeability Act of 1865 by which all poor relief was to be paid for by the union as a whole. The act removed the old disincentive to build cottages because by doing so there would no longer be the risk of creating new parochial settlements and increasing parish poor rates. This factor was reinforced by a new concern to retain an adequate labour supply in the rural sector and led to a marked increase in cottage building in many rural areas by the 1870s. This alleviated but did not entirely remove the shortage of housing in the countryside, which continued until 1900. The housing situation, the decline in rural industry, and the impact which the agricultural depression had on labourers' wages resulted in an exodus of rural population (especially of young adults) to urban, industrial areas during the late nineteenth century.

By the end of the century adult able-bodied pauperism had ceased to be a major problem in rural unions, an experience which was in marked contrast to that in many urban areas. The Royal Commission on the Poor Laws of 1905–9 found that the highest rates of pauperism were in rural unions by the turn of the century and attributed this to the migration of working people to the towns. This had left an ageing population in the countryside which was particularly liable to become dependent on poor relief. It discovered that a typical country workhouse was 'an almshouse for the aged and infirm and the children' which was administered with humanity. 'In one excellently managed workhouse the master's main scheme of classification was to put into one ward the deaf old men and those who snored.'[37]

This comparatively benevolent treatment of old people in workhouses was the result of a recent change in policy which had been forced on the Local Government Board by pressure of public opinion, by the lead given by a handful of enlightened boards of guardians, and by the work of women guardians who had been elected in large numbers in 1894 when the electoral-rating qualification for guardians had been removed. The circulars issued by the Local Government Board in the 1890s which authorised a more liberal treatment of old people in workhouses were acted upon slowly and reluctantly by some rural boards of guardians. These boards believed that a continuing rigour and economy in the relief of the aged was justified by the traditional arguments of protecting the ratepayers' pockets, stimulating private charity, enforcing the financial responsibility of children for their parents, and encouraging the young to be thrifty so that they could support themselves in old age. Both the Royal Commission on the Aged Poor in 1895 and the Select Committee on the Aged Deserving Poor four years later, condemned the continuing practice of giving inadequate outdoor allowances to many old people and of sending some deserving cases to the workhouse. In the late nineteenth century the labourer's fear that he might be one of the unlucky few who were forced into the workhouse when he was too old to work, and his resentment at the low wages which meant that this could happen after a long and arduous working life, continued to sour the relationships between the classes in the countryside.

The Royal Commission of 1905–9 stated that rural unions could be distinguished from urban ones because they were administered under the more stringent relief regulations of the Outdoor Relief Prohibitory Order of 1844, but they also noticed that the ratio of outdoor to indoor relief cases was far higher in rural than in urban unions.[38] That outdoor allowances were normal rather than exceptional indicated that the central board established under the 1834 Act was impotent to enforce its relief policies on local boards of guardians in the countryside. Since the 1860s regional Poor Law conferences had been preoccupied by the high ratio of outdoor to indoor relief and the emptiness of workhouses in rural areas. Before the end of the century pressure from the Workhouse Amalgamation Movement had led to the dissolution of some rural unions and the concentration of relief in fewer workhouses in order to cut overhead costs and rationalise the expensive administrative arrangements created by the Poor Law Amendment Act of 1834. In spite of sixty years of nominal operation the principles of the New Poor Law had not been firmly established in rural areas although the extent of the variations in regional experience can only be clarified by further local research. Both pre- and post-1834 the Poor Law in the countryside was dominated by local farmers who relieved the poor with outdoor allowances. This continuity was more striking than any differences which the 1834 Act had made.

8. The Poor Law in Nineteenth-Century Scotland

AUDREY PATERSON

THE New Poor Law of 1834 did not apply to Scotland and it was another eleven years before the existing arrangements for poor relief in the northern part of the United Kingdom were reorganised. In 1845 an Act (8 & 9 Vic. cap. 83) 'For the amendment and better administration of the laws relating to the relief of the poor in Scotland' came into force, the title itself indicating that previous arrangements had been neither adequate nor properly administered. The new system introduced a central Board of Supervision to supervise arrangements made at local level by parochial boards, a machinery which remained unchanged until 1894 and set the two-tier pattern for future developments in helping the poor.

Under the pre-1845 provisions each parish in Scotland was responsible for its own poor, the right to belong to a parish being determined by settlement – a term borrowed from English law during the eighteenth century. Although never legally defined it was understood to mean the right of a destitute person to claim help from a parish either because he had been born there, or had lived and worked there for three years or had acquired a settlement by marriage. The concept of settlement had been established not for the benefit of the pauper but for those who contributed to the poor fund, for it was hoped that it would be a means of evenly distributing the burden of maintaining the poor.

To qualify for help a claimant also had to be 'destitute' and 'disabled' (for an account of how the two terms were interpreted in the nineteenth century, see below p. 185). If these conditions could

For Notes to Chapter 8, see p. 214; for Bibliography, see pp. 202–3.

be established, the claimant was then placed on the parish poor roll
as a pauper entitled to help from the poor fund. This arrangement
derived from sixteenth- and seventeenth-century legislation, the aim
of which was to relieve deserving paupers while punishing vagrants,
the 'strong idle beggars' mentioned in the statutes.[1] Vagrants were
presumed to be fit for work but to have chosen wandering ways of
life, maintaining themselves by unauthorised begging. Theoretically
they could be punished or confined in Correction Houses, but most
of these institutions had fallen into disuse or were used to house
paupers who could not manage on the traditional outdoor-relief
arrangements. It was often very difficult to distinguish between
paupers and vagrants, as administrators of the poor fund discovered.
Those running the Poor Law were the members of the kirk-sessions
and the heritors (holders of lands and property in a parish), and there
was no central body to exercise any control over poor-relief distribution in each parish.

The poor fund was collected at church services, but it could be
augmented by legacies, bequests, money collected as payment for
religious services such as the hire of mortcloths or by the interest on
capital held in trust by the church for the benefit of the poor. It was
also possible to levy a compulsory poor rate on the heritors within a
parish, and with the growing burden on voluntary funds in many
parishes in the south of Scotland, such assessments were not uncommon by the early nineteenth century, but they were universally
regarded with suspicion. In the first place, levying a poor rate meant
taxing heritors who helped administer the poor fund, implying parsimony on the part of those who could afford and should have been
willing to make adequate voluntary contributions towards the poor.
In addition there were many who opposed rating because of its
burden on the ratepayers and its supposed demoralising effect on the
poor themselves and they were fond of quoting English experience as
proof of this belief. Such views were eloquently propounded by Dr
Thomas Chalmers, the most distinguished Presbyterian cleric of the
first half of the nineteenth century. He held that any regular
allowance encouraged the poor to dependency by reducing their
motivation towards self-help and that discrimination in the distribution of a small voluntary poor fund had a beneficial effect upon both
donor and recipient.[2] Chalmers tried out his ideas in 1819 in the
parish of St John in Glasgow where volunteers both collected the
funds and personally investigated all claimants so that only the most

deserving cases received help. Although this scheme was not entirely successful, it provided additional weight to the arguments against compulsory assessment.

Early in the nineteenth century it became increasingly obvious that, at best, the amounts collected were too small to do other than provide irregular and inadequate relief, but the sums given were regarded as supplementary to the resources provided by the family or even acquired through the pauper's own efforts. The giving of licences to beg within the parish was often part of relief arrangements. Indeed, as the numbers of paupers and vagrants increased, the proportion of beggars became cause for further concern. It was not likely that what had been devised for a poor peasant society in the seventeenth century would prove appropriate for a rapidly developing urban society in the nineteenth.

When the English system was altered in 1834 Parliament made no provisions for the introduction of the New Poor Law into Scotland, despite the growing awareness there that relief arrangements were not satisfactory. Under the Act of Union in 1707 Scotland retained her separate judicial system, and many statutes dealing with legal or administrative procedures could not be applied unless amending clauses were incorporated or a separate Scottish Act passed. Neither course of action was taken in 1834, perhaps because it was not accepted that the old system was inadequate. The existing mechanism tended to disintegrate gradually, becoming more obviously inadequate in some areas than in others. Furthermore, the effects of industrialisation developed at a slower pace compared with England and the accompanying economic and social changes had not disrupted Scottish patterns of life in 1834. Although the able-bodied unemployed in the industrial sector had been an intermittent problem since the first decade of the nineteenth century, it was not until the 1840s that their numbers became so great as to pose a substantial additional strain on society.

As the able-bodied were formally excluded from the benefits of the poor fund in Scotland, many unemployed joined the ranks of the wandering poor. It became increasingly difficult to distinguish between the idle vagrant and the tramping artisan or labourer searching for work, or even the pauper who, finding his allowance from his own parish very inadequate, wandered elsewhere hoping to augment his income. Singly or in groups the growing numbers of wandering poor were cause for alarm as they often demanded help by unauthorised begging, or they intimidated inhabitants, or they engaged in crime, all of which were difficult to control in parishes with an inadequate police organisation.

A return to the earlier principles of relieving paupers and repressing vagrancy seemed to be indicated; but what was also necessary was an adequate fund to meet growing demand, a point of view forcibly expressed by Dr W. P. Alison, Professor of Medicine at Edinburgh University.[3] He argued that existing arrangements were totally inadequate for a rapidly developing industrial society and proposed a regular rating system to provide a fund from which the poor would at last receive adequate allowances, thereby improving both their health and their welfare. Like Chalmers, Alison found many supporters. Moreover, in 1843 the Church of Scotland was broken into two halves by the Disruption. Two-fifths of the clergy left the Church of Scotland to form the Free Church and this fragmentation of church unity affected the arrangements for the poor. The old system, which entrusted care of the poor to the kirk-sessions of the established church, was no longer practical when half the populace joined the Free Church, and the new congregations could ill afford either the time or the money to organise a relief system. The effect of the Disruption was to emphasise how inadequate the existing arrangements had become and a Royal Commission was appointed to inquire into the relief system and to suggest improvements.

Its *Report* in 1844 criticised what was generally understood to be the prevailing system in Scotland, although the commissioners acknowledged that there were substantial regional differences in practice.[4] They indicated that poor relief was irregularly given and was inadequate in amount; that demand exceeded supply; and that even in areas where voluntary funds were augmented through rates there was no properly organised machinery through which relief could be efficiently distributed. The *Report* suggested a two-tier system of administration and a more extensive use of the power to levy rates, the opposition to which had been appreciably reduced by the effects of the Disruption.

The direct result of the *Report* was the 1845 Act which came into force on 4 August 1845, creating the Board of Supervision and the parochial boards. Each parish remained responsible for its own poor and the concept of settlement was retained with the period of continuous residence increased from three to five years. A parochial board was annually appointed in each parish, and was required to employ an inspector of poor as its executive officer; but each parish could itself decide whether to raise funds by imposing a poor rate or by continuing to rely on voluntary contributions. As far as relief was concerned, comprehensive, regular, adequate help had to be provided for 'paupers', but as the Act did not define this term, the previous criteria of destitution and disability remained in operation. According to Section 68 of the Act, 'nothing herein contained shall be held to confer a right to demand relief on able-bodied persons out of employment', a clause which both central and local administrators interpreted as allowing each parochial board to exercise discretionary power to give temporary help.

Relief to the entitled poor could be given in cash or in kind on an outdoor basis, or total maintenance could be offered in a poorhouse, the latter institutions being regarded as places of shelter for the aged, the young, the sick and the friendless who for some reason were incapable of maintaining themselves as outdoor recipients. Poorhouse provision was not a statutory obligation.

Within one year the Act was operational. The Board of Supervision was not an elected body but it was intended that the nine members would represent the various parts of the country. The three Sheriffs of Perthshire, Renfrewshire, and Ross and Cromarty represented the agricultural, industrial and Highland regions respectively, while the Lord Provosts of Edinburgh and Glasgow represented the two largest urban areas. In practice the Sheriffs acted as legal advisers along with the Solicitor General, and the three remaining members were appointed by the Crown, one of whom acted as the paid chairman. From 1845 to 1868 Sir John M'Neill was chairman of the Board of Supervision and on his suggestion the other two Crown appointments were made from either side of the House of Commons in an effort to promote political balance. This was certainly his intention as he stated to the Select Committee inquiring into the administration of the Poor Laws in 1868, that he felt that 'the Board of Supervision should be free from party bias and from the suspicion of party bias'.[5]

From its headquarters in Edinburgh the Board of Supervision helped to organise the appointment of a parochial board in each of the 880 parishes in Scotland. Membership of local boards was determined by two factors; whether a parish was classed as a burgh or not and the local decision whether to levy rates or rely on voluntary contributions. In unassessed parishes (where no poor rates were levied) the kirk-session and heritors arrangement continued but on a yearly basis and under a more organised procedure. In assessed parishes ratepayers elected a fixed number of representatives to the parochial board each year under a complicated procedure devised by the Board of Supervision, with variations for the burghs and for the non-burghs.

No anti-Poor Law movement developed in Scotland as it had in England, where in some areas strong opposition had impeded or prevented the implementation of the 1834 Act. This lack of organised opposition in Scotland was partly due to the cautious diplomatic approach taken by the central Board and partly to the way in which the Scottish legislation was framed to avoid at least four main areas of dispute which had occurred after the English reorganisation, namely forceful centralisation, loss of local identity, compulsory rating and emphasis on indoor relief.

As the central authority, the Board of Supervision appeared to have few powers of compulsion, its name implying it would operate as a supervising advisory board sanctioning local arrangements. It could apparently neither initiate action nor claim the power of audit. Responsibility and initiative thus seemed to lie with parochial boards, which raised the funds and distributed poor relief, using the Board of Supervision only to clarify the law or to give suggestions on request. This impression of a merely supervisory role was reinforced by the central Board itself which, in the first few years after 1845, aimed at co-operation and conciliation rather than authoritative demands or compulsion. However, the Board of Supervision came to receive a large number of complaints each year from ratepayers, local inhabitants, parochial board members and staff as well as from paupers, and as a result of the ensuing investigations it began to issue circulars to all parishes as a means both of improving relief arrangements and of preventing maladministration. By the time parochial boards realised that the Board of Supervision *did* intend to intervene in local affairs, the central administrative machinery was well established and it was difficult for one parish in which mis-management had been discovered to persuade others to oppose central authority. In any case, hostility to the Board of Supervision tended to be sporadic and, as parochial boards notoriously had dif-ficulty in co-operating with each other on any matter, they were un-able to offer concerted opposition to the central Board.

As parishes were not forced to combine into unions as they were in

England administrative boundaries generally remained unchanged, each parochial board administering a traditional area, which was usually much larger than the parish in England. There was, therefore, no compulsory loss of local identity, although the Act did allow any parish to combine with contiguous parishes for Poor Law purposes. Few took this course of action at first, which was perhaps fortunate since the Board of Supervision discovered that, while it could approve such an arrangement, it had no power to dissolve a combination in the event of it being unworkable. In 1861, however, the Board obtained this power, largely because of friction in the combined parishes of Islay. Once it was realised that combinations could be dissolved a few more parishes were willing to unite, although, generally, parochial boards preferred to retain their own identity or combine solely for the purpose of providing a poorhouse. In the city of Edinburgh, for example, there were three parochial boards, a combination of which would have resolved many administrative difficulties, but it was not until the 1870s that two of them agreed to come together.

The controversial issue of poor rates was dealt with in a very simple manner in 1845. Each parish made its own decision whether or not to impose rates, the Act demanding only that sufficient money should be available to provide regular adequate allowance to the poor. If rating was chosen, however, then a parochial board had to select one of the four specified methods of assessment. Two of these involved an inquiry into personal income, to which ratepayers soon objected, so in 1861 the more popular alternatives based on rateable value of property were adopted as the future legal basis for assessment. Rating was not a straightforward procedure in Scotland even after the Valuation Act of 1854, however, for the arrangements for levying assessment were controlled by two laws with very different purposes. The 1845 Act allowed each parochial board to assess property for rates but this gross annual rental was then subject to deductions for repairs, burdens and other items before the poor rate was levied. The Valuation Act established the annual value of property in a parish which was then used as a basis upon which each parochial board estimated the deductions and there was no uniform method of arriving at the rateable value for poor rates.

The Board of Supervision soon indicated that part of its function was to ensure more adequate relief provisions. Expenditure therefore rose after 1845, often as a direct result of the central Board's regulations for minimum standards of care and administration, a point not always understood by local ratepayers who tended to direct their criticisms at the parochial boards. An increasing number of parishes therefore found it necessary to impose rates instead of relying on voluntary contributions. In 1845, 230 (or roughly 25 per cent of) parishes imposed rating but by 1894, 840 (or 95 per cent) found it necessary to levy a regular yearly rate.[6] The Board of Supervision mentioned in its 1847 minutes that opposition to assessment was gradually being overcome partly due to the optional rating clause in the Act. Most of the continuing prejudice against rating was confined to northern rural parishes, some of which remained unassessed even in 1894.

There had been opposition in England to the emphasis placed in 1834 on indoor relief. The Scottish Act suggested that parochial boards could consider 'the propriety of erecting a poorhouse' in which medical attention could be given to the sick inmates, but there was no obligation, either on the local boards to do so, or on the poor to enter the buildings. Indeed for many years after 1845 paupers who objected to indoor relief were given outdoor help instead. English workhouses were part of the deterrent principle aimed at reducing the number of able-bodied unemployed who applied for relief. In Scotland such a consideration could hardly arise since such applicants were expressly debarred from demanding relief as a right, although until 1859 local boards exercised discretion and could give temporary help to the able-bodied. This was not as strange as it would appear because, prior to 1845, relief had often been given to the unemployed in times of famine or distress, and parochial boards continued to give interim help. A court decision in 1859, however, made it quite clear that this was not legal and the definition of pauper in Scotland continued to be confined to persons who were both disabled and destitute. There was thus no tradition of 'setting the poor on work' and for many years no organised employment was provided in the majority of poorhouses. Hence many of the complaints levied against the English workhouse were irrelevant in Scotland.

It was one thing to pass an Act of Parliament in 1845; it was quite another thing to make the law operational. The Act contained few definitions and many ambiguous phrases which could be interpreted in various ways. Unless the central Board was prepared to be authoritarian and parochial boards were willing to accept central direction without question, no uniform relief system could emerge.

Neither condition existed, so a very varied pattern of poor-relief administration resulted, but such diversity had advantages and disadvantages for both the administrators and the recipients.

The Board of Supervision was empowered to issue rules and regulations to amplify the outline in the Act and if these were forwarded to the Secretary of State for his approval, they became Statutory Instruments or obligatory extensions of the original law. The Board of Supervision could then enforce these regulations under Section 87 of the Act which gave it the power to instigate a Court of Session procedure in cases where parochial boards refused or neglected to execute the law properly. The opinion of the central Board regarding the satisfactory performance of duties by a parochial board was very important, but the Board of Supervision appeared reluctant to invoke this section of the Act, although on the few occasions it did so the legal decision was given in its favour. This was understandable because the central Board had three Sheriffs and the Solicitor General as members, ably assisted by a paid secretary with legal qualifications, and court proceedings were unlikely to be initiated unless these very experienced lawyers thought there were valid grounds. The few parochial boards, like Glasgow and Edinburgh, which could afford an expensive legal confrontation with the central Board soon realised it was more expedient to reach a compromise in the event of a difference of opinion. Furthermore, the Board of Supervision very seldom bluntly refused to consider a parochial board's alternative proposals for the administration of relief and this flexibility at local and central level became a distinct feature in Scottish poor relief.

The Board of Supervision did issue numerous rules and regulations between 1845 and 1894, usually as a result of receiving a complaint that maladministration or defective provisions for relief existed in a parish. When the central authority considered such a complaint lay within its jurisdiction a thorough investigation usually ensued. If the allegation was proven, the parochial board was informed what measures the central Board thought necessary to remove the cause, though the details were usually negotiable. If, as a result of the inquiry, the Board of Supervision then considered that similar problems might arise in other parishes, a general regulation was issued. In 1850, for example, the Board investigated many complaints that parishes were reluctant to allow Roman Catholic pauper children to attend schools appropriate to their religious persuasion and issued a regulation forbidding religious intolerance of any kind.

Since not all regulations, rules and circulars issued by the central Board were submitted to the Secretary of State for approval, parochial boards were often unsure which regulations were obligatory and which were simply the Board of Supervision's own recommendations. Clarification on this point was uncommon as ambiguity operated to the advantage of the central Board by providing the maximum flexibility, allowing adaptation to local customs and resources in the most effective manner. Variety of parochial resources was indeed a problem in a countryside where the agricultural economy was changing and in towns where there was often no consolidated local government to control piecemeal development, particularly in the absence of a compulsory poor rate. Also parishes themselves differed; some were large and populous, others small and sparsely inhabited; others again in the Highlands and Islands covered vast areas with congested agricultural population but little industrial development. The whole relief system depended upon how much a parish could (or was prepared to) raise; uniform arrangements were quite impossible. No central government grants were available under the 1845 Act to augment local poor funds and the Board of Supervision was not willing to direct parochial boards to incur large expenditure. It was impractical, for instance, to insist that every parish had a poorhouse, or that every poorhouse built had the elaborate staffing arrangements which were essential if the regulations for residential care were to be minutely implemented. In the absence of any power of audit the Board of Supervision was only prepared to ensure that sufficient funds were made available to provide minimum standards of care. Arrangements over and above these were a matter for the discretion of each parochial board, so parish finances remained a matter of local rather than national concern.

As far as administrative details were concerned, the Board of Supervision drew up a general scheme for an organised system. If a parochial board had the resources of capable members, competent staff and the necessary finances to adopt all the suggestions, then an effective management structure could indeed be developed. Edinburgh City parish with an annual income of over £25,000 from rates and other resources could afford to employ a large staff to assist its Poor Law inspector, but Canongate parochial board, in close proximity, had neither the income nor the managerial skill to follow its example. Further north, small town parishes like Elgin with an annual income of about £50 could do even less. The Highland parishes, whether assessed or not, had great difficulty financing relief let alone incurring administrative costs. The Board of Supervision did not expect its regulations would be implemented in a uniform manner, but it did expect that what was organised should be an improvement on the pre-1845 arrangements and that improvements would continue as standards of living altered in Scotland. When the Medical Registration Act was passed in 1858, for example, the Board of Supervision insisted that medical officers employed by parochial boards should be properly qualified and this was a prerequisite for obtaining a share of the medical relief grant given to Scotland after 1848. This grant of a fixed annual sum of £10,000 (increased to £20,000 a year in 1882) was shared out in a very complicated system devised by the Board of Supervision. Parochial boards could choose whether or not to participate in the grant scheme but those which did not comply with the regulation issued by the central Board received no financial help towards improving medical relief.

The crucial link between the Board of Supervision and the parochial board was the local inspector of poor, who was held responsible for the effective implementation of the law in his parish. In 1845, this was a new post in Scotland. Although the Act said a 'fit and qualified person' should be appointed by each parochial board, the term had little meaning, the appointment mainly depending on local interpretation of the job. In the absence of any formal training, 'qualified' could not involve documentary evidence of competence; it was not until the turn of the century that diplomas could be obtained by examination. As one inspector wrote in 1865, 'Twenty years ago inspectors were qualified all the same; they knew nothing.'[7] The only way to learn was by experience, yet it was a very important post. Many parochial boards had no idea how to hold meetings, appoint committees, levy rates or conduct elections, but the inspector could obtain detailed information on these matters from the Board of Supervision. He was then in a position to advise his employers (who held office for a year at a time) and on more than one occasion the Board of Supervision was forced to remind inspectors that as servants of the parochial board they must treat their employers with respect and not assume overriding authority.

In 1845 the majority of parochial boards regarded clerks as suitable for the position of inspector though few of the men appointed had proper book-keeping experience and many soon got into difficulties with the accounts. As parochial boards were not required to audit or publish their accounts many inspectors became deeply involved with improperly balanced books. The Board of Supervision, having no power of audit, could not check parish accounts and indeed refused to do so even when requested by a parochial board, fearing this was *ultra vires*. To complicate matters, however, one of the duties of the central Board was to send an annual report to Parliament in which statements of parochial finances and numbers of paupers were included. The central Board therefore required formal returns periodically from every inspector of poor, a request which could not be ignored because the local inspector was directly responsible to the Board of Supervision. Although locally appointed and paid, the inspector could only be censured, suspended or dismissed by the central Board, a safeguard which was provided in the 1845 Act to give an inspector security of tenure. Had this not been done, many inspectors would have found themselves in difficult situations, torn between providing improved relief and placating parochial board members who objected to rising costs, but the safeguard also produced conflicting situations in which inspectors found difficulty satisfying the Board of Supervision and their immediate employers. The central Board might dismiss them for neglect of duty or for actions it considered made them unsuitable to continue in office, and failure to complete the required returns could come under this heading.

Faced with a complicated return which many of them did not understand and local book-keeping which was haphazard, inspectors often sent in inaccurate data which was in turn used by the Board of Supervision to compile statistics on the state of pauperism in Scotland for national perusal. There were many complaints made to the central Board about the inspectors' financial incompetence, and sometimes an inspector so accused either resigned without waiting to be investigated or absconded with the rest of the parish funds. In these cases the Board of Supervision suggested that the parochial board should institute a regular audit to prevent irregularities in the future, but not all local boards took this advice.

The Board of Supervision also recommended that reasonable salaries should be paid and retirement pensions awarded as there was otherwise an obvious temptation for overworked and underpaid men to embezzle. From a House of Commons return in 1881, however, it was clear that this advice was also widely ignored.[8] Even at this late date few inspectors held full-time appointments. They combined their jobs with a surprising variety of other occupations, acting also as collectors of poor rates, clerks of all descriptions, bank agents or merchants. As inspectors of poor they enjoyed salaries ranging from 15 shillings to £700 a year – but very few were near the upper limit. A list of their official duties made such formidable reading that even a full-time inspector in a moderately sized parish would have found difficulty in completing all the tasks without assistance, yet very few were provided either with clerical help or with any assistance in visiting and supervising paupers under their care. It was not surprising that some aspects were neglected. The duties became even more arduous after 1854 because of subsequent social legislation, most of which gave the inspectors additional responsibilities although rarely extra payment.[9] As far as the Board of Supervision was concerned, however, the inspector was primarily engaged to fulfil his duties under the 1845 Act.

Until 1852 the Board of Supervision learned of any neglect of duty from complaints received from local citizens, parochial boards and paupers. Persons refused relief appealed direct to the Sheriff's Court but paupers had the right of appeal to the central Board if they considered their relief was inadequate. Through various channels, therefore, the Board of Supervision learned about the capabilities of the local inspectors of poor, yet between 1845 and 1851 only five inspectors were dismissed. There was a dramatic increase in the following year when six inspectors lost their posts. The explanation for the sudden increase was not that inspectors were becoming more incompetent, but that the Board of Supervision was allowed to promote one of its clerks to the post of Visiting Inspector, an omission in the 1845 Act which was rectified after repeated requests to the Secretary of State. In 1856 formal legislation enabled the central Board to appoint two General Superintendents and shortly afterwards a Visiting Officer for poorhouses was also appointed. this permanent central inspectorate of three men energetically visited all the parishes in Scotland, submitting confidential reports to the Board of Supervision to augment less detailed information sent in by local inspectors. The parochial boards and their staff developed a respect for the central inspectorate, realising that any mismanagement was unlikely to remain undetected for long.

In fact, the Board of Supervision did not always intervene in local arrangements unless the defect reported by its officials was considered a serious maladministration or was supported by a local complaint. In the 1870s, for example, the Visiting Officer repeatedly suggested to his employers that poorhouse sick wards should not be staffed by pauper nurses but trained nursing staff ought to be employed. This involved additional local expenditure and parochial boards were not convinced either that trained staff would provide the best care for the poorhouse, or indeed that nurses would be willing to attend the chronic pauper sick when their expertise was in greater demand in voluntary hospitals. The Board of Supervision was reluctant to enforce the Visiting Officer's suggestion and decided to leave the matter to the discretion of parochial boards which appeared to be justified when later events showed that the Visiting Officer had not considered all the difficulties. Edinburgh and Glasgow, for example, found it difficult to attract trained staff to their poorhouses and many inmates were quite capable of giving kindly care to the chronic sick if adequately supervised by the matron and resident physician.

It was in the sphere of the relief provisions themselves that parochial boards enjoyed most freedom of action. Indeed for many years, the Board of Supervision actually encouraged diversity in local arrangements. There was no one procedure for any single category of pauper, each application for relief being treated according to the individual circumstances and local tradition. The central Board took this line of approach when it came to consider complaints of inadequate relief. Between 1845 and 1894 more than 20,000 such complaints were lodged, over 11,000 of them being dismissed as invalid, while some 4000 were referred back to the appropriate parochial boards with suggestions for the removal of the grounds of complaint; only in 33 cases did the local Board refuse at this point to change its original decision.[10] In these cases the Board of Supervision issued a minute declaring that the applicant had just cause for legal action in the Court of Session. The pauper could then sue his parochial board and, during the hearing, both received an allowance fixed by the central Board (but paid by the local board) and obtained free legal aid to pursue his case. Not all the 33 cases reached the court, however, because once parochial boards realised that these minutes would be issued, they preferred to alter their original decision at this stage rather than incur legal expenses quite out of proportion to the increased allowances suggested. A threat that an order would be issued was usually sufficient to remove the grounds of the complaint.

The total resources of a parish obviously affected the quality and quantity of care, as the local inspector had to remember when reviewing applications for relief. As he could be held criminally liable for any breach of duty which affected the life or health of a pauper, he had to be quite sure of the circumstances before refusing an application. Although theoretically each parochial board had the responsibility of determining who was entitled to relief, how it was given and for how long, it was usually the inspector who made the initial decision, which the parochial board approved or altered at a later date. Deciding who was entitled to relief was by no means a simple matter; absolute 'destitution' was not required and 'disability' could be widely interpreted to include physical or mental illness, or even a degree of economic or social deprivation. In Edinburgh, for example, paupers were admitted even if they enjoyed casual earnings between sixpence and eleven shillings a week. Cash allowances of between one shilling and six shillings to such people were recorded but often there was no obvious correlation between earnings and the amount of relief allowed.[11] Disability could be applied to widows with or without children, deserted wives and families, single-parent families, the aged, the homeless, wives of prisoners, and so on. In fact, destitution and disability were two very elastic terms often applied differently at different times within a single parish. In a relief system covering over 800 parishes there was an infinite variety of interpretations.

Many inspectors of poor used settlement as a guide when deciding what type of relief should be offered, even though help could not legally be refused after 1845 simply because the applicant had no settlement in the parish. Ascertaining the facts of settlement as quickly as possible was important because any help given could be reclaimed from the appropriately liable parish, at least if it lay in Scotland. Unfortunately it was rarely easy to accomplish without a great deal of investigation and it often provoked hostility between parishes. The inspectors, however, gradually reached amicable arrangements between themselves, particularly after the foundation in 1856 of a Society of Inspectors of Poor with the aims of encouraging mutual support and co-operation in Poor Law affairs.

The settlement issue was not so simple to resolve for paupers with no rights in Scotland (cf. p. 38). Natives of England, Ireland and the Isle of Man could be legally removed to their own countries when they applied for relief in Scotland, but these removals were the subject of much controversy, particularly in the case of the Irish, which was complicated by the possibility of racial and religious bias. Urban parishes like Edinburgh which attracted large numbers of casual labourers and immigrants were often notorious for repatriating Irish paupers as quickly as possible. The Irish Poor Law authorities were equally notorious for returning the same paupers to Scotland just as speedily, sometimes on the same boat as the returning Scottish inspector who had delivered the paupers to an Irish workhouse. The Board of Supervision received complaints from both Scottish and Irish authorities. To prevent undue hardship the central Board devised elaborate rules for removal procedures, which, if strictly followed by any parochial board, ensured Board of Supervision support in the event of any complaint from Ireland. Realising the benefits of obeying these rules, parochial boards tried to conform, but the removal controversy was not entirely resolved and remained a bone of contention throughout the late nineteenth century.

Having decided which applications to accept the inspector had further to assess whether to give outdoor relief or offer the pauper a place in the poorhouse. Again, parish resources had to be taken into account. By 1850 there were twenty-one poorhouses in Scotland, all with varying amounts of accommodation, and parishes without a poorhouse of their own could apply to the Board of Supervision for permission to board paupers in a nearby poorhouse. None of these buildings were without some structural, sanitary or management defects, however, and the constant alterations suggested by the Board of Supervision were often a drain on local finances. The provision of outdoor relief was much preferred by both paupers and parochial boards, but some paupers often required some kind of institutional care; the sick, the homeless, the elderly and the young for example. Parishes could provide a poorhouse in their own area (singly or as a joint venture) or supervise lodging houses, or include a rent allowance in the outdoor relief. The Board of Supervision tried to control the construction and management of poorhouses, having decided in 1846 that this supervision was part of its function. It issued regulations regarding the suitability of the site, the internal space requirements and sanitary arrangements, and parochial board rules for poorhouse management also required central Board approval.

Such rules, which came to be largely based on those submitted by Edinburgh in 1846, were very elaborate and strict, but as the Edinburgh parochial board itself quickly discovered, discipline was often impossible to enforce except by discharging troublesome inmates on to the outdoor roll, a practice not endorsed by the Board of Supervision. A system of inducements developed whereby inmates received additional amenities for good behaviour and for participating in the routine work of the poorhouse. Women inmates helped in normal household management and men were offered shoemaking, tailoring or work on constructional repairs, but there was no compulsion and Scottish institutions remained 'poorhouses' not 'workhouses'. Indeed many inmates spent the day in idleness. The rules regarding specific 'liberty days' were also difficult to enforce, as, in practice, inmates could come and go as they pleased. With the development of the central inspectorate such anomalies came to the notice of the Board of Supervision and parochial boards came to realise that building a poorhouse increased the possibility of central intervention. Many parochial boards were therefore tempted to run lodging houses instead, as these were not regulated to the same extent. After frequent complaints about these establishments, however, the Board of Supervision extended its regulations to include this kind of residential care and when in 1867 it became the central authority for public health stricter control was exerted.

This additional duty brought the Board of Supervision into contact with other local authorities as well as with parochial boards and it helped to increase the central Board's prestige. New legislation which assigned duties to existing authorities at both the local and central levels was a feature of Scottish nineteenth-century administration. When this course of action was not taken, as for instance in the case of the Lunacy Acts from 1857, both central and local resentment often resulted. Assigning public-health duties to the Board of Supervision, however, meant that the General Superintendents could investigate parish arrangements for both poor relief and public health and this dual function brought increased central intervention.

Parochial boards preferred to give the majority of paupers outdoor relief anyway, mainly because it was cheaper and easier to organise than residential care. It was simply a cash allowance collected by the pauper each week, perhaps augmented by relief in kind, or by the proceeds of any self-help activities the pauper might undertake. The local inspector was required to visit paupers in their own homes at least twice a year but, as many officials worked alone in a parish, this was not always possible. In the crowded urban areas, although an inspector usually had assistants, investigating the slum tenements of the poorer sectors of large towns required a stamina and dedication to duty which not all parochial board employees possessed. In any case, regular visiting in insanitary quarters had attendant risks; a number of inspectors and medical officers contracted fever in this way.[12] On the low salaries many of the parochial boards paid their staff, it was not surprising that some employees were less zealous about visiting.

Relief in kind could be widely interpreted. It could include personal clothing, bedding, fuel, payment of rent or rates, food, medical attention, medicine, extra items to supplement the diet of the sick, and education for children of school age who were either paupers themselves or dependants of paupers. Each parish gave relief in kind on purely local criteria, so quality and quantity varied considerably. For example, northern parishes often gave allowances of meal. The Board of Supervision received periodic complaints about the quality and, as relief in kind was also part of 'adequate care', investigations ensued which sometimes disclosed that inspectors either owned the local shop or were improperly involved in selling goods to their own parochial boards. The central Board therefore prohibited any inspector from supplying goods to paupers directly or indirectly, but in remote parishes this was difficult to enforce.[13]

The provision of education for pauper children was mentioned in the 1845 Act, and hence was a statutory provision long before the 1872 Education Act, and all parochial boards had either to provide a poorhouse school or pay fees for children attending a local school appropriate to their religion (cf. Chapter 3). Boarding out children with suitable guardians was also a common feature of Scottish relief which had been in use long before 1845. The practice was extensively used by urban parishes, which sent the children into the countryside, in the belief that the scheme was of great benefit to the recipient. Apart from the advantages of a rural environment the child had the benefits of the cohesion and stability of family life, on which the Victorians placed a high value. The children took their place in the family routine, learned household duties, attended the local school and in many cases were subsequently placed in suitable employment. Many parochial boards believed that the recurrent cycle of pauperism found in successive generations of recipients could be broken if this training and supervision was offered. The Board of Supervision, at first rather dubious about the scheme, gave its full approval in 1863 after investigating a complaint in Arran and it decided that children brought up in this way had distinct advantages over children reared in institutions. The success of the Scottish scheme promoted its adoption in many English unions.

Medical attention for the physically and mentally ill pauper was also a statutory obligation under the Act of 1845 and the Board of Supervision's subsequent regulations for improving medical care were approved by the Secretary of State. Paupers obtained help from medical officers either in their own homes or as inpatients in poorhouse wards and voluntary hospitals. Sometimes the sick were boarded out with selected families though this was not common. To encourage improvement of medical relief, government grants were given to the Scottish authorities from 1848 for the physically ill, and from 1875 for the mentally ill. Parish participation in the grant scheme was not obligatory, and as it was conditional upon compliance with the Board of Supervision's regulations, not all parochial boards accepted the terms. Nevertheless, even non-participating parishes were expected to provide adequate care for sick paupers. The Board of Supervision remained the central authority for the physically ill pauper throughout the period, but the responsibility for pauper lunatics was transferred to a specially constituted Board of Lunacy in 1857. As the parochial boards and inspectors of poor were henceforth responsible for two central authorities, which had differing requirements for poorhouse accommodation of paupers and pauper lunatics, local administrators often found themselves in impossible situations. This was further aggravated in 1875 when the Board of Supervision became the controlling authority for the lunacy grant while the Board of Lunacy retained the duty of establishing the conditions attached to a parochial board's participation. Obviously this produced a very complicated situation which increased the hostility between the two central Boards. The care of pauper lunatics remained a constant anxiety to parochial boards.

From the mid-1850s, criticism of the way outdoor relief was commonly applied became more frequent in the daily press and in magazine articles. As largely unsupervised care it much resembled the indiscriminate relief Chalmers had decried. Supervised relief for both indoor and outdoor paupers was expensive and could only be properly applied where adequate resources of finance, managers and staff were available, as in the larger parishes in Edinburgh and Glasgow. During the 1860s the Poor Law inspectors in these parishes were very able men, who instituted local training schemes for clerks who could be gradually promoted to assistant inspectors. Having reached this level some trainees would leave to become inspectors elsewhere, taking with them knowledge and expertise which benefited other parishes. In addition, the formation of local branches of the Society of Inspectors of Poor enabled members to discuss and exchange ideas, and these meetings helped foster interest in supervised relief as a means of controlling and re-educating paupers. Many parochial boards thus tried to emulate the example of the larger parishes, reorganising their administrative structure and attaching conditions to the relief they offered. Pauper parents with children of school age were thereby 'persuaded' to avail themselves of the educational opportunities offered, and dissipated paupers who mis-spent their allowances were obliged to enter the poorhouse if they wished to continue receiving relief. But not all parochial boards could introduce these conditions on the same elaborate scale as the cities because their incomes were insufficient and poorhouse accommodation was limited.

By 1868 there were 66 poorhouses in Scotland with accommodation for approximately 12,000 inmates although these places were never full, the average number of inmates being between 8000–9000 each year. Although the number of poorhouses remained the same until 1894 about 3000 additional places were provided as the older buildings were gradually demolished and replaced by purpose-built institutions equipped with central heating and with sanitary facilities superior to those in the homes of the labouring class. With additional staff an increased amount of supervised care was possible in these new poorhouses since they were designed to permit differential care to various categories of inmates. There were male and female wards for the sick, the old and the young, for the 'respectable' and the 'dissolute', and, as many of the poorhouses were built in rural areas, cultivation of the surrounding land provided work for both men and women. As 'disability' was often interpreted on a social criterion and was extended to include dependants of paupers, inmates were often capable of performing useful tasks, but as no inmate could be compelled to work, the rewards system previously mentioned continued to operate.

The central inspectorate approved of the gradual move towards more supervised care believing that this kind of rehabilitation or retraining would help to reduce pauperism in the future, and the Board of Supervision encouraged parochial boards to be more discriminating in granting relief. Such encouragement became even more intense after 1868 following the appointment of a new chairman and the publication of a select committee report in which favourable comments about its operations helped increase the Board of Supervision's prestige. Furthermore, the annual report showed that the number of paupers had reached the unprecedented figure of 136,444 or approximately one pauper in every twenty-four of the estimated population and only 8794 of these were inmates of poorhouses.[14] The Board of Supervision felt that lax administration might account for some of the increase and suggested parochial boards could be more discerning in assessing applications for relief. The idea developed both that a decreased number on the parish roll indicated administrative efficiency and that if expenditure continued to rise this indicated improved relief.

Not all parochial boards were willing to assume the additional responsibility which the provision of more supervised care entailed, but many inspectors of poor appeared anxious to demonstrate their efficiency. A reduction in the number of paupers was not easy to achieve, however, and the deterrent principle used in England was aimed at able-bodied paupers, a category not entitled to relief in Scotland. If destitution was regarded as the result of misfortune, illness or improvidence, then paupers could be classified accordingly, and by giving different treatment to each group a certain amount of control and discipline could be exerted. Outdoor relief was increasingly reserved for 'deserving' paupers and, as this method of help became a symbol of respectability, the status of the poorhouse became inferior by implication. If the outdoor paupers did not continue to deserve their allowance, it could be withdrawn and an offer of poorhouse entry substituted which might be refused simply because it meant restricted liberty. If the offer was refused, however, then the parochial board could remove the pauper's name from the poor roll and show a decrease in the incidence of pauperism.

By 1894 the annual report showed that there was one pauper for every forty-four of the population, that 9212 were inmates in the 66 poorhouses and 72,891 paupers received outdoor relief, but these figures do not include lunatic paupers. The Board of Supervision considered that the decreased number of paupers was due to more efficient management and that the offer of indoor relief acted as a test of need. This was debatable, as a close examination of some of the local records reveals that discrepancies occurred between local and central figures. The voluminous tables in each appendix of the annual report only indicated the amount of information concerning parish income, expenditure and number of paupers that each parochial board was prepared to reveal to the Board of Supervision and the statements could not be checked or verified. Between 1845 and 1894, despite an increase in poorhouse accommodation, the majority of Scottish paupers continued to receive outdoor relief. By 1894 there was accommodation for over 15,000 paupers in the poorhouses, but the average number returned each year to the Board of Supervision was between 8000 and 9000 inmates. Not all parochial boards offered poorhouse entry to their paupers or even introduced a stricter regime. The Edinburgh inspector stated in the 1880s that tramps and the idle poor preferred to seek help elsewhere, which indicated that other parishes offered a less restrictive help than the City parish.

Various references have been made to the additional responsibilities given to the Board of Supervision, the parochial boards and the inspectors of poor. It seemed that having created this machinery in 1845 the government was prepared to utilise it for the implementation of subsequent social legislation. It was more common, however, to use the parochial boards and the inspectors rather than the central Board, but additional remuneration for the overworked inspectors was not awarded by parliamentary legislation. The two-tier system begun in 1845 became the general pattern for subsequent developments. In 1857 the Board of Lunacy was created to supervise and direct arrangements for the mentally ill and the parochial boards were given additional responsibilities. In 1867, however, the Board of Supervision became the central authority for public health and dealt with town councils as well as parochial boards to improve burgh and rural amenities. Education facilities after 1872 followed a slightly different pattern, for new authorities were created at both the central and local levels, but the parochial boards and their inspectors were involved in the collecting of the school rate and also with parents who could not afford school fees for their children without undue hardship.

By 1894 both the Board of Supervision and the parochial boards had increased their responsibilities. The central Board dealt with some arrangements for the mentally ill, including the sharing out of the lunacy grant. It was involved in local taxation returns, in the improvement of medical facilities and public-health duties and often collected various kinds of information for the government. The parochial boards were involved in education, public health, valuation, burial-ground facilities, the registration of births, marriages and deaths, vaccination arrangements and industrial schools for young offenders, but how many of these additional duties were assigned to a parochial board depended on the size and status of the parish. As a general rule, where no town council or comparable organisation existed, responsibility for the local inhabitants was assigned to a parochial board. The inspectors of poor were even more involved with additional duties because, apart from acting as employees for their parochial boards, they had responsibilities under legislation which did not directly concern their local boards. For instance, they investigated applicants for pawnbroker licences on behalf of the magistrates yet the parochial boards were not involved in this responsibility.

The 1845 Act was a major statute providing the administrative framework through which improved relief was given for both paupers and their families, and this organisation could be utilised to implement other legislation. Once established the machinery provided a nucleus for the development of local government and, in the major towns, the parochial boards were often in competition with the town councils. As a piece of legislation for poor relief, however, the act helped introduce a local rating system on a more regular basis, a local administrative structure in which citizens could participate, and a central authority to supervise parish arrangements. It reaffirmed that some people in society were entitled to help from the more affluent, help which was to be regular, comprehensive and available as a right, not as a charity.

The 1845 Act remained operational until 1894 when the Board of Supervision ceased to exist and was replaced by a more powerful Local Government Board directly responsible to Parliament.[15] Parochial boards were replaced by parish councils holding office for three years, but their discretionary powers were severely curtailed by giving the Local Government Board the power of audit long denied to the Board of Supervision. Relief provisions thereafter became more uniform and many English features were introduced, although the system retained some Scottish characteristics. The 1845 Poor Law Amendment Act was the foundation upon which future welfare services could be built; even the defects discovered during its implementation provided valuable lessons for those who drafted subsequent legislation.

List of Abbreviations

(for Bibliographical Notes, and Notes and References)

B.M.	British Museum
C.C.E.	Committee of the Council on Education
Ec.H.R.	*Economic History Review*
E.H.R.	*English Historical Review*
H.J.	*Historical Journal*
L.G.B.	Local Government Board
P.L.B.	Poor Law Board
P.L.C.	Poor Law Commission
P.P.	*Parliamentary Papers*
P.R.O.	Public Record Office
R.C.	Royal Commission
S.C.	Select Committee

(Unless otherwise stated, the place of publication in the ensuing lists is London.)

Bibliographical Notes

1. SETTLEMENT, REMOVAL AND THE NEW POOR LAW

1 Contemporary Material

A large amount of printed material on settlement and removal, much of it highly critical of the system, exists for the nineteenth century. Here we can only indicate the main areas where this is located. A useful introduction to the complex state of settlement law can be found in J. R. McCulloch, *Statistical Account of the British Empire*, 4th edn (1854) vol. ii, pp. 652–3. Sir George Nicholls, *History of the English Poor Law*, vol. iii by T. Mackay (reissued, 1904), ch. xvi offers a fuller but equally clear exposition of the state of the law and the problems involved in its reform, as does P. F. Aschrott, *The English Poor Law System, Past and Present*, 2nd edn (1902) part ii, ch. 1, sec. iii. Details of the various statutes affecting settlement and removal, and of some of the more important legal cases involving settlement, can be found in the numerous legal textbooks on settlement published to help parish and union officials and others involved in settlement litigation find their way through the tangle of statute and case law on the subject. J. F. Archbold, *The Poor Law Comprising the Whole of the Law of Settlement and All the Authorities*, 15th edn (1898) which went through ten editions between 1850 and 1898, J. F. Symonds, *The Law of Settlement and Removal*, 4th edn (1903) and Herbert Davey, *The Law of Settlement* (1908) are good examples of this, whilst E. Lidbetter, *Settlement and Removal* (1932) shows that, even after the disappearance of the unions and the boards of guardians, a knowledge of the law of settlement was considered essential for aspiring candidates in local government service.

George Coode, *Report to the Poor Law Board on the Law of Settlement and Removal of the Poor* (1851), and Robert Pashley, *Pauperism and Poor Laws* (1852), constitute the two most comprehensive critiques of the law of settlement as it existed at mid-century. The *Wellesley Index to Victorian Periodicals 1824–1900*, vol. i (1966) vol. ii (1972) provides a useful aid to tracking down some of the numerous articles on settlement and removal which appeared in nineteenth-century periodicals. Sir Edmund Head's article of 1848 in the *Edinburgh Review* has recently been reprinted in A. W. Coats (ed.), *Poverty in the Victorian Age*, vol. ii (1973). Discussions of settlement and removal also figure prominently in the voluminous pamphlet literature on the Poor Law.

An indispensable source of information and opinion is of course the great mass of evidence collected by the many nineteenth-century parliamentary select committees on settlement and removal, particularly those of 1847 (*P.P.*, 1847, xi); 1854 (*P.P.*, 1854, xvii); 1857–60 (*P.P.*, 1857–8, xiii); (*P.P.*, 1859 [sess. 2] vii); 1860 (*P.P.*, 1860, xvii) and 1878 (*P.P.*, 1878–9, xii), together with the evidence on, and discussion of, the problem of settlement in the reports and appendices of the Royal Commissions of 1832–4 and 1905–09.

2   Recent Works

In contrast to the spate of nineteenth-century writing on settlement and removal, the question has been relatively neglected by modern social historians, particularly with regard to developments after the 1834 Act. Inevitably S. and B. Webb, *English Local Government, English Poor Law History, Part II, The Last Hundred Years,* vol. I (1929; reprinted, 1963) provides the basic account of the reforms of the law of settlement and their effects after 1834. Arthur Redford's pioneering *Labour Migration in England 1800–1850* (1926; 2nd edn with introduction by W. H. Chaloner, 1963) contains a valuable discussion of the operation of the law of settlement and its effect on labour mobility. More recently, historical geographers and economic historians have begun to show a renewed interest in Poor Law settlement and removal as it affected the pattern of settlement and population distribution in rural areas. Dennis R. Mills, 'The Poor Laws and the Distribution of Population, c. 1600–1860, with Special Reference to Lincolnshire', *Transactions of the Institute of British Geographers,* XXVI (1959) pp. 185–95, marks the beginnings of this type of study, and chapter 8 of his *English Rural Communities: The Impact of a Specialised Economy* (1973) continues the analysis with reference to Nottinghamshire. Another article by the same author, 'Francis Howell's Report on the Operation of the Laws of Settlement in Nottinghamshire, 1848', *Transactions of the Thoroton Society,* LXXVI (1972) pp. 46–52, examines the report of one of the Poor Law Board's inspectors on the effects of settlement and removal in his area. B. A. Holderness, ' "Open" and "Close" Parishes in England in the 18th and 19th Centuries', *Agricultural History Review,* XX (1972) pp. 126–39 contains a valuable discussion of the number, distribution and effect of 'close' parishes in rural areas. Dennis R. Mills, 'Spatial Implications of the Settlement Laws in Rural England' in *Poverty and Social Policy, 1750–1870,* Open University Arts Fourth Level Course, Great Britain 1750–1950: Sources and Historiography Block IV Units 12–16 (1974) provides an excellent brief summary of the changes in the law of settlement between 1834 and 1865, and also makes suggestions as to the possible design of further local research into questions of settlement, 'close' and 'open' parishes and population distribution in rural areas, which may go some way towards remedying the relative neglect of nineteenth-century settlement and removal by historians.

2.   MEDICAL SERVICES UNDER THE NEW POOR LAW

Surprisingly, in view of its comparative neglect by social historians, the Poor Law medical service is one of the most fully documented aspects of nineteenth-century social administration. The *Annual Reports* of the Poor Law Commission from 1834 to 1846, those of the Board from 1847 to 1870, and of the Local Government Board from 1871 on provide, in addition to the texts of the relevant Orders, some basic statistics and commentary on the evolution of the service from its initiation in 1834. All these reports were printed in the normal sessional series of Parliamentary Papers. To supplement this regular series there were also, from time to time, periodic enquiries into the operation of medical relief and the state of the workhouse infirmaries. The most useful of these were the *Report of the Select Committee on the Poor Law Amendment Act, P.P.* XVIII (1837–8); the *Report of the Select Committee on Medical Poor Relief,* IX (1844); the *Report of the Select Committee on Medical*

Relief, XII (1854); the *Report of the Select Committee on the Administration of Relief to the Poor,* IX (1864), and *Report of Dr Edward Smith . . . on the Metropolitan Workhouse Infirmaries and Sick wards, P.P.,* LXI (1866). The *Reports of the Royal Sanitary Commission, PP.,* XXXII (1868–9) and XXXV (1871), contain some valuable evidence about the public-health activities (or inactivity) of the guardians.

The unprinted records of the central authorities – the Commission and the later Boards – embracing a vast mass of correspondence on matters relating to medical relief with boards of guardians, assistant commissioners and inspectors, are all preserved in the Ministry of Health series in the Public Record Office in London. At local level there is a wealth of archival material in the records of individual boards of guardians, most of it preserved and available for historians in County and City Record Offices. These extensive manuscript sources have as yet been little exploited by historians apart from a number of unpublished theses for higher degrees.

Outside the official sphere the history of the Poor Law medical service is also well served by the publications of institutions and professional associations with a close interest in the medical aspects of poor relief. The issues of the medical journals, particularly the *Lancet* from 1834 and the *British Medical Journal* from 1856, frequently contain material of direct relevance, much of it critical, while the special report of the *Lancet*'s 'Commission' of 1865 – *Report of the Lancet Sanitary Commission for Investigating the State of the Infirmaries of Workhouses* (1866) – has been explicitly referred to above. After its formation in 1857, the National Association for the Promotion of Social Science published many papers on this subject in the *Transactions* in which its annual conferences were reported.

Much information may also be found in the considerable pamphlet literature which was a principal vehicle for the campaign for reform of the Poor Law medical service. This literature is nowhere comprehensively surveyed, and it is probably most fully exploited – as are so many other areas of Poor Law pamphleteering – in the footnotes of the Webbs' *Poor Law History.* The periodical reviews – particularly the *Fortnightly, Macmillan's* and *Fraser's* – occasionally gave space to propaganda for reform of the medical service. At the most personal and intimate level, the memoirs of medical men and workhouse visitors provide some of the most revealing glimpses of the reality of the Poor Law medical service. In this class the outstanding works are Joseph Rogers, *Reminiscences of a Workhouse Medical Officer,* ed. Thorold Rogers (1889), and Louisa Twining, *Recollections of Workhouse Visiting and Management during Twenty-Five Years* (1880).

Given this wealth of source material, secondary works based on it are disappointingly few. An admirable early history of the Poor Law medical service was provided by one of the leading reformers, Dr H. W. Rumsey, in his *Essays on State Medicine* (1857) pp. 141–294. The Webbs' account of the Poor Law medical service is rather scrappy and concentrates heavily on the more immediate background to the Royal Commission of 1905–9: S. and B. Webb, *English Poor Law History, Part II, The Last Hundred Years,* I (1929; reprinted, 1963) pp. 314–19. Of recent work, Ruth Hodgkinson, *The Origins of the National Health Service: The Medical Services of the New Poor Law, 1834–1871* (1967) is comprehensive and authoritative. Its sheer bulk, however, and its remorseless pursuit of detail, makes it extremely difficult for the reader to see the wood for the trees. (The book's 400,000 words include, for example, a single, unbroken chapter of 75,000 words – as long as many whole books!) The index – an essential guide through such a wordy labyrinth – is inadequate, and the bibliographical references are often incomplete. The value of what is potentially an important work is, therefore, much diminished, and the book is unlikely to be read widely. The loss is all the greater in that there are no adequate alternatives. B. Abel-Smith, *The Hospitals, 1800–1948* (1964) – not, for example, mentioned in Dr Hodgkinson's bibliography – offers, in contrast, a succinct account of the Poor Law infirmaries. Ruth Hodgkinson herself offers a more concise account of the 'Poor Law Medical Officers of England, 1834–1871', in the *Journal of the History of Medicine and Allied Sciences,* 11 (1956) while J. E. O'Neill in 'Finding a Policy for the Sick Poor', *Victorian Studies,* VII (1963–4) provides a brief survey of the background to the 1867 Metropolitan Poor Act. Royston Lambert, whose superb study, *Sir John Simon (1816–1904) and English Social Administration* (1963) throws incidental light on some aspects of the subject, provides a useful account of vaccination under the Poor Law medical service in 'A Victorian National Health Service: State Vaccination', *H.J.,* V (1962). The development of the Poor Law medical service after its transfer to the Local Government Board in 1871 is well covered by Jeanne L. Brand, *Doctors and the State* (Baltimore, 1965) of which chapter 5 was published previously as 'The Parish Doctor: England's Poor Law Medical Officers and Medical Reform, 1870–1900', *Bulletin of the History of Medicine,* XXXV, 1961; also see Sir A. Powell, *The Metropolitan Asylums' Board and its Work, 1867–1940* (1930).

3.   PAUPER EDUCATION

There are no full studies of Poor Law education, apart from a few contemporary contributions to the nineteenth-century debate. Much detailed information can be gleaned from the standard Poor Law histories: S. and B. Webb, *English Poor Law History* (reprinted, 1963), and G. Nicholls and T. Mackay, *History of the English Poor Law* (1898–9). The administrative context in which the district-school scheme developed is described by S. E. Finer, *The Life and Times of Edwin Chadwick* (1952).

Most histories of education describe how the Poor Law schools shaped the thinking of Kay-Shuttleworth, whose semi-autobiographical *Four Periods of Public Education* (1862) is worth consulting. F. Smith, *The Life of Sir James Kay-Shuttleworth* (1923) is a good brief biography written by an educationalist. More recent discussions of the social and economic context and aims of Victorian state education include J. S. Hurt, *Education in Evolution* (1971) and R. Johnson, 'Educational Policy and Social Control in Early Victorian England', *Past and Present,* XLIX (Nov. 1970). Works which throw incidental light on facets of Poor Law schooling are N. Ball, *Her Majesty's Inspectorate* (1963) and A. Tropp, *The School Teachers: The Growth of the Teaching Profession in England and Wales from 1800* (1957).

Among official records, the annual reports of the successive Poor Law central authorities are a mine of information. So, too, are the Committee on Education's annual minutes, especially those covering parochial union schools, published separately for the years 1847 to 1858, and including the annual reports of the schools' inspectors.

Three other official reports provide valuable information for different key periods in the nineteenth century. The *Reports on the Training of Pauper Children,* House of Lords Sessional Papers, XXXIII (1841) were collated by the Poor Law Commission to support the case for district schools. Mrs Senior's *Report on the Effect on Girls . . . of Education at Pauper Schools,* L.G.B., *Third Annual Report* (1874) pp. 311–94, provides a perceptive critical survey of the barrack schools. The much more substantial report and evidence of the departmental committee of 1896 provides a comprehensive survey of Poor Law schooling at the end of the century, *Departmental Committee . . . on Poor Law Schools, P.P.*, XLIII (1896). Particularly interesting is the evidence of Will Crooks, the Labour pioneer, who had known the South Metropolitan District School as a pupil. Very few of his fellow pupils have left any published account of their schooling, with the notable exception of Charlie Chaplin.

4. THE POOR LAW AND PHILANTHROPY

As for the working of the Poor Law itself, much of the evidence for nineteenth-century philanthropy has to be sought in local collections. A great deal of this evidence has not received adequate study, and this is an aspect of social history where the work of local historians can be very useful indeed. Local newspapers, with their accounts of the meeting of societies and their lists of subscribers, form a useful starting point for any local research, while many public libraries contain annual reports or similar publications from philanthropic organisations of various kinds. A multiplication of local studies of nineteenth-century philanthropy would be a valuable addition to our knowledge of the approaches to poverty in that period.

One very good example of this kind of local study, on a larger scale than would be necessary in dealing with a smaller community, is M. B. Simey, *Charitable Effort in Liverpool in the Nineteenth Century* (1951). A discussion of early nineteenth-century philanthropy in Newcastle is included in 'Aspects of the Relief of Poverty in Early Nineteenth-Century Britain', an essay contributed to *The Long Debate on Poverty*, a volume of essays published by the Institute of Economic Affairs in 1972.

The best general account of nineteenth-century philanthropy is in D. Owen, *English Philanthropy, 1660–1960* (1965). Voluntary efforts to provide medical facilities for the poor are discussed in Ruth Hodgkinson, *The Origins of the National Health Service* (1967) ch. 16. A paper by Brian Harrison on 'Philanthropy and the Victorians', *Victorian Studies*, IX, provides a succinct and illuminating general discussion.

Much detailed evidence about the activity of philanthropic organisations can be found in various official publications of the period. Two good examples are the Appendix to the *Third Annual Report of the Local Government Board, P.P.* (1873–4) especially the evidence given by the social reformer Octavia Hill and Colonel Lynedoch Gardiner, where the relationship of official and unofficial relief activities was discussed; and the evidence taken by the *Select Committee on Distress from Want of Employment* (1895) which includes information from a multitude of places on the organisation of unofficial relief activities to meet hard times.

5. THE POOR LAW AS A POLITICAL INSTITUTION

Very little attention has been devoted by historians to the political aspects of the Poor Law. The only exception is the Anti-Poor Law Movement which is well covered by N. C. Edsall, *The Anti-Poor Law Movement* (Manchester, 1971), J. T. Ward, *The Factory Movement* (1962), M. E. Rose, 'The Anti-Poor Law Movement in the North of England', *Northern History*, I (1966), and 'The Anti-

Poor Law Movement' in *Popular Movements*, ed. J. T. Ward (1970). In passing, some glimpses of political aspects are provided in the older surveys of the Webbs and Nicholls and Mackay. Those interested in examining the political role of the Poor Law must look to local newspapers and local Poor Law records, supplemented by the national records held in the Public Record Office. For an example of a study based on such sources see D. Fraser, 'Poor Law Politics in Leeds, 1833–1855', *Thoresby Society Publications*, LIII (1970) pp. 23–49. Some of the theses listed in the appendix have something to say on politics, but not very much. One scholar who does place the Poor Law in the context of the exercise of power is Dr A. Brundage: see his 'The Landed Interest and the New Poor Law', *E.H.R.*, LXXXVII (1972) pp. 27–48; 'The English Poor Law of 1834 and the Cohesion of Agricultural Society', *Agricultural History*, XLVIII (1974) pp. 405–17; and 'Reform of the Poor Law Electoral System 1834–94' (forthcoming). A different interpretation is offered in reply by P. Dunkley, 'The Landed Interest and the New Poor Law; A Critical Note', *E.H.R.*, LXXXVIII (1973).

6. THE URBAN POOR LAW

Much of the work done on the urban Poor Law is contained in unpublished theses. Some of these are mentioned in the Notes and References, while others which have proved useful include those by Rose, Caplan, Kelly, Handley, and Midwinter.

Popular resistance to the New Poor Law and the early conflicts between the Poor Law Commission and the northern boards of guardians are dealt with in N. C. Edsall, *The Anti-Poor Law Movement, 1834-44* (Manchester, 1971), which may be supplemented by M. E. Rose, 'The Anti-Poor Law Movement in the North of England', *Northern History*, I (1966). N. McCord, 'The Implementation of the 1834 Poor Law Amendment Act on Tyneside', *International Review of Social History*, XIV (1969) reminds us that not all industrial areas stood out against the new measure.

R. Boyson, 'The New Poor Law in North-East Lancashire, 1834–1871', *Transactions of the Lancashire and Cheshire Antiquarian Society*, LXX (1960) studies the impact of the New Poor Law on seven Lancashire unions, a theme taken up by E. C. Midwinter, *Social Administration in Lancashire, 1830–1860* (Manchester, 1969). The same author's 'State Intervention at the Local Level: The New Poor Law in Lancashire', *H.J.*, X (1967) emphasises the continuity between the old and new systems of relief, while M. E. Rose, 'The New Poor Law in an Industrial Area', in *The Industrial Revolution* ed. R. M. Hartwell (Oxford, 1970), analyses the failure of the New Poor Law in the industrial north.

The central authority's attempts to regulate outdoor relief and, in particular, to eliminate the payment of relief in aid of wages, are discussed by M. E. Rose, 'The Allowance System under the New Poor Law', *Ec.H.R.*, 2nd series, XIX (1966), while W. O. Henderson, *The Lancashire Cotton Famine, 1861–1865*, 2nd edn (Manchester, 1969), describes the efforts made to deal with a massive outbreak of unemployment and the changes that resulted.

P. Dunkley, 'The "Hungry Forties" and the New Poor Law: A Case Study', *H.J.*, XVII (1974) describes how relief policy in Durham varied in response to economic fluctuations, and M. Caplan, 'The Poor Law in Nottinghamshire, 1836–71,' *Thoroton Society Transactions*, LXXIV (1970) examines poor relief in Southwell and Basford, where domestic framework knitting was a key industry. Other local studies include S. I. Richardson, *A History of the Edmonton*

Poor Law Union, 1837–1854, Edmonton Hundred Historical Society, Occasional Papers, New Series, no. 12, n.d. (1968) and E. E. Butcher, *Bristol Corporation of the Poor, 1696–1898,* Bristol branch of the Historical Association, Local History Pamphlets, no. 29 (1972) which, though concerned chiefly with the period before 1834, provides an important example of a relief authority which remained outside the Poor Law Commission's control.

General urban histories sometimes contain useful sections on Poor Law administration. Among them, R. A. Church, *Economic and Social Change in a Midland Town: Victorian Nottingham, 1815–1900* (1966); R. Newton, *Victorian Exeter, 1837–1914* (Leicester, 1968); A. T. Patterson, *Radical Leicester: A History of Leicester, 1780–1850* (Leicester, 1954); A. T. Patterson, *A History of Southampton, 1700–1914,* vol. II, *The Beginnings of Modern Southampton, 1836–1867* (Southampton, 1971); and A. Redford, *The History of Local Government in Manchester,* vol. II, *Borough and City* (1940).

7. THE RURAL POOR LAW

The rural Poor Law has received relatively little attention from historians and there is no short introduction to the topic available. On the general administrative development of the New Poor Law the standard account is still S. and B. Webb, *English Poor Law History, Part II, The Last Hundred Years,* 1 (reprinted 1963) which can be supplemented usefully by an analysis of the weaknesses of the central administration in its early years in D. Roberts, *Victorian Origins of the British Welfare State* (New Haven, 1960), and by an illuminating collection of documents in M. E. Rose, *The English Poor Law, 1780–1930* (Newton Abbot, 1971).

The formation and initial operation of Poor Law unions in rural areas has been analysed provocatively by A. Brundage, 'The Landed Interest and the New Poor Law: A reappraisal of the Revolution in Government', *E.H.R., LXXXVII* (1972). His conclusion that the 1834 Act led to an enlargement of the powers of the landed gentry has been challenged by P. Dunkley, 'The Landed Interest and the New Poor Law: A Critical Note', *E.H.R., LXXXVIII* (1973).

There is an interesting, if brief, description of protests by the poor against the imposition of the New Poor Law in the countryside in N. C. Edsall, *The Anti-Poor Law Movement, 1833–44* (Manchester, 1971). A meticulous analysis of the role which grievances about the New Poor Law could continue to play in a rural area is that of D. Williams, *The Rebecca Riots: A Study in Agrarian Discontent* (Cardiff, 1955).

The contrasting arguments of D. Roberts, 'How Cruel was the Victorian Poor Law?', *H.J., IV* (1963) and U. Henriques, 'How Cruel was the Victorian Poor Law?', *H.J., XI* (1968) give some insight into rural relief practices. The 'bastilles', symbols of the oppressive nature of the 1834 Act, receive a full-length treatment including a dispassionate account of the infamous rural workhouse at Andover in N. Longmate, *The Workhouse* (1974). A more sensationalised treatment is accorded the same topic in I. Anstruther, *The Scandal of the Andover Workhouse* (1973).

The *Report of the Royal Commission on the Poor Laws of 1832–4* is essential reading for an understanding of the over-optimism of the Poor Law Commission towards rural relief administration and it has been reprinted together with a perceptive introduction by S. G. and E. O. A. Checkland (eds), *The Poor Law Report of 1834* (Harmondsworth, 1974). The response by the Poor Law Commission to the continued problem of surplus labour through migration and emigration schemes is described succinctly in A. Red-ford, *Labour Migration in England, 1800–1850*, 2nd edn (Manchester, 1964), and the regional relief practices which were adopted by guardians to deal with rural underemployment are analysed in A. Digby, 'The Labour Market and the Continuity of Social Policy after 1834: The Case of the Eastern Countries', *Ec.H.R.*, 2nd series, XXVIII (1975).

J. Caird, *English Agriculture in 1850–1*, 2nd edn (1968) gives a masterly, contemporary account of the socio-economic problems of the countryside while a modern discussion is that of E. L. Jones, 'The Agricultural Labour Market in England, 1793–1872', *Ec.H.R.* 2nd series, XVII (1964). A com-prehensive survey of agrarian change is given in J. D. Chambers and G. E. Mingay, *The Agricultural Revolution, 1750–1880* (1966). D. R. Mills (ed.), *English Rural Communities: The Impact of a Specialised Economy* (1973), contains a lucid summary by R. Lawton on rural depopulation, and also an analysis by the editor of the impact of the settlement laws on Lincolnshire and Not-tinghamshire. An important article on the settlement laws is that by B. A. Holderness, '"Open" and "Close" Parishes in England in the Eighteenth and Nineteenth Centuries', *Agricultural History Review*, XX (1972).

The operation of the New Poor Law at the local level can be found in help-ful articles in local historical journals which include: J. A. H. Brocklebank, 'The New Poor Law in Lincolnshire', *Lincolnshire Historian*, 11 (1962) and M. Caplan, 'The Poor Law in Nottinghamshire, 1836–71', *Transactions of the Thoroton Society of Notts*, LXXIV (1970).

8.   THE POOR LAW IN NINETEENTH-CENTURY SCOTLAND

The chapter is mainly based upon Poor Law sources. Invaluable Parliamen-tary Papers include *The Report to the Board of Supervision by Sir John M'Neill on the Western Highlands and Islands*, P.P. XXVI (1851); Edwin Chadwick's *Report on the Sanitary Conditions of the Labouring Population of Scotland*, P.P., XXVIII (1842); *The Report of the Commissioners of Inquiry into the Conditions of the Crofters and Cot-tars in the Highlands and Islands*, P.P., XXXI–XXXVI (1884), all of which should be read with caution. The Board of Supervision minutes (1845–94) vols 1–23, the annual reports (1847–94) Edinburgh City Parochial Board Minutes (1845–94) and relevant committee books have all provided information, but of these only the annual reports are printed and available in the National Library of Scotland. For a fuller survey of Edinburgh, see A. Paterson, 'Poor Law Administration in the City Parish of Edinburgh, 1845–1894', un-published Ph.D. thesis, Edinburgh University (1974). The following three books by T. Ferguson have some value but the material has been taken from both other published sources and also the annual reports of the Board of Supervision: *The Dawn of Scottish Welfare* (Edinburgh, 1948); *Scottish Social Welfare* (Edinburgh, 1958); and *Children in Care and After* (1966).

For background reading the following are very useful: R. Mitchison, *A History of Scotland* (1970), and T. C. Smout, *A History of the Scottish People, 1560–1830* (1969). For regional information, J. P. Day, *Public Administration in the Highlands and Islands* (Edinburgh, 1918) contains much detailed material. The development of ideas concerning supervised relief can be found in C. L. Mowat, *The Charity Organisation Society* (Edinburgh, 1961). The following ar-ticles also provide very useful information: E. Chadwick, 'Poor Law Ad-ministration in Scotland', *Journal of the Statistical Society* (27 Apr. 1892); A. V.

Douglas, 'Historical Studies in the Development of Local Government Services in Edinburgh', *National Association of Local Government Officers* (1936); and R. Mitchison, 'The Making of the Old Scottish Poor Law', *Past and Present*, LXIII (1974) pp. 58–93.

Nineteenth-century newspapers and magazines are very valuable sources, particularly *Poor Law Magazine* published monthly after 1859, and they are essential for an accurate account of the Scottish Poor Law in this period.

LIST OF POOR LAW THESES

In recent years a considerable amount of research has been done on the history of the Poor Law. Much of this material is unpublished and remains in the university theses for which it was prepared. The list below is not exhaustive and the editor would be pleased to hear of any theses not included.

B.A. theses

G. Cadman, 'The Administration of the Poor Law Amendment Act in Hexham, 1836–40 and 1862–9' (Newcastle, 1965).

D. A. Farnie, 'The Establishment of the New Poor Law in Salford, 1838–50' (Manchester, 1951).

S. M. Morgan, 'Local Government and Poor Relief in Oldham, 1826–50' (Manchester, 1959).

J. Toft, 'The New Poor Law in Leeds' (Manchester, 1964).

J. R. Wood, 'The Transition from the Old to the New Poor Law in Manchester' (Manchester, 1938).

M.A. theses

C. F. Baker, 'The Care and Education of Children in Union Workhouses of Somerset, 1834–70' (London, 1961).

R. G. Barker, 'Houghton-le-Spring Poor Law Union 1834–1930' (M.Litt., Newcastle, 1974).

A. Becherand, 'The Poor and English Poor Laws in Loughborough Union, 1837–60' (M-ès-Lettres, Nancy, 1972).

R. Boyson, 'Poor Law Administration in North-East Lancashire, 1834–71' (Manchester, 1960).

E. A. Christmas, 'The Administration of the Poor Law in some Gloucestershire Unions 1815–1847' (M.Litt., Bristol, 1974).

A. M. Davies, 'Poverty and its Treatment in Cardiganshire, 1750–1850' (Aberystwyth, 1969).

F. Duke, 'The Education of Pauper Children: Policy and Administration, 1834–55' (Manchester, 1968).

P. J. Dunkley, 'The New Poor Law and County Durham' (Durham, 1971).

A. Froshaug, 'Poor Law Administration in Selected London Parishes, 1750–1850' (Nottingham, 1969).

D. E. Gladstone, 'The Administration and Reform of Poor Relief in Scotland with Special Reference to Stirlingshire, 1790–1850' (Stirling, 1973).

M. D. Handley, 'Local Administration of the Poor Law in Great Boughton, Wirral and Chester Unions' (Wales, 1968).

N. D. Hopkins, 'The Old and New Poor Law in E. Yorks c. 1760–1850' (M. Phil., Leeds, 1968).

C. F. Hughes, 'The Development of the Poor Law in Caernarvon and Anglesey, 1815–1914' (Wales, 1945).

T. D. Jones, 'Poor Law and Public Health Administration in Merthyr Tydfil, 1834–74' (Cardiff, 1961).

S. Kelly, 'The Select Vestry of Liverpool and the Administration of the Poor Law, 1821–1871' (Liverpool, 1972).

P. Mawson, 'Poor Law Administration in South Shields, 1830–1930' (Newcastle, 1971).

C. F. L. Pack, 'Evolution of Methods of Poor Relief in the Winchester Area, 1720–1845' (Southampton, 1967).

W. Pike, 'The Administration of the Poor Law in Rural Areas of Surrey, 1830–50' (London, 1950).

E. M. Ross, 'Women and Poor Law Administration, 1857–1909' (London, 1956).

V. J. Russell, 'Poor Law Administration, 1840–43, with Particular Reference to Cardiff Union' (Wales, 1966).

K. E. Skinner, 'Poor Law Administration in Glamorgan, 1750–1850' (Wales, 1956).

J. E. Thomas, 'Poor Law Administration in West Glamorgan, 1834–1930 (Swansea, 1951).

Ph.D. Theses

A. L. Brundage, 'The Landed Interest and the New Poor Law in Northamptonshire, 1834–40' (California, 1970).

M. Caplan, 'The Administration of the Poor Law in Southwell and Basford, 1836–71' (Nottingham, 1967).

A. Digby, 'The Operation of the Poor Law in the Social and Economic life of Nineteenth Century Norfolk' (East Anglia, 1972).

N. C. Edsall, 'The Poor Law and its Opponents, 1833–44' (Harvard, 1965).

E. Midwinter, 'Social Administration in Lancashire, 1830–60' (York, 1967).

A. Paterson, 'Poor Law Administration in the City Parish of Edinburgh, 1845–1894' (Edinburgh, 1974).

M. E. Rose, 'The Administration of Poor Relief in the West Riding of Yorkshire c. 1820–1855 (Oxford, 1965).

A. M. Ross, 'The Care and Education of Pauper Children in England and Wales, 1834–96' (London, 1956).

V. J. Walsh, 'The Administration of the Poor Law in Shropshire, 1820–55' (Pennsylvania, 1970).

Notes and References

For abbreviations used here, see page 194 above.

INTRODUCTION   *Derek Fraser*

1. For fuller discussion of these issues see J. R. Poynter, *Society and Pauperism* (1969); M. E. Rose, *The Relief of Poverty, 1834–1914* (1972); D. Fraser, *The Evolution of the British Welfare State* (1973); S. G. and E. O. A. Checkland (eds), *The Poor Law Report of 1834* (1974).
2. *Report* (Pelican edn) p. 244.
3. Ibid. p. 256.
4. Ibid. pp. 248–9.
5. J. B. Smith to C. P. Villiers (25 July 1839) Smith's Corn Law Papers, Manchester Reference Library.
6. P.L.C., *Fifth Annual Report* (1839) pp. 12–13.
7. G. W. Oxley, *Poor Relief in England and Wales, 1601–1834* (1974) p. 72.
8. *Local Government Chronicle*, (29 Oct 1910).
9. A. Austin, *Report*, (22 Apr 1847) P.R.O. M.H.12/15228.
10. P.L.C., *Seventh Annual Report* (1841) p. 11.
11. P.L.C., *Fourth Annual Report* (1838) Appendix, p. 145.
12. Ibid. p. 140.
13. L.G.B., *Third Annual Report* (1873–4) Appendix, p. 247.
14. *Report . . . of the Salford Operative Conservative Society* (Manchester, 1838) p. 16.
15. *Porcupine* (1 June 1861) p. 97.
16. *Leeds Mercury* (21 Dec 1839).
17. W. Rathbone, *Social Duties Considered* (1867) pp. 12–13.
18. Ibid. p. 87.
19. Cited in *Introduction to Historical Psephology,* Open University course D301, Unit 9, p. 25; Salford source: *A Plain Statement of Facts* (Manchester, 1837) p. 19.
20. Cited (no reference given) in J. P. D. Dunbabin, *Rural Discontent in Nineteenth-Century Britain* (1974) p. 119.
21. B. Keith Lucas, *The English Local Government Franchise* (1952) p. 36.
22. Resolution of the Manchester Churchwardens (6 June 1837) Borough Reeve's Letter Book, vol. 3, Manchester Reference Library, M9/61/3.
23. *Sheffield Times* (10 Nov 1855).
24. Rathbone, *Social Duties Considered*, pp. 48–9.
25. Manchester Guardians' Books (14 Dec 1849), Manchester Reference Library, M4/2/2; Liverpool Workhouse Committee (23 Dec 1859), cited by S. Kelly in 'The Select Vestry of Liverpool and the Administration of the Poor Law, 1821–1871', Liverpool University M.A. thesis (1972) p. 88.
26. *Report of the Sub-Committee . . . of Pauperism* (Leeds, 1850) p. 16.
27. Dunbabin, *Rural Discontent*, p. 300.
28. *Leicester Journal* (28 Feb 1838).

29. C. Clements to J. Beckwith (18 July 1845) Letters from the P.L.C. (1845) Leeds City Archives.

30. Rathbone, *Social Duties Considered*, pp. 21, 48.

31. Ibid. p. 124.

32. 60 & 61 Vic., cap. 31, clause 1.

1. SETTLEMENT, REMOVAL AND THE NEW POOR LAW *Michael E. Rose*

1. T. R. Malthus, *Essay on Population* (1798), pb. edn, ed. K. E. Boulding (Ann Arbor, 1959) p. 32. Adam Smith, *The Wealth of Nations* (1776); pb. edn, ed. E. Cannon (1961), I, p. 158.

2. George Elson, *The Last of the Climbing Boys* (1900) p. 13.

3. Only one union – Docking in Norfolk – seems to have taken advantage of this provision: *Report of Committee to Enquire as to the Effect of the Union for Settlement in the Docking Union*, P.R.O. M.H./12/8253 (11 Dec 1850). I am grateful to Anne Digby for this reference.

4. S.C., *Law of Settlement*, XI (1847).

5. P.L.B., *Report . . . on the Law of Settlement and Removal of the Poor*, P.P. 1152, XXVII (1850).

6. P.L.B., *Report of George Coode . . . on the Law of Settlement and Removal of the Poor*, 675, XXVI (1851).

7. Robert Pashley, *Pauperism and Poor Laws* (1862). Called to the bar in 1837, Pashley (1805–59) had a large practice on the Northern Circuit. He took silk in 1851 and in the following year stood unsuccessfully for Parliament at both York and King's Lynn. In 1856 he was made assistant judge of the Middlesex Sessions.

8. Sir Edmund Head, 'The Law of Settlement', *Edinburgh Review*, LXXXVII (Apr 1848); Sir George Nicholls, *Memorandum on Settlement, Removal and Rating* (Nov 1850), P.P., 90, LV, part 1 (1854).

9. S.C., *Operation of 8 & 9 Vic., Cap. 117*, XVII (1854).

10. S.C., *Operation of 9 & 10 Vic., Cap. 66*, (1857–8), XIII; Session 2, VII (1859); XVII (1860).

11. S.C., *Operation of existing Laws in U.K., relating to settlement and irremovability of paupers*, XII (1878–9).

12. For details of this scheme, see A. Redford, *Labour Migration in England*, 2nd edn (1963) ch. VI.

13. S.C., XI (1847): evidence of Edwin Chadwick, QQ1979.

14. Head, 'The Law of Settlement', pp. 472, 457.

15. P.P., 553, LXXXIV (1852–3).

16. P.L.B., *Reports* (1850); Pashley, *Pauperism and Poor Laws*, ch. 14.

17. R.C., *Poor Law*, XXXV, XXVI (1834), Appendix B(2): 'Answers to Town Queries'.

18. S.C., XI (1847): evidence of Henry Coppock, QQ5428–9.

19. P.R.O., MH12/15515 (16 Mar 1850). Pashley, *Pauperism and Poor Laws*, p. 263.

20. S.C., XI (1847): evidence of Edwin Chadwick, Q2029.

21. Volume of Poor Law Vouchers in Archives Dept, Halifax Public Library.

22. Accounts Ledger, Manchester Reference Library, M4/6/1. *Register of Non-Resident Relief* (1849–61) Leeds City Library Archives.

23. P.L.B., *Eighth Annual Report* (1855), Appendix 29.

24. R.C., *Poor Laws* (1909); *Report*, p. 543.

25. E. H. Hunt, *Regional Wage Variations in Britain, 1850–1914* (1973).

26. D. R. Mills, 'Poor Laws and the Distribution of Population (c. 1600–1860) with special reference to Lincolnshire', *Trans. Institute of British Geographers Publications*, XXVI (1959). B. A. Holderness, '"Open" and "Close" Parishes in England in the 18th and 19th Centuries', *Agricultural History Review*, XX (1972) pp. 126–39.

27. P.L.B., *Report*, (1850) p. 190.

28. S.C., P.P. XI (1847): evidence of Henry Coppock, Q5183.

29. S.C., P.P. XI (1847): evidence of William Royston, Q5057.

30. P.P., L 666 (1850).

31. S.C., P.P. XI (1847): evidence of William Royston, Q5032.

32. S.C XII (1878–9): evidence of H. J. Hagger, QQ1674, 1716, 1726, 1813–14.

33. S.C. XVII (1854) Appendix 17.

34. S.C. XI (1847) Appendix 2. S.C., XIII (1878–9) Appendix 2.

35. S.C. XII (1878–9): evidence of H. W. Higgins, QQ2137, 2182, 2216.

36. S.C., *Irremovable Poor*, P.P., 520, XVII (1860), Appendix 17.

37. S.C., XI (1847): evidence of J. Beckwith and C. Heaps, QQ3907–9, 4077. Pashley, *Pauperism and Poor Laws*, p. 279.

38. S.C. XI (1847), evidence of Henry Coppock, Q5467.

39. S.C., 282, XII (1878–9), Appendix 2: evidence of H. W. Higgins, QQ2125–30.

40. *Hansard,* Parliamentary Debates, 3rd Series, CXXX (10 Feb 1854) col. 459.

2. MEDICAL SERVICES UNDER THE NEW POOR LAW *M. W. Flinn*

1. S.C., *First Report . . . on Medical Poor Relief*, XI (1844): evidence Q2.

2. A. R. Neate, *The St Marylebone Workhouse and Institution, 1730–1965*, St Marylebone Society, Publication no. 9 (1967) pp. 6–9.

3. Joseph Rogers, *Reminiscences of a Workhouse Medical Officer*, ed. Thorold Rogers (1889) p. 250.

4. R.C., *Report . . . on the Poor Law*, XXVII (1834) pp.146, 172. R. A. Lewis, *Edwin Chadwick and the Public Health Movement, 1832–1854* (1952) p. 27.

5. S.C., *Report . . . on Poor Law Amendment Act*, XVIII (1837–8).

6. Richard Griffin, 'Poor Law Medical Relief', *Transactions of the National Association for the Promotion of Social Science* (1861) p. 376.

7. From MS. report by Tufnell, quoted in S. E. Finer, *The Life and Times of Edwin Chadwick* (1952) p. 159.

8. S.C., *Report . . . on Medical Relief*, XII (1854): evidence Q2152.

9. *Seventh Report of the Medical Officer of the Privy Council* (1865) p. 20.

10. R.C., *Sanitary Report*, XXXV (1871) p. 24.

11. Ibid. p. 21.

12. E. Chadwick, 'Administration of Medical Relief to the Destitute Sick of the Metropolis', *Fraser's Magazine*, LXXIV (1866) p. 353.

13. Memorandum by G. C. Lewis, quoted in R. A. Lewis, *Edwin Chadwick and the Public Health Movement, 1832–1854* (1952) p. 75.

14. Richard Griffin, 'Poor Law Medical Relief', *Transactions of the National Association for the Promotion of Social Science* (1861) p. 379.

15. E. Hart, 'Metropolitan Infirmaries for the Pauper Sick', *Fortnightly Review*, IV (1861) p. 461.

16. Frances Cobbe, 'Workhouse Sketches', *Macmillan's Magazine*, III (1861) p. 456.

17. Rogers, *Reminiscences*, p. 5.

18. Ibid. p. 10.

19. Louisa Twining, *A Letter to the President of the Poor Law Board on Workhouse Infirmaries* (1866) pp. 10–11.

20. S.C., *Report . . . on Medical Relief*, XII (1854): evidence Q1951.

21. S.C., *Third Report . . . on Medical Poor Relief*, IX (1844): evidence Q9087.

22. P.L.C., *Seventh Annual Report*, XI (1841), p. 11.

23. S. and B. Webb, *English Poor Law History, Part II, The Last Hundred Years*, I (1929) p. 316.

24. Hart, 'Metropolitan Infirmaries for the Pauper Sick', p. 462.

25. S.C., *Third Report . . . on Medical Poor Relief*, Q4.

26. S.C., *Final Report . . . on Poor Relief*, IX (1864), p. 45.

27. B. Abel-Smith, *The Hospitals, 1800–1948* (1964), p. 82.

28. P. F. Aschrott, *The English Poor Law System Past and Present*, trans. H. Preston-Thomas (1888), p. 233.

3. PAUPER EDUCATION *Francis Duke*

1. P.L.C., *First Annual Report* (1835) p. 98. This formula was also employed in Art. 114 of the General Order of 24 July 1847 which was the main co-ordinating regulation for workhouse administration throughout the nineteenth century.

2. This traditional view of the commissioners' role is expressed in S. E. Finer, *The Life and Times of Sir Edwin Chadwick* (1952) pp. 152–3; and D. Roberts, *Victorian Origins of the British Welfare State* (New Haven, 1960) p. 241.

3. Hall's MS. reports to the P.L.C. on attempts to form school districts in London provide the clearest evidence of the intentions behind the 1844 Act, as well as of the difficulties in applying it: P.R.O. MH32/36, especially the reports of 1 Feb 1845 and 1 Jan 1947.

4. P.L.B. letter to Committee of Council on Education (11 Apr 1853): P.R.O. MH19/15. This provided estimated average costs per head of maintenance in district schools but advised an emphasis on the longer-term benefits.

5. P.L.B. correspondence with these three schools in their early years illustrates their problems. See P.R.O. MH27, vols 68, 77 and 84 for, respectively, Farnham and Hartley Wintney, South-East Shropshire and Reading and Wokingham district schools.

6. P.L.B., *Twenty-Third Annual Report* (1870) pp. 414–36.

7. C.C.E. to P.L.B. (11 May 1849), P.R.O. MH19/14.

8. Until 1857 a Calendar of Certificates awarded was included in the C.C.E. annual minutes for Parochial Union Schools; *Minutes P.U. Schools* (1847–8–9) pp. x–xi lists the requirements for each certificate.

9. 12 December 1848, P.R.O. MH19/14.

10. *P.P.*, XXI, part 1 (1961), pp. 352–85.

11. For these four inspectors' reports, see *P.P.* XLIX, part 1 (1862), no. 150, especially pp. 5, 35.

12. Browne's views are expressed most fully in his reports for 1854 and 1855: C.C.E. *Minutes P.U. Schools* (1854–5) pp. 109–10; (1855–6) pp. 108–10.
13. L.G.B., *Third Annual Report* (1874) pp. 311–94.
14. C.C.E., *Minutes P.U. Schools* (1855–6) p. 138.
15. *P.P.*, LXIV, no. 354 (1878).
16. W. C. Glen (ed.), *The Poor Law Orders*, 10th edn (1887) p. 127 n.
17. *P.P.*, LVIII, no. 123 (1870); return of children on outdoor relief.
18. L.G.B., *Third Annual Report* (1874) pp. 335–6.
19. S. and B. Webb, *English Poor Law History, Part II, The Last Hundred Years* (1963 edn) I, pp. 281–2.
20. C.C.E., *Minutes P.U. Schools* (1852–3) p. 58.
21. Ibid. (1850–1–2) pp. 60–3 and (1852–3) pp. 134–5. L.G.B., *Third Annual Report* (1874) p. 332.
22. The tale is told in Hawley's special report for *1862*: *P.P.*, XLIX (1862), p. 35.
23. C.C.E., *Minutes P.U. Schools* (1847–8–9) p. 242.
24. Ibid. pp. 9–10.

4. THE POOR LAW AND PHILANTHROPY
Norman McCord

1. For further discussion on this point, see Norman Gash's introduction to the 2nd edition of *The Long Debate on Poverty* (1974).
2. The discussion of charitable societies is much curtailed here since the writer has discussed the subject at greater length in 'Aspects of the Relief of Poverty in Early Nineteenth-Century Britain', in *The Long Debate on Poverty*, pp. 91–109.
3. *New Statesman* review (29 Sep 1972).
4. These efforts to provide work in 1819 are mentioned in several letters in Home Office Papers at the P.R.O.: HO 41/5, HO 42/196, HO 42/197. For an early statutory attempt to provide employment in hard times, see M. W. Flinn, 'The Poor Employment Act of 1817', *Ec.H.R.*, 2nd series, XIV (1961) pp. 82 ff.
5. John Latimer, *Local Records, or Historical Register of Remarkable Events, etc.* (Newcastle, 1857) pp. 90–1.
6. *The Local Historian's Table Book*, vol. v (Newcastle, 1846) p. 28.
7. *Memoirs of John Wigham Richardson, 1839–1908* (Glasgow, 1911) p. 105.
8. Richard Redmayne, *Men, Mines and Memories* (1942), pp. 296–7.
9. David Owen, *English Philanthropy* (Cambridge, Mass., 1965) p. 218.
10. P.L.C. to Carlisle board of guardians (8 May 1844) Poor Law Correspondence Files, Cumbria Record Office, Carlisle. I owe this reference to Mr R. N. Thompson.
11. Sunderland board of guardians, Minute Books (13 July 1871) Sunderland Central Library. I owe this reference to Mr Peter Wood. In general for material on Poor Law history I am indebted to recent research work carried out by Miss G. Cadman, Miss P. Mawson and Messrs R. Barker, R. N. Thompson and P. Wood.
12. See *The Long Debate on Poverty*, pp. 105–7.
13. L.G.B., *Third Annual Report* (1873–4) pp. 134–5.
14. P. Mawson, 'Poor Law Administration in South Shields, 1830–1930', Newcastle University M.A. thesis (1971) ff. 121–2.

15. Newcastle upon Tyne Ragged School Society, *Second Annual Report* (Newcastle, 1849) p. 5.

16. See E. P. Thompson, *The Making of the English Working Class* (Pelican edn, 1970), pp. 223, 380.

17. Space does not permit a more extended discussion here of the activities of these societies. See C. L. Mowat, *The Charity Organisation Society, 1869–1913* (1961) and A. F. Young and E. T. Ashton, *British Social Work in the Nineteenth Century* (1956).

18. B. S. Rowntree, *Poverty: A Study of Town Life*, 2nd edn (1902) p. 43.

5. THE POOR LAW AS A POLITICAL INSTITUTION   Derek Fraser

1. C. Mott, *Report* (24 Aug 1841) P.R.O. MH/12/15225.

2. R. Baker to P.L.C. (18 Mar 1836) P.R.O. MH12/15224.

3. *Leeds Intelligencer* (7 Jan 1837).

4. E. Baines, Sr, to J. A. Ikin (30 Jan 1837) Baines MS., Leeds City Archives; A. Power to P.L.C. (13 Jan 1837) P.R.O. MH12/15224.

5. M. Johnson to P.L.B. (13 Jan 1848) P.R.O. MH12/15229.

6. H. B. Farnall, Report (6 Aug 1852) P.R.O. MH12/15230; *Leeds Times* (3 July 1852).

7. P.L.B. *Nineteenth Annual Report*, Appendix (1866–7) pp. 126–36.

8. Enquiry of H. Longley and D. B. Fry, P.R.O. MH12/15243 (Oct 1870) p. 385.

9. Ibid. p. 508. It would seem that electoral malpractice of this sort could yield greater political dividends than the multiple voting system inherited from Sturges Bourne, which is discussed in A. Brundage, 'Reform of the Poor Law Electoral System, 1834–94' (forthcoming).

10. For a general review of Salford's affairs, see R. L. Greenall, 'The Development of Local Government in Salford, 1830–1853', Leicester University M.A. thesis (1970).

11. *Manchester Times* (4 Apr 1835).

12. *Manchester Guardian* (4 Apr 1838).

13. C. Mott to P.L.C., (18 May 1841) P.R.O. MH12/6220.

14. F. Wrigley to P.L.C. (12 Dec 1840).

15. C. Mott to P.L.C. (4 June 1842).

16. *Birmingham Advertiser* (9 Apr 1840).

17. For further details of Nottingham newspapers, see D. Fraser, 'The Nottingham Press, 1800–1850', *Trans. Thoroton Society* (1963).

18. *Nottingham Review* (6 Nov 1840); *Nottingham and Newark Mercury* (6 Nov 1840).

19. *Nottingham Journal* (16 Apr 1841).

20. J. Sutton, *Date Book . . .* (Nottingham, 1852) p. 446.

21. *Sheffield Free Press* (24 Nov 1855).

22. J. Mainwaring to P.L.B., (21 June 1957) P.R.O. MH12/15475.

23. For Ironside's activities, see J. Salt, 'Experiments in Anarchism . . .', *Trans. Hunter Archaeol. Soc.* (Sheffield, 1972).

24. *Sheffield Times* (10 Nov 1855); cf. *Sheffield Daily Telegraph* (10 Nov 1855).

25. *To the Ratepayers of Sheffield* (Apr 1856) P.R.O. MH12/15474.

26. *Sheffield Iris* (13 Nov. 1855).

27. *Sheffield Free Press* (22 Mar 1856).

28. Ibid. (19 July 1856).

29. *Sheffield Times* (18 Sep 1858).

30. Ibid.
31. *Leeds Mercury* (13 Apr 1844).
32. *Leeds Intelligencer* (8 Apr 1843).
33. Memo to P.L.B. (15 Aug 1859); Ramsden Papers L.C.A. Box 47 B2, Leeds City Archives.
34. Cf. *Liverpool Mercury* (21 Mar and 4 Apr 1845, 13 Mar and 17 Apr 1846).
35. P.L.C. to J. Hope (26 Apr 1841) P.R.O. MH12/6220.
36. J. Hope to C. Mott (28 May 1842).
37. Ibid.
38. E. Ambler to G. Melly (13 Aug 1863) Melly Papers 1638, Liverpool Record Office.
39. Ibid. (25 July 1863) Melly Papers 1637.
40. Ibid. (21 June 1864) Melly Papers 2005.
41. *Sheffield and Rotherham Independent* (29 Mar 1856); E. Stephens to G. Wilson (4 Mar 1844) Wilson Papers, Manchester Reference Library.

6. THE URBAN POOR LAW *David Ashforth*

1. *P.P.*, Accounts and Papers, 309, 212, XLIX (1856).
2. *Bradford Observer* (14 Dec 1837).
3. A. Power to P.L.C. P.R.O. MH32/63 (25 Nov 1836); C. Mott to P.L.C., P.R.O. MH32/57 (10 Dec 1839).
4. A. Power to P.L.C., P.R.O. MH32/63 (21 Oct 1837); C. Mott to P.L.C., P.R.O. MH32/57 (9 May 1839).
5. A. Power to P.L.C., P.R.O. MH32/63 (21 Oct 1837); C. Mott to J. S. Lefevre, P.R.O. MH32/57 (15 Sep 1838).
6. P.L.C., *Fourth Annual Report* (1837–8), Appendix A, no. 7.
7. A. Power to P.L.C., P.R.O. MH32/63 (21 Oct 1837).
8. Sir J. Walsham to Durham boards of guardians (26 Dec 1836) quoted in P. Dunkley, 'The New Poor Law and County Durham', Durham University M.A. thesis (1971) p. 182.
9. R. A. Church, *Economic and Social Change in a Midland Town: Victorian Nottingham, 1815–1900* (1966) p. 115.
10. E. Senior to P.L.C., P.R.O. MH32/66 (18 Apr 1840).
11. Quoted by Dunkley, 'The New Poor Law and County Durham, p. 240.
12. *Burnley Express* (4 Nov 1869) quoted in R. Boyson, 'The History of Poor Law Administration in North-East Lancashire, 1834–1871' Manchester University M.A. thesis (1960) pp. 257–8.
13. M. E. Rose, 'The Allowance System under the New Poor Law', *Ec.H.R.*, XIX (1966) p. 610.
14. P.L.B., *Tenth Annual Report* (1857–8) Appendix no. 14.
15. P.L.B., *Thirteenth Annual Report* (1860–1) pp. 17–18.
16. Quoted in W. O. Henderson, *The Lancashire Cotton Famine, 1861–1865*, 2nd edn (1969) p. 64.
17. P.L.B., *Fifth Annual Report* (1852) Appendix no. 4.
18. P.L.C. to Bolton board of guardians (19 Jan 1843) quoted in R. Boyson, op. cit. pp. 265–6.
19. Quoted in A. T. Patterson, *A History of Southampton, 1700–1914*, II (1971) p. 129.
20. *Bradford Observer* (2 Sep 1847).
21. *Bolton Chronicle* (23 Apr 1842) quoted in R. Boyson, op. cit. p. 264.

22. *Bradford Observer* (25 Nov and 2 Dec 1847).

23. T. Davies Jones, 'Poor Law and Public Health Administration in the Area of Merthyr Tydfil Union, 1834–1894', University of Wales M.A. thesis (1961) pp. 131–2.

24. E. E. Butcher, *Bristol Corporation of the Poor, 1696–1898*, Bristol Branch of the Historical Association, Local History Pamphlets no. 29 (1972) p. 16.

25. A. Froshaug, 'Poor Law Administration in Selected London Parishes between 1750 and 1850', Nottingham University M.A. thesis (1969) p. 627, n. 25.

26. P.L.C., *Seventh Annual Report* (1841) p. 332.

27. S.C., *Poor Removal, P.P.* XIII (1854–5): Manchester evidence QQ2957, 3105, 3109, 3155, 3168; Liverpool Q2957; Bradford QQ1294–6.

28. J. Wagstaff to P.L.B., P.R.O. MH12/14726 (26 Feb 1848); J. Darlington to P.L.B., P.R.O. MH12/14729 (1 Mar 1852).

29. S.C., *Poor Removal, PP.*, XIII (1854–5): QQ3123, 3127; Q2953.

30. H. Farnall to P.L.B., (20 May 1854) P.R.O. MH12/14770.

31. P.L.B., *Twenty-Second Annual Report* (1869–70) p. xv.

32. Quoted in P. Mawson, 'Poor Law Administration in South Shields, 1830–1930', Newcastle University M.A. thesis (1971) p. 62.

33. P.L.B., *Twenty-Second Annual Report* (1869–70) p. x.

7 · THE RURAL POOR LAW   *Anne Digby*

1. P.L.C., *Report . . . on the Continuance of the P.L.C., P.P.*, XVII (1840) p. 212.

2. P.L.C. *First Report, P.P.*, XXXV (1835) p. 122.

3. Lord George Hamilton, 'A Statistical Survey of the Problems of Pauperism', *J. Royal Statistical Society*, LXXIV (1910–11) pp. 30, 33.

4. A. Brundage, 'The Landed Interest and the New Poor Law: A Reappraisal of the Revolution in Government', *E.H.R.*, LXXXVII (1972) pp. 34, 41.

5. Correspondence of E. Parry with P.L.C., P.R.O. MH32/60. Correspondence of J. Kay with P.L.C., MH32/48. Kay to P.L.C., P.R.O. MH12/8185 (17 Mar 1836).

6. Kay to P.L.C., P.R.O. MH12/8455 (28 Apr 1836); *Norwich Mercury* (25 Mar 1837); Wayland Minutes (22 Oct 1835) Poor Law Catalogue, Norfolk Record Office, Norwich; N. C. Edsall, *The Anti-Poor Law Movement, 1833–34* (1971) pp. 27, 29–30, 38.

7. Edsall, *The Anti-Poor Law Movement*, pp. 39–41; M. E. Rose, 'The Anti-Poor Law Agitation', in *Popular Movements c. 1830–1850* ed. J. T. Ward (1970) pp. 81–2, J. A. H. Brocklebank, 'The New Poor Law in Lincolnshire', *Lincolnshire Historian*, II (1962) pp. 25–6, 30–1; A. Digby, 'The Operation of the Poor Law in the Social and Economic Life of Nineteenth-Century Norfolk', East Anglia University Ph.D. thesis (1972) ff. 170–5.

8. P. G. Rogers, *Battle in Bossenden Wood* (1961) pp. 86, 93, 104; H. Fearn, 'Chartism in Suffolk', in *Chartist Studies*, ed. Asa Briggs (1962) pp. 153–6.

9. P. Dunkley, 'The Landed Interest and the New Poor Law: A Critical Note', *E.H.R.*, LXXXVIII (1973) pp. 836–41; Brundage, 'The Landed Interest and the New Poor Law', pp. 28–30, 43–7; Norfolk Union Minutes (1835–8), Poor Law Catalogue, Norfolk Record Office, Norwich.

10. R.C., *Poor Laws Report* (1834), Cd. 2728, 4th edn (1905) p. 364.

11. A. Redford, *Labour Migration in England, 1800–50*, 2nd edn

(Manchester, 1964) p. 109; *Return and Correspondence on Emigration, P.P.*, XL (1836) pp. 476, 481; *Report from the Agent for Emigration in Canada, P.P.*, XLII (1836) pp. 30, 32.

12. Petition to P.L.C., P.R.O. MH12/8616 (25 Mar 1837).
13. P.L.C., *First Report*, XXV (1835) pp. 118–19.
14. Ibid. pp. 266, 311, 260, 344; Redford, *Labour Migration in England, 1800–50*, pp. 105–8.
15. Redford, *Labour Migration in England, 1800–50*, p. 108.
16. Correspondence of R. M. Muggeridge with P.L.C., P.R.O. MH32/58; P.L.C., *Second Report*, XIX (1836) Part 1, pp. 409–42; P.L.C., *Third Report*, XXXI (1837) pp. 220–9; P.L.C., *Fourth Report*, XXVIII (1837–8) p. 183.
17. P.L.C., *Second Report*, XXIX (1836) Part I, p. 211.
18. P.L.C., *Seventh Report*, XI (1841) p. 428.
19. P.L.C., *Report . . . on the Continuance of the P.L.C., P.P.*, XVII (1840) pp. 280–347.
20. S.C., *Settlement and Removal, P.P.*, XI (1847) QQ 2103–4.
21. *Letters Addressed by the Poor Law Commissioners to the Secretary of State Respecting the Transactions of Business of the Commission* (1847), pp. 51–2; S.C., *Settlement and Removal*, XI (1847) QQ 2103–4.
22. P.L.B., *Twenty-Third Report, P.P.* XXVII (1871) pp. 202, 204, 222; Walsham to P.L.B., P.R.O. M.H.32/83 (7 Jan 1856).
23. L.G.B., *Tenth Report, P.P.*, XLVI (1881) p. 21.
24. S.C., *Andover Union, P.P.*, V (1846) Part 2: QQ 24541–7, 24677–8.
25. D. Williams, *The Rebecca Riots: A Study in Agrarian Discontent* (Cardiff, 1955), pp. 139–46, 205–9, 224; A. E. Davies, 'Sir Hugh Owen and the New Poor Law', *Bulletin of the Board of Celtic Studies*, XXI (1966) pp. 166–70; D. W. Howell, 'The Agricultural Labourer in Nineteenth Century Wales', *Welsh History Review*, VI (1973) pp. 276, 280.
26. L.G.B., *Twenty-Fifth Report, P.P.*, XXXVI (1896) p. 221.
27. S.C., *Andover Union, P.P.*, V (1846) pp. 5–6.
28. D. Roberts, 'How Cruel was the Victorian Poor Law?', *H.J.*, VI (1963) pp. 97–103; *Sixth Report of the Medical Officer of the Privy Council, P.P.*, XXVIII (1864) pp. 234–60.
29. L.G.B., *Twenty-First Report, P.P.*, XXXVIII (1892) p. 157.
30. J. Caird, *English Agriculture in 1850–1*, 2nd edn (1968) p. 517.
31. Tufnell to Lewis, B.M. Add. MSS.40587 (25 May 1845); P.L.C., *Twelfth Report, P.P.*, XIX (1846) pp. 87–96.
32. P.L.B., *Reports . . . on Laws of Settlement and Removal, P.P.* XXVII (1850) p. 329.
33. A. Digby, 'The Labour Market and the Continuity of Social Policy after 1834: The Case of the Eastern Counties', *Ec.H.R.*, XXVIII (1975).
34. B. A. Holderness, '"Open" and "Close" Parishes in England in the Eighteenth and Nineteenth Centuries', *Agricultural History Review*, XX (1972) pp. 136–7; D. A. Mills (ed.) *English Rural Communities: The Impact of a Specialised Economy* (1973) pp. 95, 186–8.
35. Caird, *English Agriculture in 1850–1*, p. 518.
36. M. E. Rose, *The English Poor Law, 1780–1930* (Newton Abbot, 1971) pp. 195–8; C. S. Read, 'Recent Improvements in Norfolk Agriculture', *J. Royal Agricultural Society of England*, XIX (1858) p. 292.
37. R.C., *Poor Laws Report* [Commission of 1905–9] (1909) Cd. 4499, pp. 53–6, 174.
38. Ibid. pp. 187–8, 195.

8. THE POOR LAW IN NINETEENTH-CENTURY SCOTLAND   *Audrey Paterson*

(The writer would like to thank Professor T. C. Smout for his critical comments on an earlier draft of this chapter.)

1. Acts of Parliament of Scotland: 1579, cap. 74; 1597, cap. 272; 1661, cap. 38; 1698, cap. 21.

2. Thomas Chalmers (1780–1847); pamphlets later published in book form, for example *Problems of Poverty* (Edinburgh, 1908); for brief summary, see T. Ferguson, *The Dawn of Social Welfare* (1948) p. 189.

3. W. P. Alison, *Observations on the Management of the Poor in Scotland* (Edinburgh, 1840). See also supporting views in G. Bell, *Day and Night in the Wynds of Edinburgh* (Edinburgh, 1849; republished 1973 with introduction by G. H. Martin).

4. *Report from H.M. Commissioners . . . into . . . the Poor Law in Scotland, P.P.,* xx (1844).

5. S.C., *Report . . . into Operation of the Poor Law in Scotland, P.P.,* 301, xi, 1 (1868–9).

6. Unless otherwise stated detailed information has been extracted from the Board of Supervision minute books in which data was often at variance with the information published in the annual reports.

7. *Poor Law Magazine* (Mar 1866) p. 320.

8. *P.P., Accounts* (1881) vol. 242. The questionnaire was inaccurately completed because it asked inspectors to state their yearly income, not just the salary as inspector of poor. The return shows that 100 inspectors were paid less than £10 per annum as Poor Law officials; the lowest paid was 82 years of age and had worked for the same board for 35 years. The rest were paid as follows: 232 at £10–19; 174 at £20–9; 129 at £30–8; 66 at £40–9; 50 at £50–9; 27 at £60–9; 20 at £70–9; 13 at £80–9; 9 at £90–9; 37 at £100–99; 8 at £200–99; 10 with £300 or more.

9. For example, to accept accounts of registrars: 1854 Act; to enforce vaccination of defaulters: 1855 Act; to deal with lunatics: 1857 Act *et al.*; to sign pension forms and post notices for militia: 1854 Act; public-health duties: 1867 Act; to investigate persons applying for licences to trade as pawnbrokers: 1872 Act; duties under Education Act: 1872 etc.

10. The Board of Supervision could not deal directly with complaints that relief had been refused; this appeal was dealt with directly by the Sheriff, whose decision was final.

11. Detailed information of this nature is taken from Edinburgh City Parochial Board minutes in the possession of the Town Council.

12. For details of conditions in Edinburgh, see H. Littlejohn, *Report on the Sanitary Conditions of the City of Edinburgh* (Edinburgh, 1865).

13. The Board of Supervision devised a long list of prohibited occupations for inspectors, usually on the basis that the posts would have conflicting interests. Parochial boards were not permitted to appoint women inspectors.

14. Figures before 1868 are complicated and vary according to sources: for example in the Board of Supervision annual report (1877) a table shows 134,410 paupers and dependants for 1868, but a Local Government Board source (1895) provides a table which shows 136,131 paupers and dependants for 1868. Official returns were frequently altered in the way information was collected. Poorhouse returns were not given in detail before 1864, and the comparative statement of paupers in January of each year was not published before 1878.

15. 57 & 58 Vic. cap. 58: Local Government (Scotland) Act.

Notes on Contributors

DAVID ASHFORTH graduated from Emmanuel College, Cambridge, and has pursued research into the Poor Law as a postgraduate student at Bradford University. His doctoral thesis is on 'The Poor Law in Bradford c. 1837–1871'.

ANNE DIGBY is Senior Lecturer in History at Homerton College, Cambridge. She has published a paper on the labour market and the New Poor Law. Her book on the economy and the Poor Law is nearing completion.

FRANCIS DUKE is Senior Lecturer in History at Thames Polytechnic. He has published an article on the Poor Law Commission's role in the provision of education in the *Journal of Educational Administration and History*.

MICHAEL FLINN is Professor of Social History in the University of Edinburgh. He has published many books and articles on British social and economic history in the eighteenth and nineteenth century. He is the general editor of the series *Studies in Economic and Social History*.

DEREK FRASER is Senior Lecturer in History in the University of Bradford. He has published articles in the field of nineteenth-century urban history and a general social history, *The Evolution of the British Welfare State* (1973).

NORMAN McCORD is Reader in Economic and Social History in the University of Newcastle. His publications include books and articles on various aspects of nineteenth-century British history, especially the history of north-east England.

AUDREY PATERSON is Lecturer in Social Administration in the University of Edinburgh. Her doctoral thesis on the Poor Law in Edinburgh is being expanded into a book on the Scottish Poor Law as a whole.

MICHAEL ROSE is Senior Lecturer in Economic History in the University of Manchester. His publications include *The English Poor Law 1780–1930* (Newton Abbot, 1971) and *The Relief of Poverty 1834–1914* (1972). He is at present engaged on a study of attitudes towards poverty and its relief in mid-Victorian England.

Index

Common terms which are frequently used throughout the book are excluded from this index. They include Poor Law Commission/Board, poor relief, workhouse, guardians, officials, rates, unions, etc.